The Cotton Patch
5417 Main Street
Williamsville, New York 14221
(716) 634-4544

ALBUM QUILT

This colorful quilt is made up of twenty appliquéd blocks, each with a different design. The traditional log cabin appears on one block, and the others include wreaths, baskets, floral sprays, and geometric designs. See color reproduction on the cover of this book.

THE STANDARD BOOK OF
QUILT MAKING
AND COLLECTING

by

MARGUERITE ICKIS

Author of *Handicrafts and Hobbies for Pleasure
and Profit, Arts and Crafts, Working in Leather,
The Square Weaver and Pattern Weaving, The
Christmas Book, Knotted and Braided Belts,* etc.

DOVER PUBLICATIONS, INC.
NEW YORK

Published in Canada by General Publishing Com-
pany, Ltd., 30 Lesmill Road, Don Mills, Toronto,
Ontario.
Published in the United Kingdom by Constable
and Company, Ltd., 10 Orange Street, London
WC 2.

This Dover edition, first published in 1959, is an
unabridged and unaltered republication of the work
originally published by the Greystone Press in 1949.

Acknowledgments

Grateful acknowledgment is due to the following organizations for illustrations, drawings, and other material:

Agriculture and Home Economic Extension Department of Purdue Uni-
versity, Indiana; Brooklyn Museum; Cooper Union Museum; Honolulu
Academy of Art; Index of American Museum of Art, National Gallery of
Art, Washington, D. C.; New York Historical Society; North Carolina
Historical Society; *Old-Time New England Bulletin,* Boston, Mass.; The
Smithsonian Institution; *Woman's Day* Magazine.

This book also owes much to Mrs. Charles Rankin, for photographs of
traditional quilts; Mr. Herbert S. Lutz, for quilt designs and patterns;
Dr. William Rush Denton, for photographs, advice and valuable consulta-
tion; Mrs. Anna Klostermeier Price, for photographs of historical quilts;
Mrs. Lloyd Miller, for drawings; the Spool Cotton Company, for quilt
patterns; Mr. Egbert Guy Hillegas, for his splendid photography; Isabelle
Stevenson, Frederick Drimmer and Grace Gorner, for helpful editorial
suggestions; R. L. Meyer, who designed this book, and Lester Leventhal,
who worked with him.

Standard Book Number: 486-20582-7
Library of Congress Catalog Card Number: CD62-222

Manufactured in the United States of America
Dover Publications, Inc.
180 Varick Street
New York, N. Y. 10014

"How much piecin' a quilt is like livin' a life! Many a time I've set and listened to Parson Page preachin' about predestination and free will, and I've said to myself, 'If I could jest git up there in the pulpit with one of my quilts, I could make life a heap plainer than parson's makin' it with his big words.'

"You see, to make a quilt you start out with jest so much caliker; you don't go to the store and pick it out and buy it, but the neighbors give you a piece here and there and you'll find you have a piece left over every time you've cut out a dress, and you jest take whatever happens to come. That's the predestination.

"But when it comes to cuttin' out the quilt, why, you're free to choose your own pattern. You give the same kind of pieces to two persons and one'll make a 'Nine-Patch' and the other one'll make a 'Wild-goose-Chase' and so there'll be two quilts made of the same kind of pieces but jest as different as can be. That's the way of livin'. The Lord sends us the pieces; we can cut 'em out and put 'em together pretty much to suit ourselves. There's a heap more in the cuttin' out and the sewin' than there is in the caliker."

From AUNT JANE OF KENTUCKY
by Eliza Calvert Hall

AN INVITATION
TO QUILTING

Almost every woman at one time or another has had the urge to quilt—
many have the proud results in their bedrooms for all to see and admire.
A great many more have felt that perhaps it was too difficult to attempt, too
long and involved a process, and they didn't know exactly how to go about
it. For these women, the step-by-step instructions clearly illustrated in this
book are planned to take all the doubts out of quilt making.

This book is designed for two purposes: (1) to provide an understandable
guide for the beginner and (2) to offer a greater number of lovely designs
for the experienced quilt maker and needlewoman.

If one has inherited a well-patterned quilt, there is pride in the fine needlecraft and the pattern so suggestive of the life and times of our grandmothers.
There is an even greater satisfaction derived from a quilt made with one's
own hands—and in the colors and designs of one's choice. Although machine-
made quilts come in many styles and colors, nothing can surpass the charm
and beauty of a handmade quilt with appliquéd or patchwork motifs and swirls
of quilting in the background.

Quilt making is a simple art and lends itself to many pleasant interludes—
while listening to the radio, chatting with friends, or as a bit of "pick up"
work between household chores, for a quilt will be made during a period of
time and not at one sitting. If the patches are cut and the blocks prepared for
stitching ahead of time, it will be easy to piece them into a block a few at a
time, and then set the blocks together when the sewing is completed. There is
a wide variety from which to choose, ranging from the simplest patchwork
to the more elaborate patterns.

The art appeals to all ages. The very young girl will want to make a quilt
for her doll, with mother's help. If in your 'teens, you may learn to take real
pride in fine stitches for the first time. The housewife and mother, intent on
the comfort and attractiveness of her home, could find no better way of
achieving that aim than by making a quilt. Grandmothers, whose own children
have found a home of their own, have time to while away and they can find

no pleasanter pastime than quilting. So you see this ageless craft of quilting holds an interest for everyone because of its rich tradition, the beauty of its colors and fabrics, and the memories it revives. Above all, there is the particular practicality of the quilt itself.

Your artistic talents will be stimulated by the interesting and ever-changing balance and shaping of the patterns, and the harmony and contrasts of the colors. Or you may be one of the thousands who find relaxation in quilting—the restful repetition of the stitches in lovely material, and the satisfaction of sewing a fine seam.

The quilting craft, which is so deeply rooted in the home, offers a binder to hold its conflicting interests together. Father and the boys will find pleasure in making the quilting frame and its supporting stands, and in keeping them in top-notch condition. The girls can easily join in making the quilt blocks, and will enjoy stories about the pieces and patterns. Nor need the pleasure of group accomplishment be confined to the home. Quilting parties are just waiting to be revived and social groups can join in creating modern versions of the old friendship quilts. In making these quilts, friends vied with each other to create patterns of beauty and integrity, and today a quilt is most appropriate for a special occasion.

For welfare work, few things will bring more aid and comfort to a needy household than a warmly lined quilt. Parent-teacher groups or women's clubs will find in this craft a chance for satisfying a common effort toward a worthy goal.

With all these advantages, quilting stands high among the handicrafts. As a means of enjoyable self-expression, providing practical results at the same time, you will find it second to none.

MARGUERITE ICKIS

CONTENTS

THE STANDARD BOOK OF

QUILT MAKING
AND COLLECTING

1.

Planning Your Quilt

Y OU HAVE MADE UP YOUR MIND to make a quilt. But what *kind* will it be? Take a good look at your bed, and that will help you decide the whole matter. The kind of bed you have will determine the size of the quilt, the preferable number and size of its blocks, and the best-looking pattern for it.

THE BED, LARGE OR SMALL

If the bed is large, the quilt must be of generous proportions—perhaps the old-fashioned kind, but long enough to tuck up over the pillows— and it can show off to advantage the larger blocks with a design that is bold and lusty.

You may have a narrower, modern twin-size bed. Then a quilt with a smaller-scale design, smaller blocks and a slender border will be more appropriate. The motif should never be so emphatic in size and color as to dwarf the bed. There are so many ways to combine blocks, strips and borders, that it is easy to pick the right grouping to get the best relative effect for the shape of the bed.

Consider the Period

The period of your furniture must be considered, too. If your suite is French Provençal the bed would not look right covered with a sharp geometric Pennsylvania Dutch design. One of the softly wreathed figures with smaller blocks would be more suitable. And if you have a slender, carved-stem poster bed, you will not select a sturdy, "crazy-quilt," but a dainty appliqué pattern instead.

Not Too Dramatic

The quilt should take its proper place in the whole decorative scene of the room. It should accent but never drown out the other beauty spots about it. As a covering for the bed, it plays a dramatic role, but must harmonize in color and refinement with the color and proportions of the bedroom. In other words, your quilt must blend into its surroundings.

THE IMPORTANCE OF COLORS

Select your quilt colors carefully. You will use and live with this piece of your handiwork for a long time. It even pays to choose colors which you will enjoy sewing on, for colors *do* have their influence upon us, though they work quietly and subtly. Haven't you heard of colors affecting our emotions—by irritating or soothing, depressing or cheering us?

A color scheme works out in any one of these four ways:

1. The principles of color harmony in relation to other colors in the room.

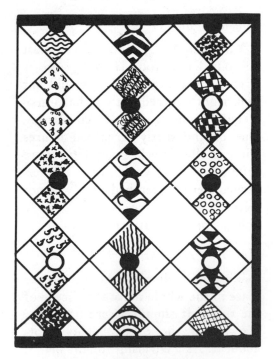

THE NECKTIE QUILT

Blocks are set diagonally, with pieced squares of Necktie pattern alternating with squares of solid color. The colors should harmonize with the color scheme of the bedroom.

2. According to the exposure of the room. A dark room needs light or warm colors.

3. Colors should harmonize with the period and the wood colors of the furniture.

4. Colors should repeat or blend with colors and designs of wallpaper and other decorations.

Color Harmony

After making a study of the colors in your room, you may have decided what will best harmonize with them. But what will be the proportion of the colors which you will introduce with your new quilt? A good plan is to have: (1) one dominant color, (2) one subordinate color, (3) one or more accent colors. In order to carry this out, you will like to have some knowledge of the color spectrum.

COLOR WHEEL

The Color Wheel (page 6) helps us to understand the relations of the various colors and how to combine them to best advantage. On the outer edge of the wheel we find standard colors arranged in order as they occur in the spectrum, and the more grayed ones as we approach the center which is neutral gray.

We see the order of the colors on the wheel. Red, yellow and blue are the *primary* or basic colors, and from them all others are made. The *secondary* colors stand between the primary colors on the wheel. Orange falls between red and yellow because it is a combination of the two; violet is a combination of red and blue, and

4

ROSE AND OAK LEAF QUILT

A modern setting is enhanced by the beauty of this quilt, owned by Gertrude Lawrence. The simple appliquéd pattern of red roses and green leaves on the white background is striking when displayed against the red leather upholstery of the head board. The famous Rose and Oak Leaf originated in the Ohio Valley, and is one of the most popular patterns copied today by modern quilt makers.

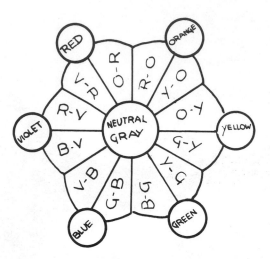

COLOR WHEEL

green of blue and yellow. The secondary colors then combine to produce *tertiary* colors.

Naming Colors

Going from red to orange on the wheel, we have orange-red until the half-way point is reached; then approaching orange we find red-orange. Thus, the predominating element of the color is named last.

WARM AND COOL COLORS

Warm. Red, orange, yellow and their variations. They are also known as the advancing colors.

Cool. Violet, blue and green. They are also called the receding colors.

Warm colors are more cheerful and stimulating than the cool colors, which, in turn, are calm and restful. It is possible to combine warm and cool colors, as long as the principles of harmony are employed. This may be done by choosing a pale shade of one of the primary colors—light blue, pink or yellow—for the background of the quilt and making the design of more striking colors.

The old appliquéd coverlets were usually made on a white background, and that simplified things, but this was because materials were scarce and the stores did not have the beautiful pastel shades we find today. We are really unlimited now in the possible play on color combinations.

Room Exposures

A room's exposure is a factor in deciding between a warm or cool effect in any decorating plans. North rooms have no direct sunlight, hence are said to have cool exposure: also northeast rooms because they have sun only during early morning hours. South and southwest are warm exposures. Rooms with both north and west windows have warm and cool light together; hence there is less need of definite attention to warm and cool effect.

Rooms on the north, and those on any side of the house which are deprived of light by shade trees or porch roofs can be helped immeasurably by throwing the emphasis on a cheerful, warm note in your decorative colors. It is surprising to see what the warm or cool colors can accomplish, and the colors of your quilt should be chosen accordingly.

Woods and Woodwork

The color tones in a room's furniture and woodwork are important. Maple, cherry and mahogany reflect warmer shades of color than oak and thus require a different selection of

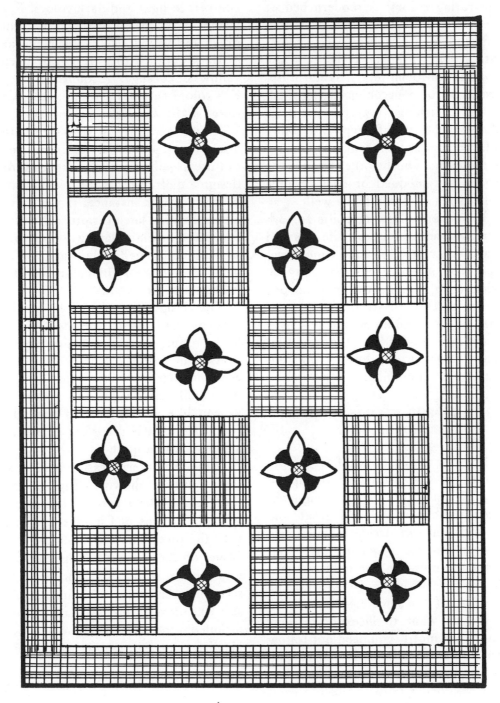

APPLIQUÉD ROSE PETAL DESIGN

This is an attractive quilt for a single bed, combining appliquéd floral blocks with delicate-toned plain blocks. It may be made in both the warm and cool colors of the room.

7

decorating colors. A modern bed of the new blond-wood finish looks better with a covering of deep colors rather than with neutral. If the woodwork is too definitely striking in appearance for a becoming background to the furnishings, it may be put in its place by the use of deep, rich colors splashed about the room, particularly in the quilts. On the other hand if the woods are subdued or dark, then a buff, peach or green looks well.

If you are planning quilts for adjoining rooms, it is desirable to avoid sharp contrasts, yet have enough variety for interest. A good way to achieve an easy transition from one to the other is to see that they have one color in common. It is clever sometimes to utilize the identical color combinations but in different patterns in the quilts.

QUILTS FOR ROOMS ALREADY DECORATED

For the room which has definite motifs in the wallpaper or upholstery, a quilt with a contrasting elaborate pattern would add great confusion. You can decide between two answers to the problem: carry out the same motif in the quilt pattern, or use a very simple design with one or more of the same colors.

If you want to incorporate your wallpaper motif, you need not follow out its minute details. It can be simplified by using the general outline and employing only one color; or it can be enlarged and used just once as the center design on the quilt.

You may also want to consider

contrast in light and dark colors. For instance, if the wallpaper is light green and yellow, your quilt could be of dark green with a design of deep yellow or orange. A quilt of deep rich colors enriches a room with pale tinted walls and light woodwork.

If your furniture is decorated with flowers or provincial patterns you can use a quilted white bedspread, or design a quilt that fits the decorations or period. For instance, if you have Pennsylvania Dutch furniture—either decorated or plain dark wood of that period, it immediately suggests a quilt of strong bright colors in red, yellow, blue or green.

The designs found on old chests, cabinets and quilts include hearts, birds, tulips, roses and quaint figures dressed in native costume. All these combine attractively in one design. Your quilt can be gay and elaborate as you like and still blend with the room, for that is the great charm of a Pennsylvania quilt.

A modern interpretation of one of these quilts is shown in Fig. 5, and there are quite a few of the Pennsylvania designs in Chapter 4, along with the directions for making them. Many of the old quilts were divided into squares with a different motif or scene in each block. The finished result was pleasing because each square included the same colors which blended them all together as a whole.

PERSONAL COLOR PREFERENCES

Color preferences of the individual are a large factor in deciding upon bedroom color schemes. One for a girl will be more or less feminine in taste according to her personality. For a boy, a more virile, masculine atmosphere is established. The "Neck-tie Pattern" is a popular one with boys. The room for parents usually shows some concessions to the tastes of each.

PENNSYLVANIA DUTCH QUILT

This well-known pattern is appliquéd in primary colors, using a peasant motif in the central wreath with hearts in each corner. The background is white, and the border very narrow. It is well suited for use in a room with plain dark woodwork.

EARLY CHINTZ QUILT

Blocks are pieced with chintz patches, and border and central cross design are appliquéd on white background.

2.

How To Make Your Quilt

AMONG THE FOLK ARTS, QUILT-ing is centuries old and yet it lives today with great vitality. That is because it is useful, economical and decorative. Any woman can make a quilt. All she needs is the ability to sew an ordinary seam, just a plain running stitch, done neatly and accurately. Even though you may be a beginner you will find it easy to make your first quilt. From then on you will constantly be on the lookout for new patterns and will have started saving your pieces for the next adventure.

Here are the most common terms used in quilt making:

Comforter. A quilt of one-color material. It consists of three layers of cover, fluffy wool or cotton inner lining and the back. The three are quilt-stitched together, in a simple or elaborate design.

Appliqué. This is sometimes called a "laid-on" quilt because the pieces in the design are cut out of different materials and laid on the plain background. They are secured in place with a fine hemming stitch, such as is used in hemming a skirt, and sometimes with the buttonhole stitch.

Patchwork. This usually refers to a "pieced" quilt, with the pieces cut in squares, triangles or diamonds and sewed together to form a design in a larger block.

Quilting stitch. This stitch serves to hold firmly together the three parts of the quilt—cover, lining and back (as in the comforter). It is made decorative by stitching in various patterns.

Block. Quilts are usually divided in parts to simplify sewing. The exception is the comforter. There may be four units or blocks, or many more. The block is a square, rectangle or hexagon. It is sometimes called a "patch" in a pieced quilt.

Setting. After the blocks are appliquéd or pieced, they are sewed together to form the quilt's design as a whole, and this is known as "setting" the quilt.

RUNNING STITCH

Begin at right, sewing toward left. Knot of thread is on under side of material. In quilting, take stitches about $\frac{1}{16}$ inch and space evenly.

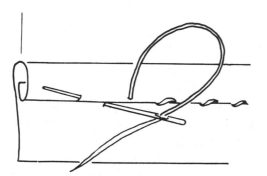

HEMMING STITCH

Sewing from right to left, the needle catches folded edge of hem to the material. Spacing varies according to material.

Blocking. This is simply pressing the quilt or its parts before and after its "setting."

MATERIALS

The amount of material you will need depends on the size of the bed. Old quilts were often square in shape —not easily adapted to a modern bed —and not made to pull up over the pillows. (If you have an old quilt, you may lengthen it by adding border strips to the top and bottom edges.) There must be enough material for the design pieces and the background of the cover and enough for the back of the quilt. Beds today are of standard size and the measuring can be done scientifically. In general, the decorated area comes to the edge of the bed on each side. It should be long enough to cover the pillows and hang down over the foot the same distance as it does on the sides. The width of the border will be according to taste. It can be very deep, medium or narrow, depending on the style of the quilt's design.

Not only the size of the bed but also the width of the material will govern the amount needed. Beds of standard sizes come in the following widths:

Double bed	54 inches
Three-quarter	49 inches
Twin bed	39 inches
Single bed	36 inches

Almost all materials suitable for making quilts come in a width of 36 inches. (Occasionally you find muslin that is 39 inches wide, and if you buy sheeting by the yard, you can get it as wide as 72 inches.)

As for the width of the border, three factors must be considered to determine the best measurement. The border should be wide enough but not too wide to "balance" or look suitable with the quilt's design. You will need a wider border if the springs and mattress of the bed are deep. Also the most economical use of your material is desirable.

An Estimate

Now let us see, having stated the problem, if we can get an estimate of material required. As a start, we might begin with the standard length of a sheet, which is usually 108 inches, and figure on a border 18 inches wide. Suppose the quilt is to be divided into blocks each 14 inches square. This is a good size for distributing the blocks in a quilt designed for any type of bed.

Double bed. Four squares will be needed to fit across the quilt and five to cover its length, making 20 in all.

Three-quarter bed. The same measurements as for the double bed's quilt will fit this size, for the extra 3-inch drop over the sides will make little difference in its appearance.

Twin bed. A good division for this bed is 3 blocks across and 5 for the length, making 15 in all.

Single bed. The same measurements as for the twin bed will approximately fit this size.

After determining in the manner just explained how many blocks it will take to cover the bed, you can estimate the amount of background material you will need.

Double or three-quarter bed. 4¼ yards to cut 20 squares. (There will be an 8-inch waste on one side.)

3 yards to cut an 18-inch border for each side, and an additional 54 inches for the border on the two ends.

This makes a total of 8¾ yards plus 2 inches. To allow for seams, you will need 9 yards.

Twin or single bed. 3⅛ yards to cut 15 squares. (There will be an 8-inch waste on one side.)

3 yards to cut an 18-inch border for each side, and an additional 39 inches for the border on the two ends.

This makes a total of 7¼ yards needed, allowing several inches for seams.

In computing the amount of material needed in any quilt, you must first divide it into units as we did above and estimate the number of yards it will take to cut each size block. This is because there is usually a certain amount of waste in order to cut the blocks to proper size.

To estimate the amount of material needed for each color in the design, take the following steps:

1. Make a paper pattern of each unit of the block design, allowing ¼ inch for seams.

2. Divide patterns according to the colors in the design.

3. After the colors are separated, take a piece of paper a yard wide and trace as close together as possible the number of pieces of one color you need for one block. Trace in the same way the pieces for the other colors, each on a separate piece of paper.

4. Measure the space it takes for each color and multiply by the number of blocks in the quilt.

KINDS OF MATERIALS

The first rule to observe in selecting material for a quilt is to combine the same kinds of fabrics together on any one design. For instance, linens and cottons go together, silks and satins, and so on, to achieve an overall effect of regularity. If you choose a fabric that can be laundered, be sure that it is pre-shrunk and all the colors are *fast.* If you are in doubt, test a small piece in the tub.

For your convenience in sewing, select a soft material, not too closely woven, both for the background and for the design part of your quilt. Closely woven cloth makes the needlework more difficult and is no stronger than thinner goods. There are more threads in each inch of cloth but the threads are of equal strength. Materials that are stiff because of being "treated" with a dressing are also difficult to work on.

In general, the following materials are a good selection for any patchwork quilts:

Body of quilt. Muslin (first choice), linen, broadcloth, cambric or percale.

Designs. Gingham, percale, calico, shirting, or broadcloth.

Of course you may make your quilt of silk, woolen, or sateen. The block background and pieces in the design must be of the same material. One last word of warning: measure all your materials carefully and be sure that you have too much rather than too little. Colors are exceedingly hard to match, even in the same shade from another bolt.

CUTTING

Cutting is one of the important steps in making your quilt. You must be precise and accurate in order to have the pattern perfect and to avoid wasting your goods. Lay the pattern on carefully. Also have sharp scissors, with blades at least 4 inches long. You will need a ruler for marking straight lines, and a pencil with hard lead to avoid blurry marks around the pattern. With these tools at hand, proceed as follows:

1. Cut a cardboard pattern ¼ inch larger than the design you have traced to allow for seams. (See directions for drafting pattern on page 16.) Smooth edges with sandpaper. Mark the number of pieces you need in each block on top of pattern to save referring to design while in the process of cutting.

2. Press all materials perfectly smooth to eliminate wrinkles. That includes small scraps as well.

3. Lay cardboard pattern on material and trace around it with pencil. Be sure the long part of the pattern runs with the warp thread—lengthwise threads (Fig. 1).

Fig. 1

TRACING DESIGN ON MATERIAL

Long part of design pattern must run with the warp thread—lengthwise of the material.

4. Allow ⅛ inch between pattern pieces for space in cutting as you repeat the marking of the pattern. Begin at one end of material and continue marking by going from left to right (Fig. 2). If the design parts are irregular, fit them together as economically as possible, always allowing for cutting space between.

5. Be sure your warp and weft

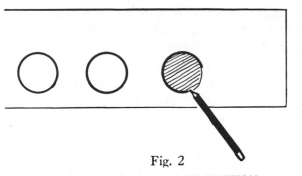

Fig. 2

REPEATING DESIGN ON MATERIAL

Begin at left end of goods and move towards right. Leave enough space between marking to give ease in cutting.

threads always run the same way, particularly if the material is striped.

6. After pattern is traced, cut pieces out carefully along your penciled lines.

7. Divide all patches according to shape and color and string them together by running a single thread through the center of each (Fig. 3). This will keep them from being lost, and will aid your sewing.

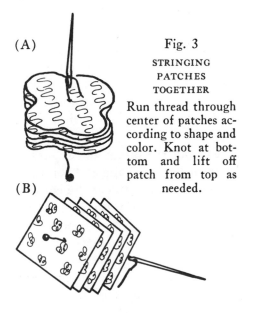

(A)

(B)

Fig. 3

STRINGING PATCHES TOGETHER

Run thread through center of patches according to shape and color. Knot at bottom and lift off patch from top as needed.

8. Cut out the entire quilt before sewing if you are in doubt as to the amount of material in any one color.

To cut stems such as are used in appliqué, cut bias strips 1 to 1½ inches wide after drawing diagonal pencil lines across material (Fig. 4). Your ruler will be helpful. Turn the edges of the strips down and baste in place. Press with warm iron before sewing.

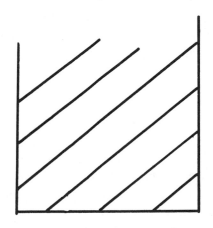

Fig. 4

BIAS STRIPS FOR STEMS

Draw diagonal pencil lines on material with help of ruler. Turn down and baste edges of strips before appliquéing.

It will help you in all these steps if you have ample space for spreading out your materials, such as a table or bread board. The tracing of the patterns will be more accurate if you have a surface to work on which is smooth and hard to resist the pressure of the pencil. A good light is also helpful. The accuracy of the tracing and cutting is very important to the quality of your finished design.

SEWING

We have discussed the simple stitches employed in quilt making—the running stitch used in piecing parts of the design together and also used as the quilt stitch, and the hemming stitch used in appliqué work. Occasionally the buttonhole stitch is substituted for this hemming stitch if you wish to emphasize a part of the appliquéd pattern.

As for using the sewing machine, old-time quilters frown on anything but the finest hand sewing. However, it may well serve a purpose after you have finished the individual blocks by hand. If you use the machine to set the blocks together, it will save time and will strengthen the long straight seams. You will find that the tiny pieces are difficult to handle on the machine, and also machine stitches make your quilt stitching almost impossible later on. Your quilt stitching will usually follow the seams between the patches as you finish the quilt, and the needle cannot penetrate the close stitches made by the machine.

The directions for sewing the quilt will be simpler to understand if we consider the two types—appliqué and patchwork—separately, for each kind involves a different technique. The appliquéd quilt is often inspired by a flower or fruit motif and there is greater freedom of design than in the piecing of small parts of the patchwork block.

DIRECTIONS FOR MAKING AN APPLIQUÉD QUILT

Appliqué is the method of applying one material to another by means of the hemming, appliqué stitch. The stitches are taken only after the edges of the pattern are turned under and basted in place neatly and evenly and after they have been pressed smooth. After you have mastered this simple technique, no quilt is too difficult to make, if you follow the directions in detail. If you choose your colors successfully and cut and sew the pattern carefully, you will have a beautiful design. It is the accuracy and delicacy of your appliquéing of each patch which will distinguish your work.

Drafting the Pattern

The first step in appliqué is to draft a pattern for the design. We have explained the use of carbon paper in tracing the pattern and getting it on to a substantial piece of cardboard. Smoothing the cardboard edges with sandpaper makes it easier to use in all your subsequent steps. You proceed as follows:

1. Make sure that you have allowed ¼ inch on all sides of each part of your cardboard design. You will need that for turned in edges. Lay them on your material and trace around the outside edges with a hard lead pencil.

2. Cut out the pieces and separate them according to shape and color. It is just as important to cut the correct size and shape for the appliquéd pieces as for the patchwork pieces.

3. Turn down the edges of each patch ¼ inch and crease the turned edges in place with the thumb and forefinger. On corners and sharp

turns you will have to make small cuts or notches about ⅛ inch deep in order to keep the outline of the design from stretching (Fig. 5). Baste the edges as you turn them, using a fairly long loose stitch. Press smooth with a warm iron. See Fig. 6. Since the bastings must be removed, always have the knot in the thread *on top* of the patch so that it may be pulled out easily. The bastings are easier to see if you use white thread.

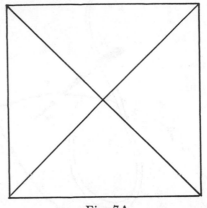

Fig. 7A

FOLDING BLOCK FOR CREASES

After folding block diagonally, press creases in with warm iron. The center point of the block is thus placed.

Fig. 5—NOTCHED EDGES

Tiny notches are snipped in places for ease in turning.

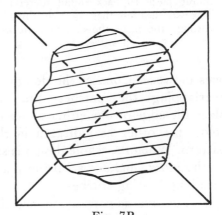

Fig. 7B

PLACING DESIGN CORRECTLY

Creases help to correctly place design in center of block.

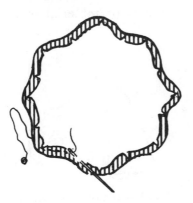

Fig. 6—BASTING TURNED OVER EDGES FOR APPLIQUÉ

Baste fairly loosely, and have knot on top side of material.

4. Next, the design parts must be assembled on the block and attached in the right place. In order to achieve uniformity on each block, crease the block square and press with the iron (Fig. 7). Creasing will divide the block into four equal parts and the lines will serve as a guide of laying on the patches. Always place the large patches first and fit the smaller

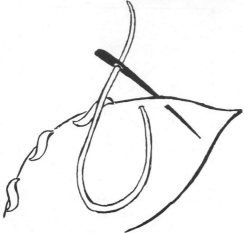

Fig. 8—APPLIQUÉ STITCH

Sew as in the hemming stitch, right to left, and catching folded edge of appliqué piece to background material. Take stitches less than $\frac{1}{8}$ inch, thread through top piece showing as little as possible.

ones between. Connect the design by overlapping the patches—that is, place the edge of one either above or below the other as indicated in the pattern. When the whole design is set on the block, make it secure in place with long basting stitches.

5. You are now ready to sew the patches to the background material. Use a short needle, size No. 8, and sew with small appliqué stitches, having the longer part of the stitch on the wrong side and barely catching the edge of the patch (Fig. 8). The buttonhole stitch is often used to emphasize an important feature of the design (Fig. 9). Sew down patches first which are supposed to come underneath another part. Use thread in color matching the patch.

6. For stems and connecting lines, bias strips are used and no pattern is necessary. The bias strip should be cut the width needed for the design with the usual $\frac{1}{4}$ inch on either side for turning under. When a bias strip is applied on a curved line, it is best to baste first along the inside edge. The material can then be stretched until it lies flat along the outer edge and will be smooth and even, without gathers.

7. After the sewing is completed, press the block on the underside with a warm iron. Use a soft pad or Turkish towel for the pressing to keep the design from flattening.

DIRECTIONS FOR PATCHWORK

Patchwork is the art of joining small pieces of material in patterns

Fig. 9—BUTTONHOLE STITCH

Begin at left and sew toward the right, looping thread below needle on each stitch.

CONVENTIONAL TULIP PATTERN

This colorful quilt has large blocks appliquéd with rose and pink tulips, with formal green leaves. The border is of exceptional interest, and the appliqué pattern joining the blocks is unusually effective.

using diamonds, triangles, squares, and similar shapes. It is important that all pieces are cut accurately, allowing ¼ inch for seams, and that they are joined together with the run-

ning stitch as evenly as possible. The success of the finished design depends not only on careful cutting and sewing together but on the color harmony of the whole. If scraps from

19

mixed colors are used they should be chosen with taste and equally distributed in all sections of the quilt.

Here are a few simple rules for the patchwork quilt:

1. Draft your pattern, allowing ¼ inch all around for the seams.

2. Use a No. 60 thread and a short needle, No. 8. A long needle is not necessary, for very few stitches are taken on such small pieces before drawing the needle through the material. Use white thread unless the patches are cut from very dark cloth. Unlike appliqué, patchwork does not require thread in matching colors.

3. It is important to have small pieces pressed smoothly to facilitate cutting as well as stitching together. Place pattern on cloth and trace around the outline with a hard lead pencil. Cut out each piece as accurately as possible.

4. Separate the patches according to size and shape, and string them together (Fig. 3). Some quilt makers prefer to sort them as they will be needed in assembling each block.

5. Sew patches together with small running stitches and secure each short seam as it is finished with at least two back stitches. The seams should be ¼ inch deep, and sewed as straight as possible.

6. In piecing the block, sew several patches together at a time to form a small section of the design. Fit sections together and see that the corners of adjoining pieces match exactly. In order to have it perfectly accurate, tack the corners together with a few over-stitches. Sew the sec-

tions together with the usual ¼ inch seam.

7. After the block is pieced, press it on the wrong side with a warm iron. Press the seams flat—not open.

If the quilt is made from many colored scraps, remember to alternate light and dark shades. Distribute patches according to color rather than print of material. It is better to finish sewing all the separate blocks before setting them together. In that way, you may be surer to get a uniform distribution of the colors.

SETTING THE QUILT

Press the blocks and lay them out on the bed to get the final effect before setting them together. If they do not cover the entire area of the bed, you will have to do something about it: (1) If the quilt is not wide enough, strips of material of white or colors may be used. Perhaps you have enough material left to piece and add an extra row of blocks. (2) If the quilt is too wide, use as deep a seam as possible in sewing blocks together. Be careful not to take the seams in the design of the blocks.

Next check your border to see if it is correct for width. It should be in balance with the design, and neither add to or detract from the main decorative part of the quilt. As you survey the blocks laid out on the bed, remember they are not yet sewed together and that the seams, when they are finished, will each account for taking up ¼ inch. This affects the fitting of the border, both as to length and breadth.

If you are satisfied with the blocks

and the measurements of the border, you will proceed with setting the blocks together. The best way is to join all the blocks of one row, sewing them with a ¼ inch seam. Continue joining blocks in one row at a time. This should really be done by hand, especially if you are sewing a pieced block. It is easier to keep the pattern accurate and the corners matched by hand, rather than on the machine. Sewing the rows of blocks can be successfully done by machine if you tack the corners together ahead of time with several overcast stitches. You may like to baste the long seams before using the machine.

In sewing on the border strips, begin with the shorter pieces of the top and bottom first. Baste them before stitching. Baste the side border pieces and stitch on.

BLOCKING THE QUILT

The term "blocking" means keeping the edges straight on all sides of the quilt so that it will be a perfect rectangle when finished. The term applies to the quilt's divisions and blocks, and also to the border, so the process of blocking is a continuing process from start to finish.

Right at the start, it will help your blocking if you have cut the pieces and blocks according to the warp and weft threads in the material, as we discussed it in the section on Cutting. Observance of this rule eliminates the tendency to pucker. It is helpful, if your material tears easily, to tear off strips the width of the blocks, then separate into individual blocks. For ease in cutting, draw a

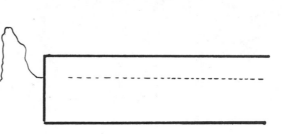

Fig. 10

DRAWING THREAD IN MATERIAL

By drawing out one or two threads of material, cutting in a straight line is made easier.

thread out where your scissors will have to cut (Fig. 10).

Pull the edges of the block straight with the fingers and pin the corners to the ironing board to hold them rigidly in place. Cover the block with a damp cloth and press with a warm iron. Do not iron the cloth *dry,* but use it more for steaming instead. Press the edges until they are perfectly straight and of equal measurements. The center is pressed last.

Plenty of Pressing

It is a good idea to press your blocks before the design is attached and then after the sewing is completed. This is also true of the border and of any section of the quilt. This means quite a lot of pressing, but it assures you of more accuracy in the final measurement of all units. After the quilt is set together, it will need a final blocking before it is ready to be quilted to the lining and back.

There will be an entire chapter to explain quilting, lining and binding the quilt.

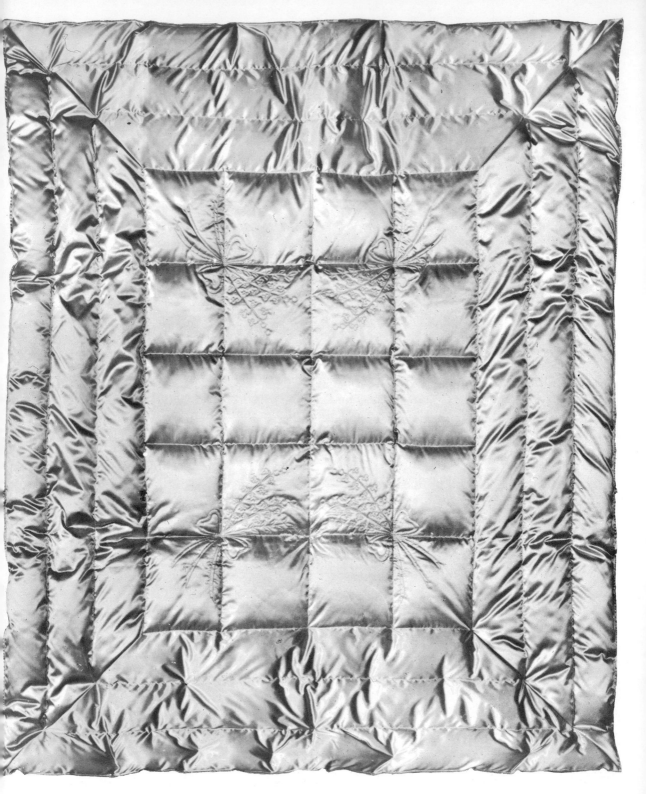

FINE SILK COMFORTER

This downy comforter is quilted in straight border lines, with squares in the center decorated with quilted bows and blossoms.

3.

The Quilt's Design and Its Parts

WE HAVE CONSIDERED MANY points which influence the choice of design in planning a quilt—the size and type of the bed, the period of the furniture, the color scheme and decorative designs of the bedroom, and even the light and exposure of the room.

You may know now exactly how long and how wide your quilt is to be, and the colors which you will use. The design may be a dainty one or bold and striking, according to its suitability. But before going any further, perhaps there are some elements in design which you would like to use in carrying out the details of your quilt. The details of appliquéd and patchwork quilts have been explained, but there are many interesting ways of using these methods.

Elements of Design

Entering into your general artistic design will be the elements of rhythm, balance, repetition and suitability.

For *rhythm* you must have lines or curves, or you can combine the two if you do it wisely. A wreath of flowers or a spray of feathers has rhythm, but you would not combine either with a straight-lined border. Nor would a pieced quilt of geometric lines look well set in a border of curves and circles.

The design of the quilt has *balance* if the sides match and the ends are alike. If there is a square figure or floral pattern in one corner, the same figure is placed in each corner to give balance to the whole. Our grandmothers made quilts of good design because they seemed to possess a native sense of balance. They also used *repetition* of their patterns to the best advantage. Even a poor design becomes pleasing in the orderly repetition of its color and motifs.

The *suitability* of any object of art or utility is a question of its looking right in its surroundings. Does its design suit its use and purpose? Anything which takes weeks to make, as a quilt does, is worth planning care-

WREATH AND STAR QUILT

This pattern of central floral wreaths and eight-pointed star is entirely appliquéd and its flow of rhythm is carried out in the curves of border sprays. The flowers are rose colored and leaves are green. As shown here, the quilt is beautifully suited to the modern bed.

fully and your good taste will reap its reward if your quilt turns out to be "at home" in your bedroom.

THE SOURCES OF DESIGNS

Our grandmothers were not always fortunate in their choice of designs. There are old quilts resting in museums which portray events of a presidential campaign, or some unusual happening of state or home county. They sometimes used subjects such as animals, birds, houses or vegetables, but you will agree that these designs look more appropriate when applied to the kitchen curtains or a luncheon cloth.

When grandmother went into the garden or even the barnyard for her designs the results were more appealing. The flowers, vines, trees and leaves from the garden were beautiful creations when transferred to the quilts in her bedrooms. And the rooster's feather developed into one of the most favored of all ideas, for from it came the basic scroll or wreath-like spray. The "feather" is seen in borders and odd shaped areas where a more formal design would not be acceptable. Also, there is the picket fence, the sunflower and the trellis—all from the familiar backyard.

Making Your Own Designs

You may be clever enough to make up your own patterns. There are many ways of folding paper and experimenting with trick cuts. Cut a square of paper the size of the design you want and fold it through the center each way, to form four small squares. Either draw a design in one corner or make random cuts with the scissors. Cut all four corners at the same time and when it is unfolded you will have a design repeated four times. Copy the figures from a print dress or necktie. These are usually simple and easy to enlarge. There is no limit to design sources, if you have ideas and imagination.

SPACE FOR QUILTING

In the master plan for your quilt, keep in mind the space where there will be no decoration except the quilt stitching. After your blocks are pieced they will be set together with plain blocks or strips, sometimes allowing a wide area between the center design and the border. Because the cotton interlining must be held firmly in place, the quilt stitching must be quite closely designed to hold it. There should be no large areas without quilt stitching. In quilting the pieced blocks remember not to quilt *over* the pieced design, but around the outline to make it stand out somewhat in relief. Do not worry about the seams in the back of your quilt, as they will all disappear when the quilt stitching is done. The pattern for the quilting should harmonize with the pieced or appliqued pattern.

HOW TO AVOID SEWING PROBLEMS

All your sewing problems will be simpler if you pick an easy design for your quilt. Too often an elaborate design presents difficulties which an

THE PATTERN SHOWING BALANCE

An appliquéd central figure of tulips is repeated in each corner to give balance to the whole. The scalloped border reflects the curving lines of the flower theme, maintaining the element of rhythm.

expert needlewoman could not master. In appliqué, a design with long lines and gentle curves is easy to turn down and baste, whereas small cut outs and tiny pieces are hard to handle.

Soft materials, too, make sewing easier. Avoid too closely woven cloth or fabric which has been treated with a dressing. Each stitch of the needle is made difficult with such material. There are also some materials which have a thin warp thread and heavy weft thread, and these fray badly when they are cut. You will remember to keep to the same materials throughout the quilt.

A MODERN TYPE OF QUILT

Perhaps the best choice for a *modern* type of quilt is the large center design. It can be feminine and dainty or bold and striking. It calls for a matching border, often in scallops.

You may like a large oval as the center design, with flowers and leaves at intervals around the edge. The two ends must balance, as do the two sides. The center of the oval is quilted as a rule, and you may include an initial in the center of the quilting design. Using a pattern scattered at intervals in the border is a time saver and still gives an attractive effect.

For the twin or single bed, a very suitable design is the rectangle, with small rectangles in each corner. A large square design in the center similarly calls for small squares repeated in the corners.

It is always an excellent idea to try out a paper design on your bed, to get an idea of the best size and shape. Cut a piece of paper for the center design. Fold it in quarters and draw the pattern on the top fold. After the pattern is drawn, cut around the edge and be sure to cut all four folds at the same time. Unfold it and see how it looks for your center design.

A Basket of Flowers

A basket of flowers is a favorite pattern for the center of a quilt, and it will give you a chance to be original and run riot with colors. Draw the basket first and proportion it so that it covers not more than ¼ of the whole design. The body of the basket should be open lattice work made of bias tape in a color that will harmonize with the background of the quilt and not be repeated in the flowers. A solid basket is too heavy unless it is made small. Fill the basket with any flowers suggested by the size and color of your scraps. Remember the arrangement of the blossoms in the basket is important—they are there to stay. They should be large and small, tall and short, and have a few sprays to balance the design. It also gives balance if you use the same colors on each side of the basket. Repeat some of the blossoms in the border design and bind the finished quilt in the color of the basket.

The basket design is not only attractive but it serves in an artistic way as an effective focal point. In using other large center designs—the oval, square or rectangle—it is sometimes necessary to find a way of making it seem related to the quilt as a whole. Otherwise, the appearance is that of being laid in the center as an unrelated piece. This can be done with an oval design by drawing an outline of the oval itself, an inch or ¾-inch wide, and attaching flowers and leaves to the stem. If the pattern is a square or rectangle, it can be "framed" with a narrow straight piece around the outer edge, or have connecting lines in the center.

Dividing the Quilt in Four Squares

Many of the old quilts were divided into four squares that called for a large, elaborate pattern. This provided space for a design that could be broken up into a number of units, or a single motif to be repeated several times, as shown in the beautiful "Maiden Hair Fern Quilt" see page 254). Quilts of this kind are striking and especially effective on a poster bed. Any of the patterns given in the next chapter are adaptable for this type by using enlarged squares, but only the more elaborate designs should be chosen. In general, wreath designs are not too successful used this way, except the "Wreath of Grapes" which works out very well.

PLAIN QUILTED AREAS

Since using four squares makes a square quilt, you will have to add a plain piece of material at the top and bottom to make it long enough to cover the pillows and still hang over the foot of the bed. This plain area can be quilted and will lend interest to the entire design. There will also be quite a large plain space in the center of the quilt where corners of the

four squares meet, and this calls for a special quilting design.

To decide on the size of each square, measure the width of the bed and divide it in half. Cut four squares to this measurement. The edge of the design should come to the edge of the bed. Make the border at least 18 inches wide and decorate it in a design adapted to the one used in the squares.

SETTING QUILTS IN SQUARES

The majority of quilts are made in square blocks and sewed together after they are completed. Each block may have a pieced design or it may be alternated with a plain block. You will find both types interesting. The quilts in squares are popular because they are easy to handle and sew. A small design is less difficult to cut and stitch, and a 14-inch square is easy to hold while stitching.

Diagonal Blocks

In some patterns the squares of the quilt are set diagonally because of the nature of the design. This is illustrated in the "Necktie Quilt." The bows of the ties are less confusing if they are set in a straight line up and down the quilt. If the squares were set straight, the ties would fall diagonally. This is true of many patchwork quilts and of a few in the appliqué section, so you should study the design before deciding on the setting. The plain squares used for alternating are cut the same size as the decorated ones, and the triangles that fill in the outside edge are made

THE FOUR-BLOCK QUILT WITH BORDER

Four large rectangular blocks make up this quilt. They are appliquéd with formal flowers and leaves in light and dark shades, and the border is a narrow strip of contrasting material.

by folding a square diagonally and cutting along the crease.

THE BORDER

Your border may be planned in a number of ways—there is no set rule. Many old quilts simply had an extra row of blocks added to each side, making a continuous design with no set border. A narrow binding in one of the colors used in the design served as an edge. Quite often they had a border decoration altogether foreign to the one in the quilt as shown on page 31, such as streamer of ribbons with bow ties, or curved lines with leaves on either side.

However, there are several basic rules to follow in planning the border: (1) Separate the quilt top and the border with a strip 2 inches wide (½ inch is for seams) in one of the design's colors. (2) Cut the border a few inches wider than one of the squares to give a better balance to the design. (18-inch borders go well with 14-inch squares.) (3) If the border decoration is in a continuous line, you must adapt the design to connect at the corners in some appropriate manner.

QUILTS SET WITH STRIPS

Some patterns are enhanced by sewing a colored strip from 3 to 5 inches wide between the blocks, particularly if more is needed in the quilt. The strips also serve to tie the whole design together. After cutting the strips, sew them between the blocks and around the edge next to the border, making a frame work all around the blocks. This makes the design in the central area rather heavy, and, in order to lighten it, you may add a plain, wide border. Use a plain band at the bottom for binding in the same width and color as the center strips. If the pattern in the squares is light and feathery, a plain scalloped border should be used to continue its delicate nature.

Variations

You may use a plain white material for cutting the strips, or any color which you wish to emphasize in the quilt. In colors, a lighter shade is preferable to a darker if you do not want the whole to be too striking. You may like the strips in a light color with a small square in a darker shade placed at the corners of the blocks where the strips cross. Another variation is to set the blocks together with white strips and place a square of print material at the intersections.

Not Enough Blocks?

Using strips often solves the problem when you do not have sufficient blocks. Suppose you find a partially pieced quilt left by your grandmother and have no matching material to finish it. This is a good time to use strips. Count the number of blocks you have and estimate the width of the strips you will need to make a full width quilt.

If the design in the blocks is simple, the connecting strips may be decorated with patchwork or appliqué, but the whole scheme should be kept simple rather than complex, with a repeat of one or more colors found in the design. In this way the whole design

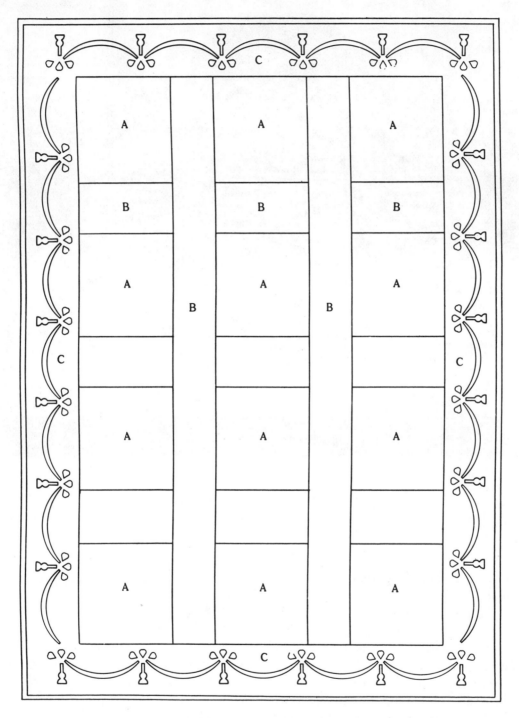

A DIAGRAM FOR BLOCKS, STRIPS AND BORDER

The square blocks (A) are put together with short and long connecting strips (B), and the border (C) is a narrow band of appliquéd ribbons and bows.

QUILT WITH CONTRASTING STRIPS

The large appliquéd pattern blocks are joined together with three strips of white and figured material. Smaller squares are set at the strip intersections.

will be blended together and not divided up into units.

Another advantage of using strips for setting blocks is to give a plain area for quilting designs. Old quilting stitch patterns such as the "Feather," "Pumpkin Seed," and "Cable" are adaptable for long, narrow spaces. Small formal designs are also good for the squares at the strip intersections.

QUILTS MADE IN STRIPES

It is surprising how few of the old quilts were made in stripes that run lengthwise with the bed. You will find a striped effect very suitable for a modern bed, looking more in place than the squared or continuous patterns. The general plan for making a striped quilt is to cut strips of white muslin 10 or 12 inches wide and use

RECTANGULAR BLOCKS WITH JOINING STRIPS

The small appliquéd flowers are made of light and dark scraps from the rag bag.
The nine blocks are joined by strips of a contrasting color, and the border has three
bands of alternating material.

them for a running appliquéd design. After the sewing is completed, they are set together with alternating strips of plain material such as pale blue, pink, green or yellow. This quilt requires no border. It will harmonize perfectly with the long, low lines and simplicity of modern furnishings.

Fine Effects

An exceptionally fine example among famous patterns is the "Wild Geese Quilt" in Chapter 4. The pieced stripes are made of a row of succeeding triangles that represent geese in flight. The large triangles can be of one color set together with two white ones between, or they can be cut from mixed prints and calicos. In fact, this is an excellent pattern for using up your scrap pieces, for the broad plain alternating stripes will neutralize the colors and give an unusual effect to the quilt as a whole.

USE OF SCRAP MATERIALS

A jumbled assortment of fabrics can be reduced to order and, with forethought, can be used in an effective design. On the subject of assorted fabrics, the nearly forgotten "rag bag" comes to mind—that Victorian collector of odds and ends of materials of all sizes, shapes and colors, which the twentieth century quilter might revive with profit.

Each patch must be placed carefully according to color and print in order to achieve a design of beauty and dignity. The first step is to sort the scraps according to light and dark shades and then again into various colors. Your problem will be to fit them into a design without disturbing the balance—that is, there must be an equal number of dark and light pieces. The proportion you use of each will determine whether your quilt is bold and striking, or of a more delicate design.

Contrast in Patches

If the design is restless, you might alternate the mixed patches with ones in a plain color. Print material, such as old-fashioned calico, may be used for the same purpose if the figure is small and on a colored background. If the design itself is made entirely of mixed patches you should inject one color, preferably of plain material that will appear in the same position on each block. For instance, in the fan design, mixed materials are cut into small pieces to form the fan, but all the handles should be the same color, thus tying the design together as a whole.

4.

Patterns and How To Use Them

THERE ARE OVER 40 FULL-SIZED patterns of outstanding quilts in this chapter. Each quilt is described and instructions are given fully for making it, but before you undertake your favorite pattern these general suggestions will be helpful:

DRAFTING THE PATTERN

The patterns given on the following pages usually fit on a block 14 inches square. You should cut a paper square of this size and then cut a paper pattern of each design unit and place them on the block to be sure they are the correct size.

After you have selected a quilt you wish to make, cover the pattern with a piece of tracing paper and draw around the outline with a soft lead pencil (Fig. 1).

Transfer the pattern to a piece of thin cardboard by placing a piece of carbon paper between the tracing paper and cardboard. Remove the tracing paper and carbon, and draw a line ¼ inch from the outer edges on all sides to allow for turnins or seams (Fig. 2).

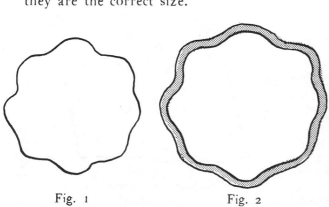

Fig. 1   Fig. 2

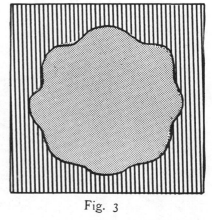

Fig. 3

Cut out the cardboard pattern and smooth the edges with sandpaper. Lay the pattern on the material you wish to use for each unit and trace around the edge with a lead pencil (Fig. 3).

ESTIMATING AMOUNT OF MATERIALS

The amount of material suggested for each quilt is for a *double bed*. If you want to make a quilt for a twin or single sized bed, you will need 1½ yards less of white background material and you will have to estimate the amount to deduct for each color used in the design.

The amount of background material suggested is for a quilt made up of twenty blocks, 14 inches square, with an 18-inch border around the edge. The outside measurements for the finished quilt would be 88 inches wide and 108 inches long.

The quantity of material suggested for the design includes an extra amount in the main colors for use in the border decoration.

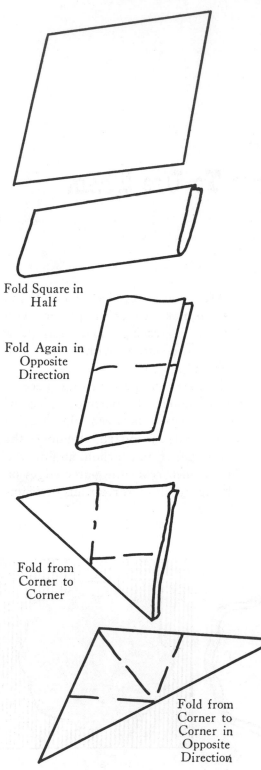

Fold Square in Half

Fold Again in Opposite Direction

Fold from Corner to Corner

Fold from Corner to Corner in Opposite Direction

Creases Shown from Various Folding

PLACING DESIGN UNITS ON BLOCK

In order to place the units in a uniform position on each block, you must fold it (sometimes diagonally) each way through the center; or some patterns require second center folds. The folds are creased with a warm iron and the lines will serve as a guide for placing the units. See diagrams on page 36 for making the folds.

Always place the large or most important units on the block first and then add the smaller units, using the background creases as a guide.

It is important that the patches are placed in exactly the same position on each block throughout the quilt.

BASKET PATTERN QUILT

BASKET PATTERNS WERE PRIME FAvorites among the quilt designs of the last century. In a great majority of these designs, the basket itself and the intricacy of its woven structure were considered interesting enough in themselves to make the picture pattern complete. Some of the traditional baskets had handles and some did not.

The quilt illustrated is a fascinating and colorful variation of the basket pattern and, from the geometric quality of its design, is a quilt that would be surely as at home on a bed of modern design as it was on a simple four-poster.

This particular design combines two quilt techniques, that of the pieced pattern and the appliqué. Here we find the body of the basket pieced and then, together with the handles and the flowers, appliquéd to the plain background block.

The selection of flowers to ornament the basket is at the discretion and taste of the designer. All the flowers in the baskets can be the same but some people prefer a variation of flowers in each of the baskets in the quilt or in a section of the quilt. A variety of flowers will test the skill and the color sense of the designer. Some knowledge of color values and harmonies will be of great aid when planning this quilt.

Knowledge of flowers, their form and size, height and disposition of their foliage and some attention to traditional flower arrangement will be of assistance in assuring symmetry and harmony in the over-all basket quilt. Your own garden and the easily procured seed catalogues will provide numerous and authentic details for transfer into quilt design.

Materials Needed

9 yards white background material
3 yards material for basket (blue, green, brown)
Scrap materials for flowers

Units in Each Square

Unit No. 1 . . . 11 colored triangles and 7 white triangles
Unit No. 2 . . . 1 colored handle (Bias strip)

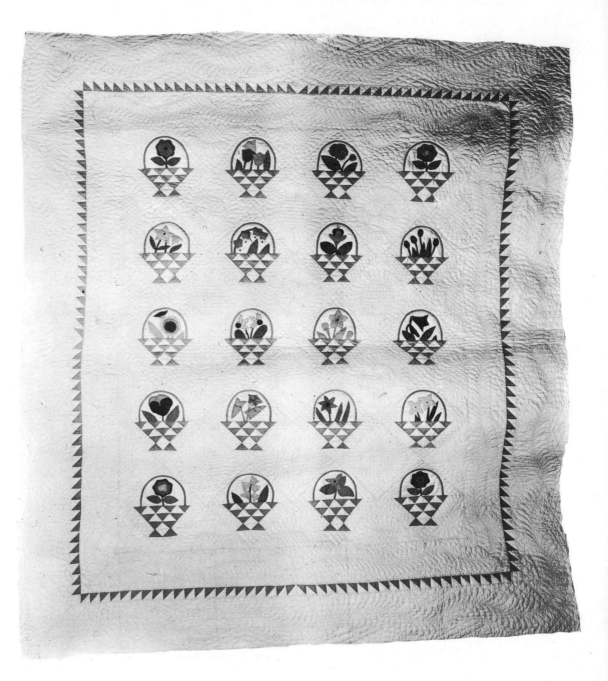

BASKET PATTERN QUILT

Sewing Directions

Sew together alternating dark and white triangles with ¼ inch seams to form the basket. Turn in outside edges and baste in place on the block.

Cut a bias strip ¾ inch wide for a handle. Turn in edges on both sides and baste in place on the basket. Baste the *inside* of the handle in place first and stretch the outer edge to make it lie flat.

Fill the baskets with any flowers you choose, cut from scrap materials. Keep the designs balanced and place only a few flowers in each basket.

After all units are assembled, ap-pliqué the basket, handle and flowers to background block with thread in matching colors.

Border

The saw tooth row between the quilt and border is made from triangles of white and colors to match the basket. Piece the triangles together and sew to the quilt edge. Add border strips in any width you need to hang over the edge of the bed. We suggest you add another row of pieced triangles along the outer edge to give a finished effect to the quilt.

Quilting Suggestions

Since there are large white areas between the baskets, a quilt stitching wreath of feathers or leaves can be used as shown in the photograph. Quilt around the outside edges of the flowers and basket handles and along the seams of the triangles in the basket. Fill in background with small quilted diamonds or squares.

TREE OF LIFE QUILT

THE TREE OF LIFE QUILT

IN EARLY AMERICAN DAYS CLIPPER ships brought cargoes of Indian and Persian cotton prints into western Atlantic ports and these fabrics enjoyed a great vogue. When quilt designers were casting afield for pattern ideas, the Tree of Life design from the Orient was conventionalized and used as a quilt motif.

The appeal of this ancient design is liked not alone for its intrinsic beauty but also for its quality of faith and belief in eternal life. The design rapidly became a favored one among the religiously inclined settlers of the New World and their descendants.

Many variations of this design are found among antique quilts but the distinguishing feature of all the Tree of Life patterns is the patchwork of the tree foliage and the trunk which is appliquéd on.

The favored material for these old quilts was a figured calico in green tones with a darker green or a brown fabric for the tree trunk. While the foliage was always figured material to imitate the play of light and shadow in the leaves, the trunk was invariably of plain fabric.

The illustration shows an old quilt in the usual square dimensions of those days, but for *modern* use, the designs will be more effectively displayed if they are used vertically down the long, narrow quilt of today. Accompanying this pattern, other tree patterns are also given.

The simple striped border as shown in the photograph fits very well into the general decoration of this pattern.

Materials Needed

9 yards white background material

6 yards plain or figured green material

1 yard brown for tree trunks (optional)

Units in Each Block

Unit No. 1 . . . 40 plain or figured green material

Unit No. 2 . . . 40 white material

Unit No. 3 . . . 1 dark green or brown

Sewing Instructions

Cut twenty white background blocks 14 inches square. Fold each block lengthwise through the center and press in crease with a warm iron.

Cut the green and white triangles that form the tree and sew them together as shown in the illustration. Next, cut the trunk of the tree, turn in the edges and baste in place.

After the triangles in the tree are pieced together, turn in all outside edges as the tree must be appliquéd to the block. Place it on the block (the center crease will guide you), baste to the background and add trunk to the lower half. Appliqué with small hemming stitches.

Border

Use border as shown in the illustration. Make the green bands about 2½ inches in width.

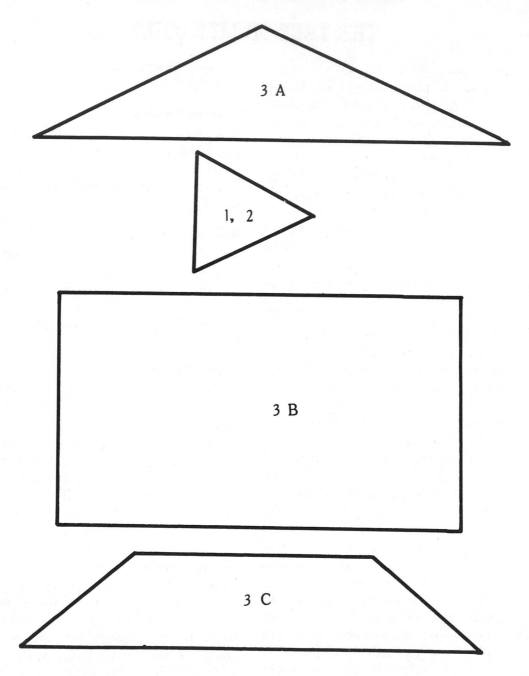

3 A

1, 2

3 B

3 C

Quilting Suggestions

Quilt along the seams of the triangles in the tree and around outside edge of trunk. Use a wreath of feathers on the background between the trees. Fill in background with stitches forming diamonds or squares.

OTHER TREE PATTERN BLOCKS

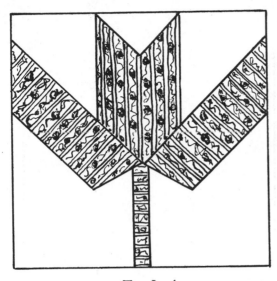

1. Tea Leaf

2. Live Oak Tree

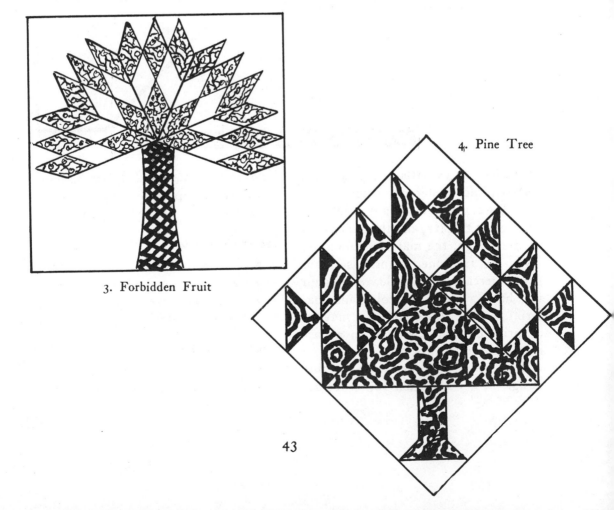

3. Forbidden Fruit

4. Pine Tree

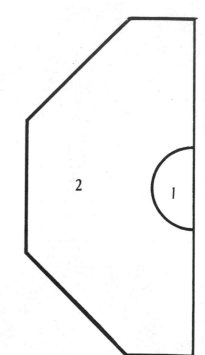

FLOWERS IN A POT DESIGN

THE DESIGN IN THIS QUILT IS MADE from old fashioned print calico. The flowers may be in any color you choose but to carry out the quaintness of the design, the material should be in an old fashioned print. Use plain green percale for the leaves. Again you have a choice of color and material for the flower pot—it may be of print or plain material in a harmonizing color.

You may find other uses for this design as a decoration for other articles in the household. It can be used as a cushion top, wall hanging, or appliquéd on the kitchen curtains.

Materials Needed

9 yards white background material
3 yards print material for flowers
3 yards plain green percale
1½ yards material for flower pot

Units in Each Block

Unit No. 1 . . . 3 green
Unit No. 2 . . . 3 yellow or red

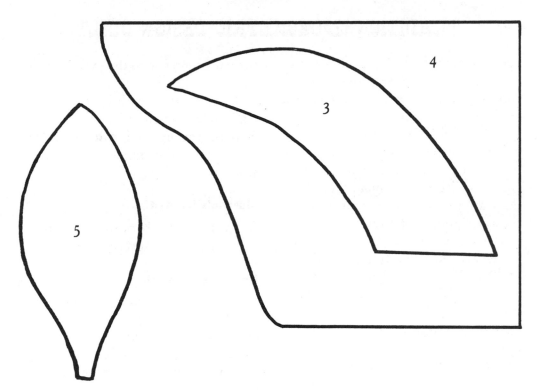

figured calico

    Unit No. 3 . . . 2 green
    Unit No. 4 . . . 1 flower pot
    Unit No. 5 . . . 2 green

Sewing Instructions

Cut 20 white background blocks 14 inches square. Fold them across the center each way and press in creases with a warm iron.

Cut out all units of block and turn in edges for sewing. Appliqué centers on each flower.

Place the units on the background block as shown in the illustration.

Baste them in place and appliqué to the background with small hemming stitches.

Border

Cut white border strips the width you need to hang down over the edge of the bed. Cut narrow bands of the green and the material used in the flower and sew them through the center of the border.

Quilting Suggestions

Quilt around the outlines of the units and fill in the background with diamonds or squares.

TRADITIONAL GEOMETRIC DESIGN QUILT

T HE ANTIQUE QUILT ILLUSTRATED shows a traditional American design in a completely conventionalized manner and intended for appliqué work in one color only on a solid color background. Many of the quilts in this pattern were made with a chalk white background and the decorations were cut out of calico in the then popular turkey red.

Each motif is a single cut out. The edges are then carefully turned and appliquéd to the background. In adapting this pattern for use in a room of today, the single color may well be maintained and any of the pastel or decorators' colors, tints or shades, can be used as the dominant note.

Another variation for modern use can be to take a more realistic approach in using this design. The central square of the figure can be cut separately to represent a flower, the four triangles on the diagonals may be cut out of green to reproduce the effect of leaves and a central dot of yellow for stamens placed in the very heart of the motif.

The border on the pictured quilt has especial distinction, though there is no particular connection with the central motif. It is composed of scallops separated by conventionalized tassels, gracefully girdling the quilt edges in harmonious color and balance.

This border can be adapted to many styles of quilts and will harmonize with many patterns from the formal geometric to the exactly realistic.

Though this quilt pattern is a traditional design it has much of the modern feeling and will blend perfectly into the modern decorative scheme.

Materials Needed

9 yards white background material
8 yards red or green calico

Units in Each Block

The original quilt is made of a single unit design in one color. However, you can make a conventional flower by making the center unit in red or any flower color and making the corner units in green to represent leaves.

Sewing Instructions

Cut 20 white background squares 14 inches square. Fold the block diagonally each way and press in creases with a warm iron.

Cut the design unit, turn in the edges and baste in place. Lay the design on the background block using the diagonal crease as a guide for centering it. Appliqué with small hemming stitches with thread in a matching color.

Border

Since the design shown in the illustration is large and bold, you will need a border 18 inches wide. Appliqué the design to the background be-

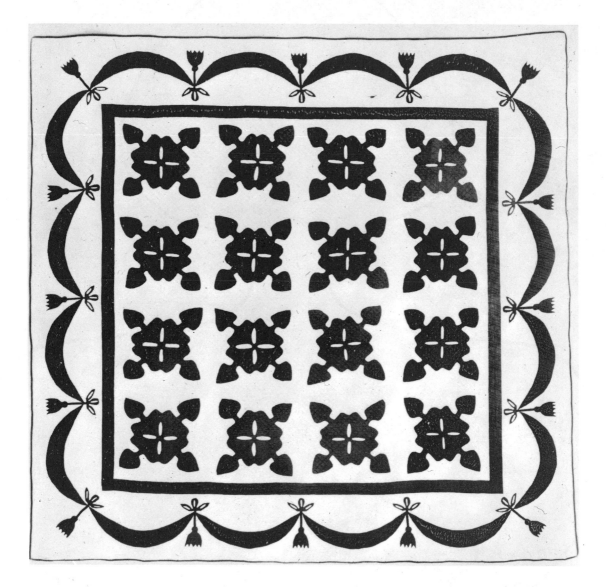

TRADITIONAL GEOMETRIC DESIGN QUILT

fore sewing the border to the center of the quilt.

Quilting Suggestions

Quilt around the outline of the de-sign unit and fill in the background with diamonds, shells or parallel lines.

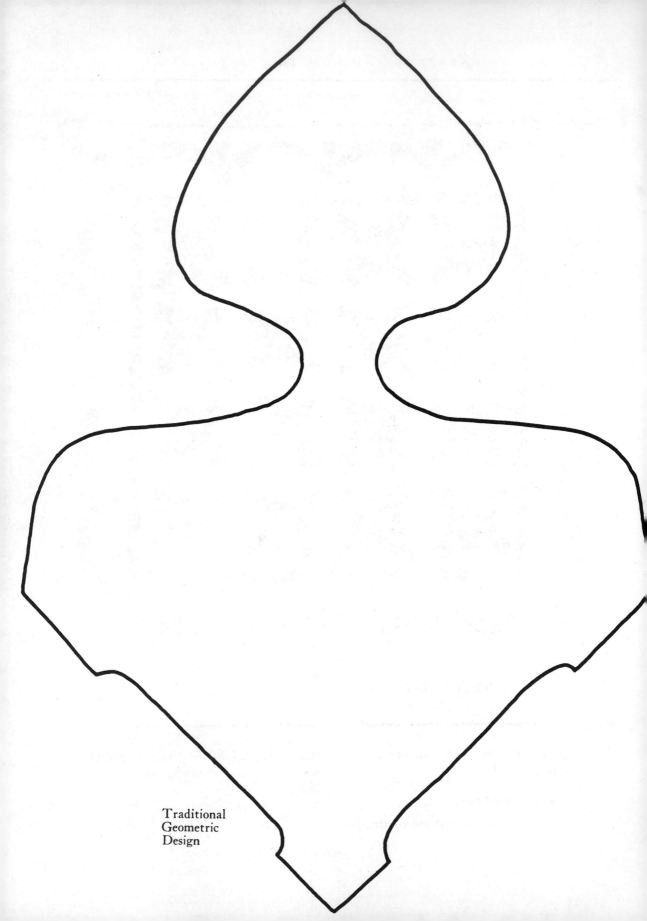

Traditional
Geometric
Design

THE TULIP QUILT

THOUGH FAR FROM REALISTICALLY presented, because of the resemblance to the early spring flower, the motif of this well known quilt is usually called the Tulip design. This is probably the most photographed and publicized quilt pattern among the many American designs being found illustrated in most articles and volumes on the lore of quilting. Around this pattern there is an appealing quality that has kept it alive and interesting to many generations of American quilters.

The original quilt was executed in red and green decorative details on a homespun background but as is the case of many other American designs,

49

this one will continue to thrive artistically, even when other colors than the original ones are used.

The lattice work effect is obtained by sewing strips one and a half inches wide (½ inch for the seams) between the blocks and between the blocks and the border to frame each block. A small triangle of the same color as the strip is cut and appliquéd to each corner of each block so that in the over-all picture of the quilt, small squares are shown at the meeting of the diagonals.

As shown in the photograph, the border with motifs is broken at the quilt corners. On modern quilts borders should be continuous around the entire edge of the quilt. To achieve the best decorative result the border should run in an unbroken design around the four sides and should round the four corners.

Materials Needed

9 yards white background material
4 yards green percale
2 yards red calico

Units in Each Block

Unit No. 1 . . . 1 green percale
Unit No. 2 . . . 3 green percale
Unit No. 3 . . . 1 green percale
Unit No. 4 . . . 1 green percale
Unit No. 5 . . . 1 red calico
Unit No. 6 . . . 1 green percale
Unit No. 7 . . . 1 red calico

Sewing Instructions

Cut 20 white background blocks 14 inches square. Fold them across the center each way and press in creases with a warm iron.

Cut units in each block and turn in edges ready for sewing.

Assemble units on block as shown in the illustration. Lay the units according to creases in the block in order to have the design in a uniform position throughout the quilt.

Appliqué to block with thread in a matching color.

Border

To draft a pattern for the border shown on the quilt, reduce the size of Units 6 and 7. Cut a bias strip ¾ inch wide for the vine and turn in edges on each side. Arrange the design as illustrated except if it is to be continuous at the corners.

Quilting Suggestions

There is no opportunity to use a special quilting design on this quilt. Quilt around the edges of the design units and fill in the background with diamonds or parallel lines.

THE FRIENDSHIP QUILT

THERE IS A GROUP OF ANTIQUE quilts we know today as the Friendship Quilts. They were made by exchanging patterns among a circle of friends, each one of whom would complete a batch of blocks using her own individual design made on a basic motif that had been chosen for the quilt as a whole.

In the quilt illustrated, the basic design selected was that of the wreath and we can see in the quilt that five separate wreath designs were employed. When the quilt was assembled the finished blocks were balanced around a central block decorated with a different wreath design used but once in the quilt.

While the individual quilters might have chosen different colors to make up the blocks they sewed, over-all color harmony was achieved by employing the same type of texture in the fabrics and by the use of green foliage to effectively blend the separate blocks into a whole. Because a general basic motif was chosen for these quilts—in this case the wreath —the general color value of the quilt can be maintained.

There is a definitely artistic quality in the individual motifs of this quilt. For that reason separate patterns are given so that they may be used either to reproduce the illustrated quilt or used singly in other quilt designs. Repetition of any one of the wreath designs of this quilt, will make an effective pattern for a bed covering.

THE FRIENDSHIP QUILT

OAK LEAF WREATH QUILT

THIS IS PROBABLY THE MOST STRIK-ing and decorative design used in the Friendship Quilt, employing as it does the four balanced oak leaves with smaller leaves to define the circle of the wreath and with the fruit of the oak tree—the acorns—used as the decoration of the inner circle of the wreath.

The leaves of the oak permit a wide color and fabric choice to the quilt designer. Two tones of green for spring and summer leaves may be used or the autumnal tones of the fading leaves may be chosen which will call into play a whole range of brown shades from light to darker, even the vivid scarlet of the pin oaks in the fall can be employed for accent if they will add to the decorative scheme. The acorns are always cut from two tones of brown or a beige and brown, blending with both the leaves and the background.

Fabrics can also be varied. Plain or figured materials can be used for the leaves but the acorns should always be of plain fabric to show their smaller dimensions to better advantage. Few quilts can employ chintz patches happily but this Oak Leaf design is the rare pattern to which chintz adds effectiveness to the design.

A quilt of this pattern makes one of the best choices for use in a man's room; it has strength, dignity and simplicity in its favor.

The border with a design of scattered oak leaves will add just the de-sired element to complete the picture.

Materials Needed

9 yards background material in white

5 yards dark green or dark red material

1 yard light green or yellow

½ yard light brown or tan material

Units in Each Block

Unit No. 1 . . . 4 dark green or dark red

Unit No. 2 . . . 4 light green or yellow

Unit No. 3 . . . 4 light brown or tan

Sewing Instructions

Cut 20 background blocks 14 inches square. Fold diagonally each way and press in creases with a warm iron.

Cut out units, turn in edges ¼ inch and baste in place. Make ⅛ inch cuts along the edges of the leaf in order to turn the curves and acute angles.

Lay units on block by placing each leaf on the diagonal creases. Baste in place for sewing.

Appliqué units to block with small hemming stitches using thread in a matching color.

Border

As suggested before, you may cut border strips of the white material and appliqué scattered leaves around the edge. However, this quilt looks

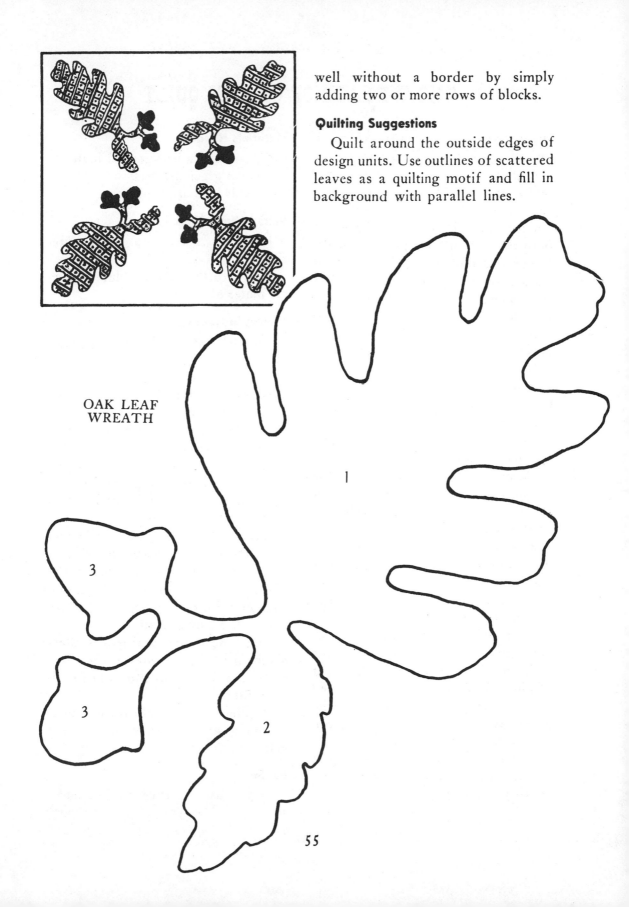

well without a border by simply adding two or more rows of blocks.

Quilting Suggestions

Quilt around the outside edges of design units. Use outlines of scattered leaves as a quilting motif and fill in background with parallel lines.

OAK LEAF
WREATH

1

3

3

2

THE WREATH OF GRAPES QUILT

THE MAKING OF THIS EXQUISITE quilt should only be attempted by the quilter after success with other quilts, and should be considered as a reward for doing simple work well and skillfully. This pattern is a test of both the skill and the patience of designer and quilter and should never be attempted by the novice. After skill is acquired, however, the beauty and decorative value of the finished quilt are so great that the effort in the making will reap a rich reward.

This is a design of such delicacy and grace that the workmanship must be on a high level and the fabrics chosen of fine texture and close weave, both for the background and the materials used in the designs.

Because of the deep notches in the grape leaves and the small circles of fabric used for the grapes, selection of the right materials is vital to success. A fabric must be chosen whose warp and weft are of equal thickness and so closely woven that the cut edges will not fray when the edges are turned for sewing.

Colors used in this Grape Wreath Quilt must be naturalistic to be most effective. The grapes should be cut of blue, bluish purple or purplish red like the grapes of nature, and the grape leaves of the rich, deep green that harmonizes.

A lattice border around the quilt can be used to represent the arbor on which the grapes grow.

Materials Needed

9 yards white background material
4 yards green material
3 yards blue or purple material

Units in Each Block

Unit No. 1 . . . 12 green material
Unit No. 2 . . . 12 blue or purple material

Sewing Instructions

Cut 20 background blocks 14 inches square.

Cut out units for each block, turn in edges ¼ inch and baste. You must make ⅛ inch cuts frequently on edges of the leaves in order to make the turns on curves and acute angles.

A bias strip is used for stem of wreath and bunch of grapes. Cut it ¾ of an inch wide and turn in edges on each side.

Draw a large circle on background block the size of wreath you wish to make. Baste bias strip around the line and be sure to baste the inside edge *first*. Pull outer edge until it lies flat on the background.

Place the grapes and leaves alternately around both sides of the circle to form a wreath as shown in the illustration.

Appliqué units to block with small hemming stitches, using thread in a matching color.

Border

If you use a lattice border, make

WREATH OF GRAPES

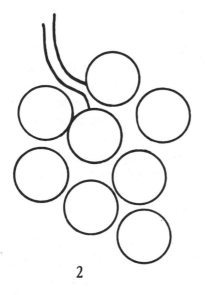

2

the lattice work with green bias tape carried in most department stores. This quilt is most effective made up entirely of decorated blocks and finished around the edges with a narrow band of green or blue material.

Quilting Suggestions

Quilt around the outside edges of the grapes and leaves. Fill in the background with diamonds to represent a lattice on which the grapes are displayed.

WREATH OF ROSES QUILT

MANY QUILT PATTERNS SHOW THE rose design, both realistic and conventionalized, some are in the wreath arrangement but there are few which equal for delicacy and artistic interest the motif of roses, leaves and buds balanced so truly in this particular wreath pattern.

As found in the flower garden, the roses of this quilt may be a study executed in two tones of pinks or yellows, the lighter tone for the flower and the deeper shade for the bud just as nature reveals on the rosebush.

In assembling this wreath pattern, the foundation upon which the flowers, leaves and buds are entwined, is a narrow bias strip laid down in a circle on the background block. The procedure should be to place the bias strip in a circle on the block before the rest of the patches are evenly distributed around the circumference.

Fabrics should be chosen carefully for this quilt and fine textures selected to accent the delicacy of the design. This pattern would be appropriate on a silk background with silk patches but less expensive materials, like finely woven, high-count sateen or the fabric known as Glosheen, will be decorative and adequate.

The border can be designed with running vines or a running leaf design completely encircling the quilt.

Materials Needed

9 yards white background material
4 yards green percale
1 yard rose percale
½ yard yellow percale

Units in Each Block

Unit No. 1 . . . 4 yellow
Unit No. 2 . . . 4 rose
Unit No. 3 . . . 8 green
Unit No. 4 . . . 8 green

Sewing Instructions

Cut units for each block. Turn in outside edges and baste in place. Appliqué unit No. 1 to center of unit No. 2.

Fold block across center each way and press in creases with a warm iron. Draw a large circle on block where wreath is to be formed being sure it is equal distance from all outside edges of the block.

Cut a bias strip ¾ inch wide and turn in edges on each side. Lay it around circle drawn on block and baste in place. Baste the inside edge first and then pull the outer edge until it stretches flat on the block.

Assemble the units around the wreath as shown in the illustration. Lay the roses on first, according to the center creases in the block, and then distribute the leaves evenly around the wreath. Baste in place.

Appliqué to block with small hemming stitches.

Border

You may use an extra row of blocks on each side and eliminate a border. Bind it in green or rose used in the wreath design.

Quilting Suggestions

Quilt around the outside edges of units in the design and quilt a small wreath of feathers in the center of each block. Fill in the background with small diamonds or squares.

WREATH OF ROSES

THE FOLIAGE WREATH QUILT

FOR USE IN A ROOM DELUGED WITH warm southern or western sun, this quilt with its motif of green leaves and buds around a conventionalized center of balanced leaves will supply the correct note of cool and comforting decorative value.

The Foliage Wreath design is based upon a narrow bias band laid in a circle on the background block. The leaves and buds are then twined around the outer rim of this circle while the four conventionalized leaves are placed along the horizontal and vertical division lines to form the central feature of the design.

The complete motif may be made of tones of green, but if a color accent is desired, the small apex of the buds may be made of rose or yellow whichever is most appropriate in the room.

A variation of this pattern may be made by eliminating the four central leaves and making the wreath itself more delicate and distinctive. Several harmonizing tones of green from palest leaf green to the deep sage green, may be used to add to the decorative values.

Another variation is to enlarge the background block and to appliqué in each corner one of the conventionalized leaf forms. This will show up in the finished quilt as a repeat of the central figure of the main wreath design.

The leaves and buds of the design can be formed into a running vine design to decorate the border and should go continuously around the entire outer edge of the quilt.

Materials Needed

9 yards white background material

5 yards green percale

Units in Each Block

Unit No. 1 . . . 4 green

Unit No. 4 (from Wreath of Roses pattern) . . . 8 green

Unit No. 3 (from Wreath of Roses pattern) . . . 8 green

Sewing Directions

Cut out units for each block. Turn in edges ¼ inch and baste in place ready for sewing.

Fold the block through the center each way and press in creases with a warm iron. Draw a circle for the wreath, being sure it is the same distance from the edge of the block on all sides.

Cut a bias strip for the wreath ¾ inch wide and turn in the edges on each side and secure with basting threads. Lay it on the circle drawn on the block and sew in place by sewing the inside edge first. Stretch the outer edge in order to make it lie flat on the block.

Assemble the units around the circle or wreath as shown in the illustration. Appliqué with green thread.

Border

Use a continuous border of leaves as shown in the Border Chapter, or use the units as shown on the outside of the wreath.

Quilting Suggestions

Since decoration on the blocks covers most of the area, quilt around the outline of the units and quilt in the background with diamonds or parallel lines.

FOLIAGE WREATH

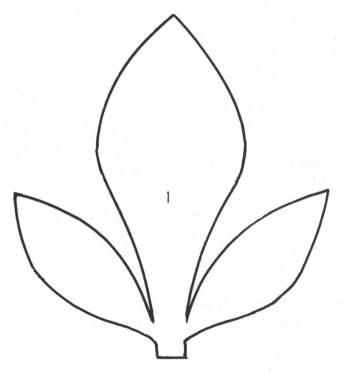

1

THE TRIPLE SUNFLOWER QUILT

THE QUILT ILLUSTRATED IS A COM-
bination of pieced and appliqué
work. Each block of this pattern is
divided into four equal squares. Three
of these squares are pieced, each with
a sunflower motif, and the fourth
square is plain. Across this plain
square the stems and leaves of the
sunflower are appliquéd.

The most appropriate fabric to select for this quilt is old-fashioned figured calico. The most effective coloring to choose is one of the yellow
tones for the print and a plain green
material for the leaves and stems.
Plain green or brown material should
be used for the center of the flowers.

When making this quilt block, the
three pieced squares should be sewed
first and the fourth square appliquéd
after the pieced squares are finished.
The three pieced squares are completed and set together with the plain
square to form the large quilt block.
The stems and leaves are cut out of
the plain green material, their edges
are turned and they are then appliquéd to the fourth square of the
block. The flower centers are cut out
and after their edges are turned
down, they are placed over and sewed
down over the triangles of the sunflower patches.

The large blocks may be alternated
with plain background blocks or they
may be joined to each other by narrow strips of green or yellow colored
material.

A border for this quilt can be selected from those given in the Chapter on Borders but it will be found
that a simple border of colored strips
of the two tones employed in the quilt
and undecorated, will be the most effective.

Materials Needed

2½ yards yellow print, 2½ yards
rust, 6½ yards green, 2 yards brown,
and 6 yards of white material.

Four blocks (3 sunflower and 1 appliqué block) are joined to make a
12-inch block. Each sunflower block
is made of 4 different units. A pattern
is given for unit Nos. 1 and 5; units
Nos. 2, 3, and 4 are respectively a
1½-inch square, a triangle 2³⁄₁₆ inches
across long side and 1½ inch on short
side, a circle 2¼ inches in diameter.
Appliqué block is made of a 6-inch
white square.

Units in Each Block

Unit No. 1 . . . 4 rust
Unit No. 1 . . . 4 yellow
Unit No. 2 . . . 4 white
Unit No. 3 . . . 4 white (trian-
gle, half 3-inch square)
Unit No. 4 . . . 1 brown (cir-
cle)
Unit No. 5 . . . 2 green
Appliqué block is 6-inch white
square.

THE TRIPLE SUNFLOWER QUILT

Setting the Quilt

Place blocks as shown, having 3-inch strips (allowing for seams) of green between blocks. Fill in corner with a Four Patch, 2 green and 2 white 1½-inch squares.

Border

Use strips 4½ inches wide for long sides and 6 inches wide for top and bottom. Quilt around patterns.

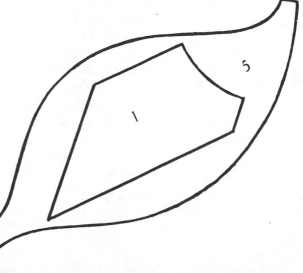

THE SQUARE AND CROSS QUILT

THE QUILT PICTURED IS ONE OF small dimensions meant originally to be used to cover a crib or a trundle bed. The trundle beds of early American days were intended for the children of the family and the bed itself small, narrow and low, slid under the great four-poster.

The pattern of this quilt, however, was often used on regular sized beds and particularly when it is developed in blue and white calico patches on a white background, it is reminiscent of the old handspun coverlets.

The needlework of this quilt design combines pieced patches with some appliqué work.

The cross and square motif should be pieced first and these set together with octagon-shaped blocks of white background material. On these blocks, small rectangular patches are appliquéd to form a broken circle with a cross at the center. The pieced cross and square motif is then joined to the octagon-shaped appliquéd blocks, using ¼ inch seam in the joining and then small squares are appliquéd diagonally along the line of the seam.

This quilt is most effective when a single color is used for making the motifs, deep blue or red, on a white background.

The design may be continuous to the edges of the quilt but if the quilter wishes to use a border, an interesting effect can be had by using two rows of broken rectangles matching the design of the broken circle. If no border is used, quilt edges should be bound to match the color of the motifs.

Materials Needed

9 yards white background material
5 yards blue percale

Pieced Block

Unit No. 1 . . . 8 blue and 8 white squares
Unit No. 2 . . . 4 blue and 4 white rectangles
Unit No. 3 . . . 1 blue square

Octagonal Block (appliquéd)

Unit No. 2 . . . 20 blue rectangles
Unit No. 3 . . . 4 blue squares
Cover each seam between squares with four small squares (Unit No. 3).

Sewing Directions

Cut 20 octagonal-shaped white blocks. Piece 1 block with squares and rectangles and measure 1 side of the finished block. Each of the 8 sides of the octagonal block should match the pieced block in size.

Piece the center squares and appliqué the rectangles onto the large octagonal block. Sew together and appliqué 4 small squares diagonally over the seams as shown in the illustration.

Border

This is an all-over design and requires no border.

Quilting Suggestions

Quilt around the design units and fill in the background with small quilted squares to match those covering the seams.

THE SQUARE AND CROSS QUILT

1

2

3

WILD ROSE WREATH QUILT

A ROSE WREATH HAS ALWAYS BEEN a choice design for modern quilters. This wreath has smaller leaves for foliage than many of the patterns, and the buds offer an opportunity to use two tones of the same color for the roses.

Delicate pastel shades should be chosen for the design and the flowers may be made in two shades of rose or yellow. Since the foliage is rather heavy around the wreath, it should be in a light shade of green.

Materials Needed

9 yards white background material
3 yards rose or yellow percale
3 yards green percale
½ yard yellow percale

Units in Each Block

Unit No. 1 . . . 4 yellow
Unit No. 2 . . . 20 rose or yellow
Unit No. 3 . . . 8 green
Unit No. 4 . . . 12 green
Unit No. 5 . . . 8 green
Unit No. 6 . . . 8 deep rose or yellow

Sewing Instructions

Cut 20 blocks of white background material 14 inches square. Fold block across center each way and press in creases with a warm iron.

Draw a large circle on the block the size of the wreath, being sure it is equal in distance from all outside edges. Cut a green bias strip ¾ inch in width and turn in edges on both sides. Baste in place around line of circle.

Cut out all units in block and turn in edges ready for sewing. Assemble around wreath as shown in the illustration and baste in place.

Appliqué all units to block with small hemming stitches. Sew inside of wreath *first* and stretch the outer edge until it lies flat on the background.

Border

This quilt may be made entirely of decorated blocks with no definite border. However, there are a number of border patterns in the Chapter on Borders that may be applied to this quilt.

Quilting Suggestions

Quilt around the outside of the design units and use small feather wreaths between the squares. Fill in the background with diamonds or parallel lines.

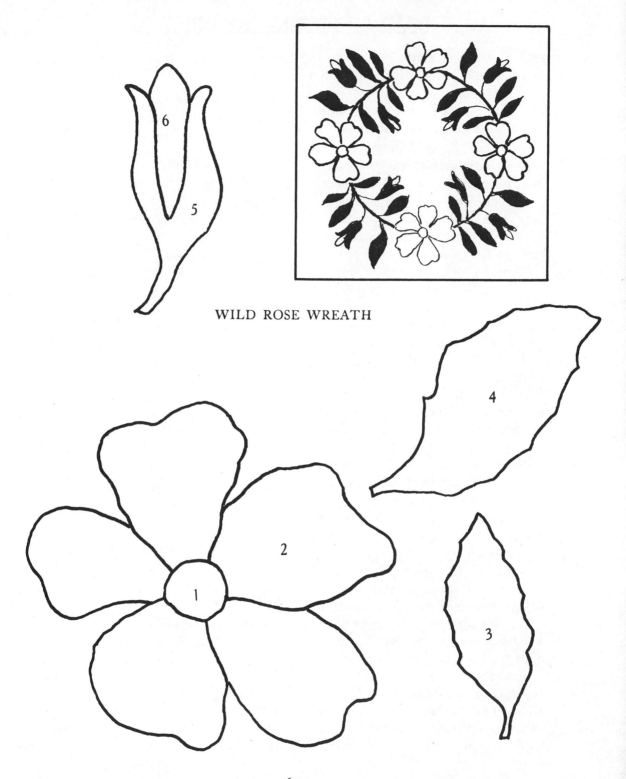

WILD ROSE WREATH

STAR OF BETHLEHEM QUILT

THIS QUILT IS TRADIONALLY MADE with the motifs developed in either plain or figured calico of blue tones on a white background. Some of the stars used in these quilts are six pointed but the quilt illustrated uses an 8-pointed star in the design thus increasing the size of the quilt motif.

For modern use other colors may be chosen besides blue, some shades of green, rose and yellow are effective but for the best decorative value, one color should be used throughout the quilt, to contrast with the background.

In piecing this quilt pattern, it will be noted that each large star motif is divided into 8 diamond-shaped sections made up of smaller diamond-shaped patches pieced together. The 8 sections are then sewed together to form the star as shown in the drawing.

Pieces of white background material are then cut to fill in between the points of the star and are then sewed into place. On the larger plain areas the quilter will have space to use both skill and artistic discrimination in the designs of the quilt stitching. To make a contrast to the straight edges of the diamond patches, feather designs of quilting stitches arranged in wreath form, make a very beautiful quilt.

For the border, a choice can be made from the number shown in the Chapter on Borders. The most effective one for this quilt will be found to be one or two rows of diamond shaped patches entirely surrounding the quilt.

Materials Needed

9 yards white background material
5 yards blue percale

Units in Each Block

Unit No. 1 . . . 64 white diamonds
Unit No. 2 . . . 64 blue diamonds

Sewing Instructions

Cut out the number of units needed for each block. You will note that each star has eight points with eight white and eight blue diamonds. Each point should be pieced separately and then set together to form the star.

After the stars are pieced, lay them out on the bed and measure the size squares you will need of white background material to set them together. You will note you will need 2 size squares, 1 large and the other smaller. Be sure to allow 1/4 inch all around for seams.

Border

Use a plain white border with 2 rows of blue diamonds running through the center. Bind the edge with a bias blue binding.

Quilting Suggestions

Quilt along the seams of diamonds in the star. Quilt a wreath of feathers in the plain white blocks. In the large square, you might tie the quilt pattern and quilting design together by quilting a small star in the center of the feather wreath.

STAR OF BETHLEHEM QUILT

THE SAW TOOTH PATTERN QUILT

THE INDIVIDUAL QUILTER MAY AC-complish much using this old and basic pattern with variations in the size, color and materials to produce either a dainty figured quilt or a boldly patterned one.

The pattern is particularly good for the use of chintz fabrics or for the old-fashioned printed calicos. Colors may be mixed throughout the quilt cover but the same color must be used in each individual block to carry out the idea of the saw tooth.

Each block of the quilt is made up of one triangular piece of white material undecorated and an equal sized pieced half of the block broken down into 1 large isosceles triangle, surrounded by twenty small isosceles triangles of the same size, half cut from figured material and half of plain fabric.

One variation of this quilt cover can be the alternation of the pieced block with a plain one, thus reducing the handwork on the quilt by half.

This quilt calls for a border of two rows of saw teeth as illustrated in the Chapter on Borders. The saw teeth or triangular patches in the border should be the same size as the smaller triangles of the motif in the body of the quilt.

Materials Needed

8 yards white background material
6 yards figured material for design
Note: This pattern is usually made from scrap material, each block being cut from a different print.

Units in Each Block

Unit No. 1 . . . 10 white triangles
Unit No. 2 . . . 9 colored triangles
Note: Cut one large white triangle and one colored triangle the same size according to directions below.

Direction for Cutting Pattern

We have given you two different size triangles as patterns. The large one is for a block 14 inches square and the small one for a 7½ inches square. Cut a paper pattern of the size block you wish to make and draw in the triangles along two sides. Divide the large square remaining in the block diagonally across and you will have a pattern for the large triangle.

Directions for Sewing

Cut the units in each block and sew together with straight even seams. If a different material is used in each block, arrange them so the colors harmonize throughout the quilt and sew them together.

Border

This quilt may be an all-over design with no definite border. A plain border of white may be used with a double row of colored triangles running through its center (Chapter on Borders).

Quilting Suggestions

Quilt around the small colored triangles and repeat the same design in the large white triangle. Fill in the center with parallel lines running diagonally across the quilt.

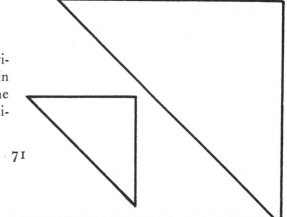

71

COCK'S COMB PATTERN

THIS VIVID PATTERN IS DESIGNED for a room with dark furniture where the quilt is the main decoration. As the name indicates, the four cock's combs form the center motif of the design with four conventionalized leaves in the diagonal corners. Since the design is meant to be striking, you should use vivid colored material.

The quilt may be made entirely of decorated blocks with no definite border and bound with a narrow band of either red or green. If you prefer a separate border, we suggest a plain white one with red and green bands running through the center. Make each band 1½ inches wide.

Materials Needed

9 yards white background material
3 yards green percale
1 yard red printed calico
1 yard plain red calico

Units in Each Block

Unit No. 1 . . . 4 dark green
Unit No. 2 . . . 4 red printed calico
Unit No. 3 . . . 4 plain red calico

Sewing Directions

Cut 20 white background blocks 14 inches square. Fold them diagonally through the center each way and press in creases with a warm iron.

Cock's Comb Pattern

Cut out units in design and turn in edges ready for sewing. Appliqué unit No. 1 to unit No. 2.

Assemble the units on background block, placing the leaves along the diagonal creases. Baste in place and appliqué with small hemming stitches.

Quilting Suggestions

Quilt around the outside edges of the design units. There will be a large plain area between the combs after the blocks are set together in which you can use any wreath design you choose. Fill in background with diagonal lines.

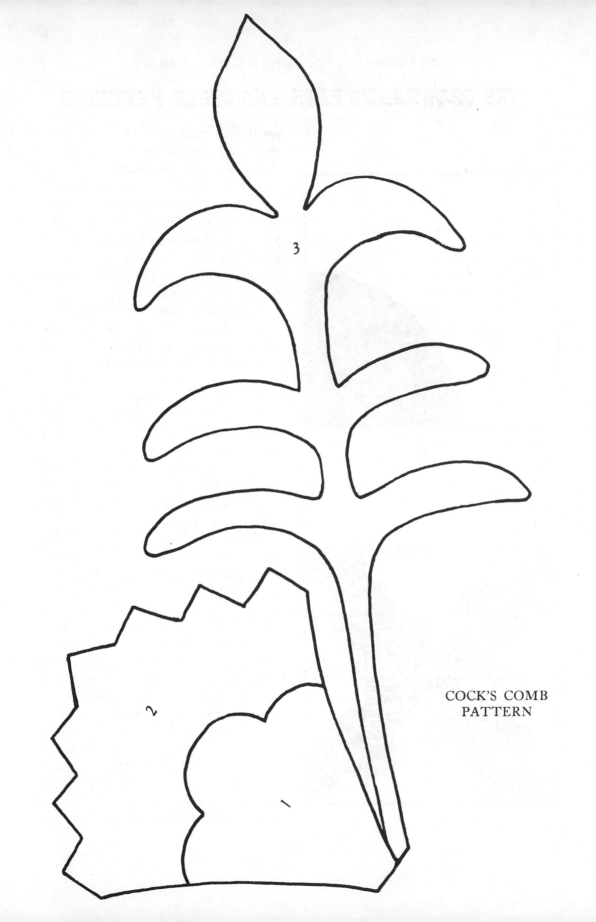

COCK'S COMB
PATTERN

3

2

1

THE DRUNKARD'S PATH AND OTHER PATTERNS

Fig. 1

THE DRUNKARD'S PATH IS A FAVORite old patchwork pattern, easily made but very confusing to set together. It will be necessary to refer often to the illustration while setting the block units until you have the pattern memorized. Piece 16 small blocks at a time and sew them together to form a large square, then set them all together to make the quilt.

The block is made up of two units —a small square with a fourth-circle set in one corner. This is a pieced block, so draft a pattern allowing ¼ inch around the circle for the seam and at the corner of the block where it is to be sewn. The seam will be circular in shape but will lie flat when pressed with a warm iron.

You can easily draft this pattern yourself. Cut a paper square the size you wish the small block to be and make a fourth-circle in one corner by marking around a cup. Cut out the circle unit and transfer the pattern on a piece of cardboard by tracing around the edges and adding ¼ inch at the curved sides for a seam (do not add ¼ inch on the other sides). Repeat the process with the square allowing ¼ inch at the curved corner where the seams join. The large block pattern should be large enough to allow a ¼ seam on all sides.

This quilt may be an all-over design with no definite border. Bind the edges with a narrow bias strip cut from the design color. A plain white border may be used with a 2-inch band of the design color set between

Fig. 2

the quilt and the border and another band of the same width placed around the outside edge.

Other Patterns

Other famous patchwork designs were made from the same basic pattern of a square with a fourth-circle set in one corner. By using mixed colors and arranging the blocks in various orders, a person with imagination can work out any number of designs.

In the illustrations you will find a number of variations of the pattern. The Drunkard's Path is usually made of 2 colors—a red or blue circle on a small white block. The illustration uses figured and plain material in the design so that you can follow the pattern more easily. By studying the blocks carefully, you will see that they are made from same basic pattern:

Figure No. 1 . . . Basic Patch

Figure No. 2 . . . Drunkard's Path

Figure No. 3 . . . Fool's Puzzle

Figure No. 4 . . . Falling Timbers

Figure No. 5 . . . Design of figured and plain colored material

Figure No. 6 . . . Design made of striped material

Figure No. 7 . . . Arrangement for figured material

Figure No. 8 . . . Wonder of the World Pattern

Figure No. 9 . . . Arrangement for large blocks

Figure No. 10 . . . Lone Ring

Figure No. 11 . . . Reverse arrangement of Fig. No. 9

Figure No. 12 . . . All-over Pattern

Fig. 3

Fig. 4

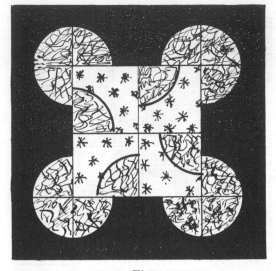

Fig. 5

Fig. 7

Fig. 6

Fig. 8

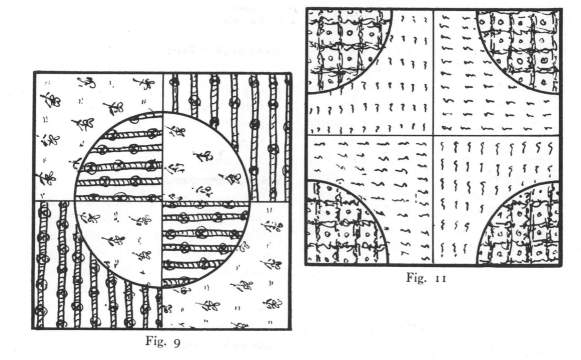

Fig. 11

Fig. 9

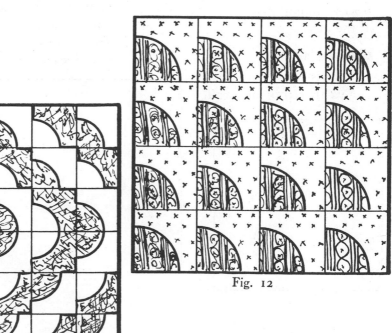

Fig. 12

Fig. 10

77

GOOSE TRACKS

THIS POPULAR OLD PATTERN IS often used today and is one of the few patchwork designs that will lend dignity to a bedroom. Perhaps it is because it is always made of a single color combined with white—the favorite, of course, being either red or dark blue.

It is a good choice for a novice at quilt making as the patches are easily combined and there are no sewing problems involved. If you do not care for the small squares set between the blocks, they may be omitted and plain white strips used instead.

Do not plan a special border for this quilt. Make the entire area of pieced blocks and have a band the same width as the strips between the blocks running around the outer edge of the quilt.

Materials Needed

5 yards white material
5 yards red or blue calico

Units in Each Block

Unit No. 1 . . . 1 white and 4 red or blue

Unit No. 2 . . . 4 white and 4 red or blue

Unit No. 3 . . . 8 red or blue and 24 white

Sewing Instructions

Cut out all units and separate them according to color and shape. Sew patches together in each block as shown in the illustration. After the blocks are pieced, set them together with a 2- or 3-inch white strip between with a colored square between the blocks.

Quilting Suggestions

Quilt along the seams between the patches. The Quilting Chapter has a number of patterns for quilt stitching the narrow strips running between the blocks.

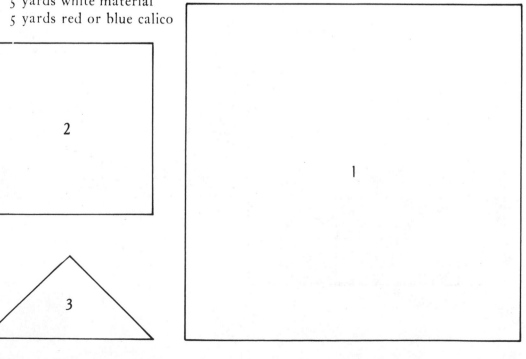

THE DOUBLE IRISH CHAIN QUILT

THIS UNIQUE QUILT AS PICTURED IS made by piecing small squares of alternately light and dark fabrics, diagonally into strips that criss cross over the quilt surface.

The pieced strips are set together with plain background blocks which are quilted in squares the exact same size as the square patches of the pieced strips, giving the over all effect of a solidly pieced quilt.

Two tones of the same color may be used for the patches or two harmonizing colors.

This quilt does not call for a border but should have a narrow binding of the darker tone or color used in the quilt.

The quilt illustrated shows the large white blocks decorated in embroidered designs. Each block has a different motif made with an outline stitch. The design should be made with cotton embroidery thread in a harmonizing color with the patches in the quilt.

Materials Needed

9 yards white material
3 yards light tone percale
5 yards dark tone percale

Sewing Instructions

This quilt can be pieced two different ways: (1) You may piece the squares together to form crossing strips and fill in the edges with small white triangles. They are then joined to a white central block. (2) Make an entirely pieced quilt as shown in the photograph.

A still simpler method of piecing this quilt is to piece a block of 25 squares and set them together with a plain white block with a square appliquéd to each corner. To do this, arrange the colored squares in each block as follows:

Row 1 . . . light, dark, white, dark, light

Row 2 . . . dark, light, dark, light, dark

Row 3 . . . white, dark, light, dark, white

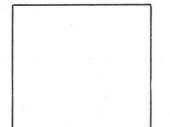

Row 4 . . . repeat row 2

Row 5 . . . repeat row 1

Cut white blocks equal in size to the pieced blocks. Appliqué a dark square in each corner. When the blocks are set together they will form the Irish Chain.

Border

This quilt may be an all-over pattern with no border. However, you will have enough material left to add a plain white border with a band of each color running through the center. This arrangement is effective and will save many hours of cutting and sewing.

Quilting Suggestions

Quilt the entire quilt in squares the same size as the patches.

PINEAPPLE DESIGN QUILT

THE PINEAPPLE IS ONE OF THE most striking and favored of the early American patterns. The design is made of one color and can be in either figured or plain material. Many of the old quilts were made in red and white, but blue or yellow can be equally effective.

If you want to be realistic, make the center unit of figured yellow or orange material and the surrounding units in plain green. The sections in the pineapple can be emphasized by quilting in small diamonds with one or two tiny stitches in the center.

This quilt is usually made up of continuous decorated blocks with no definite border.

Materials Needed

9 yards white background material
6 yards colored material for design

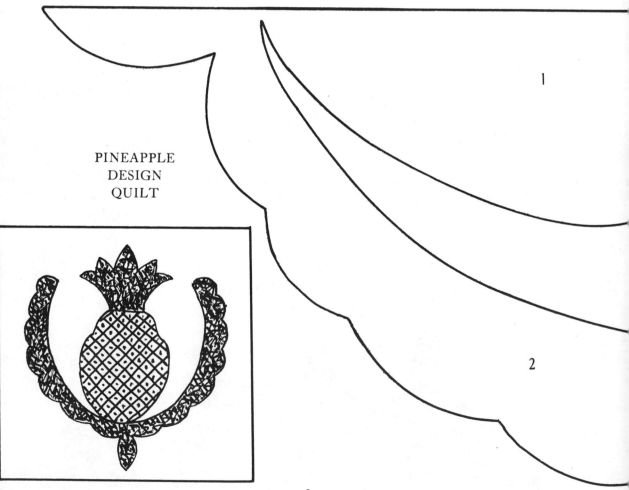

PINEAPPLE
DESIGN
QUILT

Units in Block

You may consider the center motif of the design as Unit No. 1 and make it one color and the surrounding motifs as Unit No. 2 and make them green. However, the pattern is usually cut from a single color.

Sewing Instructions

Cut 20 white background blocks 14 inches square. Fold them across the center each way and press in creases with a warm iron.

Cut out design and turn in outside edges ready for sewing. Lay the design on the background block, using the center crease as a guide for placing it.

Appliqué the design to the block with small hemming stitches using a thread in a matching color.

Quilting Suggestions

Quilt around outside edges of the design. The pineapple should be quilted in small diamonds as shown in the illustration. Use the Pineapple Pattern given in the Quilting Chapter for quilt stitches in the plain areas.

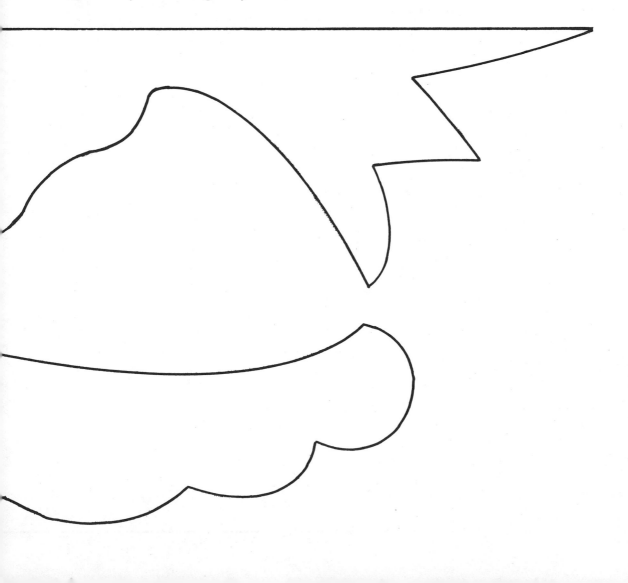

THE TWINKLING STAR QUILT

THE DISTINCTION OF THIS QUILT lies in its unusual and decorative color background being made up of light grey plain blocks alternating with the patched blocks. The original quilt was made using a dark blue figured material set together with white giving a pleasing contrast of light and shade between the pieced blocks and the grey background blocks.

The decorative values of this quilt make it useful to the designer for matching or harmonizing colors and fabrics in the patches, employing those which will tie the quilt into the scheme of the room in which it is used.

Pastel tones for the central square in the pieced blocks will make the quilt less bold and striking but no less decorative. The paler central square will emphasize the feathery or twinkling quality of this star pattern and will make the star more distinct and dominant in the over-all design.

The border may be either white or grey—a strip along top and bottom of the border width with a row of small triangles running entirely through the center of the border.

Materials Needed

8 yards light grey percale

4 yards dark blue calico

3 yards white muslin

Units in Each Block

Unit No. 1 . . . 1 dark blue

Unit No. 2 . . . 8 white

Unit No. 3 . . . 56 dark blue and 56 white triangles

Note: Cut white squares to fill in the corners.

Sewing Directions

Cut out units for each block and sew together as shown in the illustration. Be sure the patches are cut accurately and to exact size. Piece the small colored and plain triangles together first and sew to large white triangles. Sew to large center square and add a small plain square to each corner.

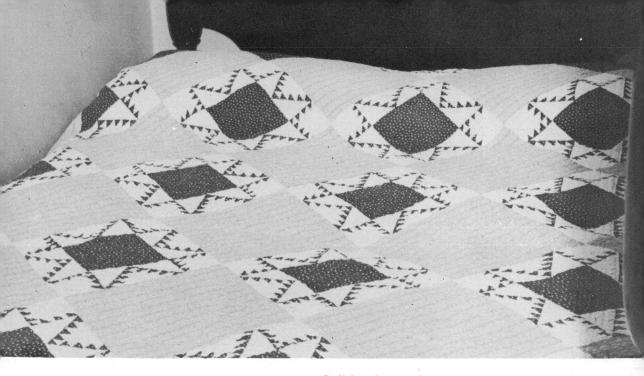

Border

Add a plain grey border with a row of small blue triangles running along the top and bottom. Bind the edge with a narrow band of dark blue.

Quilting Suggestions

Quilt around the units in the pieced blocks. Use a wreath of feathers in the large grey blocks or any special design given in the Quilting Chapter.

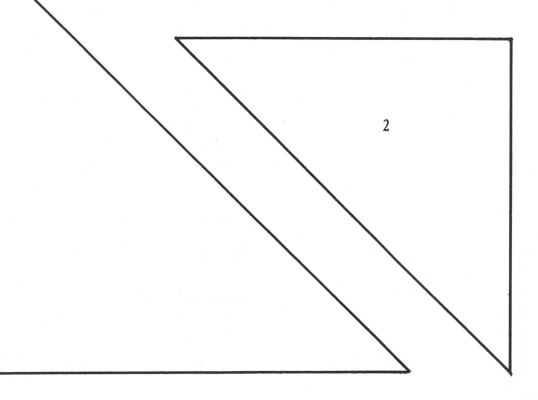

2

THE LOG CABIN QUILT

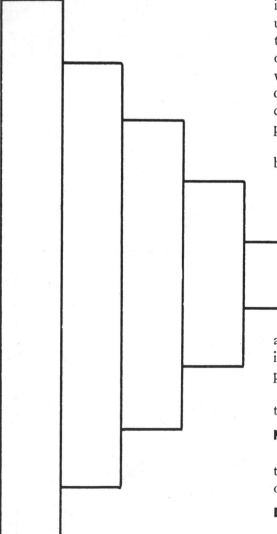

ANOTHER AMERICAN QUILT WHICH may be found in many variations is the popular Log Cabin design which uses contrasting rectangular patches of light and darker patches pieced throughout the quilt cover.

The pattern of each block is built around a central square with narrower rectangular pieces surrounding this center. These narrow pieces of varying lengths are laid end to end and represent the overlapping logs in the cabins of the early settlers. Some of the old quilts may be found with a chimney added at the appropriate spot on the design to add realism to the "cabin" on the quilt cover.

Figured materials are used in making the patches and light tones are used on two sides of the block while the dark patches are all used on the other two sides. Woolens were a favored fabric for the earliest log cabin quilts, but later the finer woolen-like challis and silk patches were employed to great effect.

Variations of the pattern are brought about by differences in the arrangement when the pieced blocks are assembled for the finished cover. In the quilt illustrated the light and dark sides are placed together thus forming large squares at the diagonal intersections.

If turned around the pattern will show alternating triangles of light and dark pieces forming a stepping stone or flight of stairs pattern.

Traditionally no border is used on this quilt.

Materials Needed

This quilt is made from scrap material. You will need an equal amount of light and dark shades.

Directions for Making Quilt

The pattern given here is for ¼

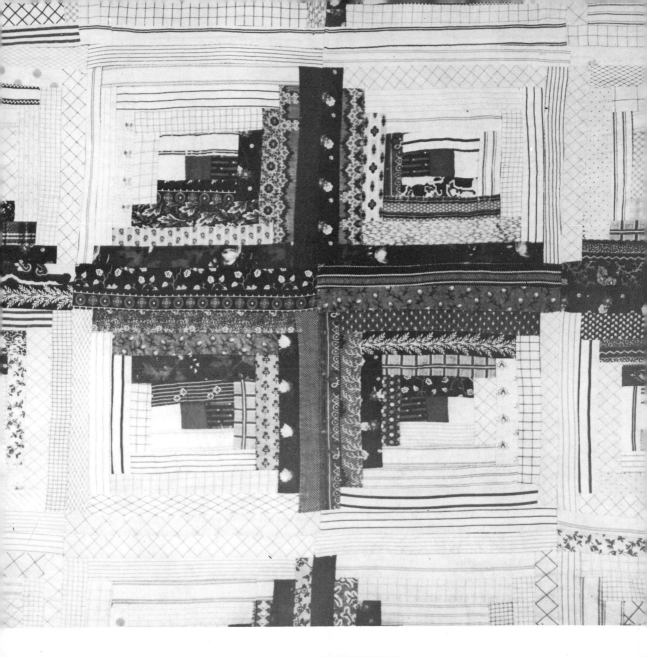

THE LOG CABIN QUILT

of the block. You will need to cut two light and dark rectangles of each size and only one center square. Allow ¼ inch all around for seams when you draft your patterns.

Sew the rectangles together as shown in the illustration. Be sure to press your scrap pieces before cut-ting as all the patches must be accurate. Arrange the dark and light tones according to taste.

Quilting Suggestions

Quilt along the seams between the patches. This quilt does not require a special quilting design.

THE CORNUCOPIA QUILT

THIS BRIGHT AND ATTRACTIVE OLD pattern shows so definite a modern tendency that it will fit very well into a bedroom planned for the home of today. The needlework is all of the pieced variety and the fabrics used for the patches are both plain and figured ones.

The quilt pictured shows one large motif on each decorated block alternating with the plain background blocks set diagonally. The flower part of the cornucopia motif is cut out of figured material. The patches for the flower are 6 equal-sized diamonds and for the leaves 4 smaller diamond-shaped patches are cut from plain green material. A holder for the flowers and foliage is in the shape of a horn or cornucopia cut from the same green used for the leaves and forms the base of the motif.

The flowers in the cornucopias may be the same throughout the quilt or each motif may be developed in a different color provided that care is taken to use the same size print with tone values constant in all the different fabrics.

The border illustrated is a band of plain material matching the leaves and the horn in width and color.

Materials Needed

9 yards white background material

4 yards green percale

Printed scrap material for flowers

Units in Each Block

Unit No. 1 . . . 1 green percale

Unit No. 2 . . . 5 green percale

Unit No. 3 . . . 6 printed material

Directions for Sewing

Cut 20 blocks of white material 14 inches square. Fold them diagonally across the center each way and press in creases with a warm iron.

Piece units together to form cornucopia as shown in the illustration. Turn in outside edges and baste in place ready for sewing.

Lay the design diagonally on the block using the creases as a guide. Appliqué in place by using small hemming stitches.

Border

Add a plain white border in any width you need to hang down over the bed. Cut a wide strip of green material and sew to the edge as shown in the illustration.

Quilting Suggestions

Quilt around the design units in the decorated blocks. You may repeat the cornucopia design in the plain block or select a design from the Quilting Chapter.

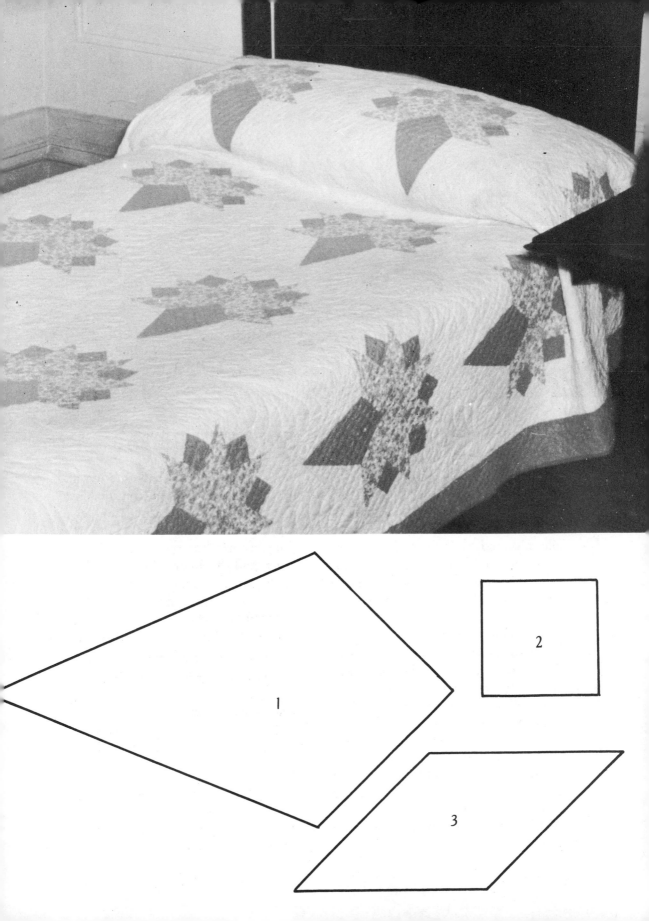

1

2

3

THE NORTH CAROLINA LILY QUILT

THIS IS A PATTERN WHICH TESTS the skill of the needlewoman for it uses both pieced patches and appliqué in the decorated blocks. In the example pictured the lily plant and pot form the motif in the decorated block which is set diagonally with alternate plain blocks when the cover is assembled.

The flowers may be cut from either plain or figured fabrics if small design old-fashioned calicos are used. The color range which may be used for this quilt is very wide, indeed, for lilies in nature may be found in many hues from the deepest red through palest yellow or cream.

The stem and leaves, as well as the flower pot, should always be cut from a plain fabric in a pleasing shade of soft green. The flowers are first pieced and then the leaves, stem and flower pot are appliquéd on the block.

The border can be the triangles as shown in the illustrated quilt, of a green fabric but two-tone stripes of green and the color used in the flower patch will prove more decorative,

Materials Needed

9 yards white background material

4 yards green percale

1 yard old-fashioned yellow calico

Units in Each Block

Unit No. 1 . . . 3 green percale

Unit No. 2 . . . 12 old-fashioned yellow calico

Unit No. 3 . . . 1 green percale

Unit No. 4 . . . 2 green percale

Unit No. 5 . . . 1 green percale

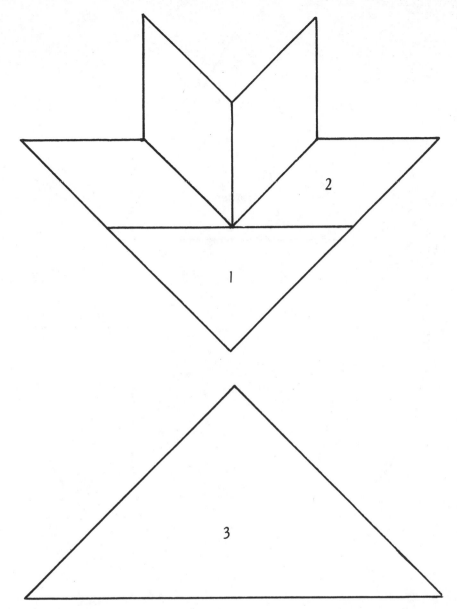

Directions for Sewing

Cut 20 white background blocks 14 inches square. Fold them diagonally each way and crease with a warm iron.

Cut out units for each block. Piece units together to form the three lilies, then turn in outside edges and baste in place. Cut bias strips ¾ inches wide for the stems and turn in edges on both sides.

Turn in edges of the three leaves and flower pot, and baste ready for sewing.

Assemble the design units on the white background block using the di-

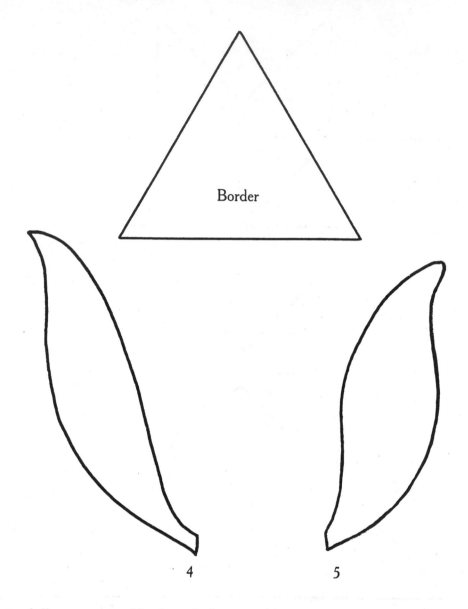

Border

4

5

agonal lines as a guide for placing them. Baste in place and appliqué design to block with small hemming stitches.

Border

Cut the border in any width you need to hang down over the edge of the bed. Add a row of green and

white triangles through the center as shown in the photograph of the quilt.

Quilting Suggestions

Quilt around the edges of the units in the quilt design. Repeat the lily design in the plain blocks, or you may use a feather wreath if you desire.

THE SUN BURST PATTERN QUILT

ONE CORNER OF AN OLD QUILT OF this pattern with its festooned border is illustrated, showing the dramatic design that can be made when this motif is employed.

The needlework of the quilt is appliqué. Cut-out patches are sewed to the quilt cover and border and a wider range of color can be used than is advisable for most quilts. The central "eye" of the sun burst motif is of course yellow. Tints and shades of three colors may be used for the triangular cut-out rays and plain or figured or both plain and figured, fabrics can be used attractively. The same colors used in the body of the quilt are repeated in the border festoons.

Each block for the entire cover can be decorated with the appliquéd motif or the appearance of the quilt may be varied by alternating the decorated blocks with plain background ones. For the quilt stitching of the plain blocks a sun burst motif in the same size as the appliqued one will be very effective.

Materials Needed

9 yards white background material

5 yards green percale

5 yards figured or plain rose percale

1 yard light pink percale

½ yard yellow percale

Units in Each Block

Unit No. 1 . . . 1 yellow

Unit No. 2 . . . 8 figured material or rose

Unit No. 3 . . . 8 green

Unit No. 4 . . . 16 light pink

Sewing Directions

Cut 20 white background blocks 14 inches square. Crease them diagonally several times and use the lines as a guide for placing the units.

This is an appliquéd quilt. Cut out all units for the block, turn in the outside edges and baste ready for sewing.

Assemble the units on block as shown in the illustration. The tips of the sun burst form a circle in the block. Begin with the outside triangles and build the design by working *toward* the center. Place the center circle in place last. Baste all units in place for sewing.

The order of appliquéing the units is in reverse to that of assembling

them on the block. Begin by appliqué-ing the center first and then sew each succeeding row of triangles, sewing the outside ones last.

Border

Cut your border strips and appliqué the design before attaching it to the quilt. However, the corner bow must be left free until border is set and then appliquéd as the final touch to the quilt.

Quilting Suggestions

A small sun burst design used on the white background between the squares will be most effective and will tie the quilt and quilting design together. Quilt around the outside edges of the units in the Sun Burst.

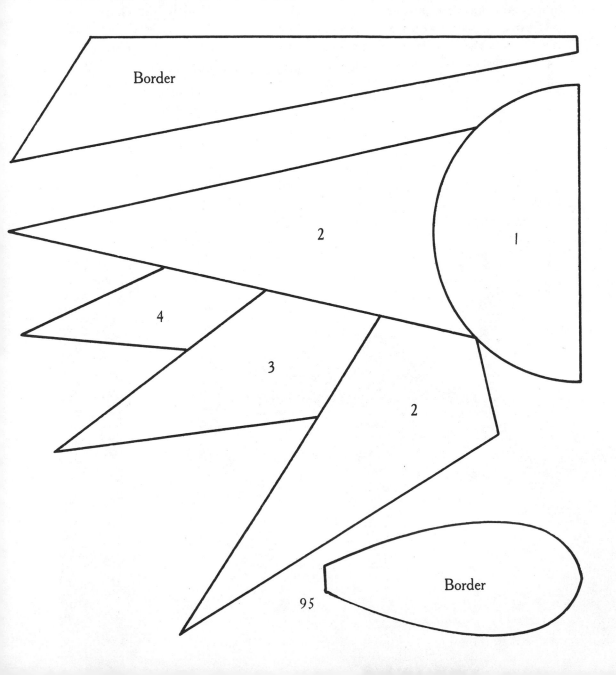

THE NORTH CAROLINA ROSE QUILT

THE QUILT DESCRIBED HERE IS UN- usual and effective, not only because of the very pleasing motifs of the design, but also through the unique unity achieved from the arrangement of stripes between the separate blocks and between the blocks and the plain border.

Two shades of a color are used in the design, the darker tone for the large center of the rose with lighter middle circle and a repeat of the dark tone in the outside circle of the inner rose. Light tones are used in the buds and plain green fabric for the leaves. The flowers, buds and stems are cut from a figured fabric with a very small design, and are appliquéd to the block.

The connecting stripes can be of the plain green of the leaves or can match the darker shade of the fabric used in the flower.

Since there is little opportunity for the expert quilter to make an elaborate quilting design in the central blocks, the border with special designs to be found in the chapter on Quilting, will add a distinctive finish to the appearance of the quilt.

Materials Needed

9 yards white background material

2 yards plain green percale

5 yards light rose or yellow (cut strips from this color)

1½ yards deep rose or yellow

Units in Each Block

Unit No. 1 . . . 1 deep rose or yellow

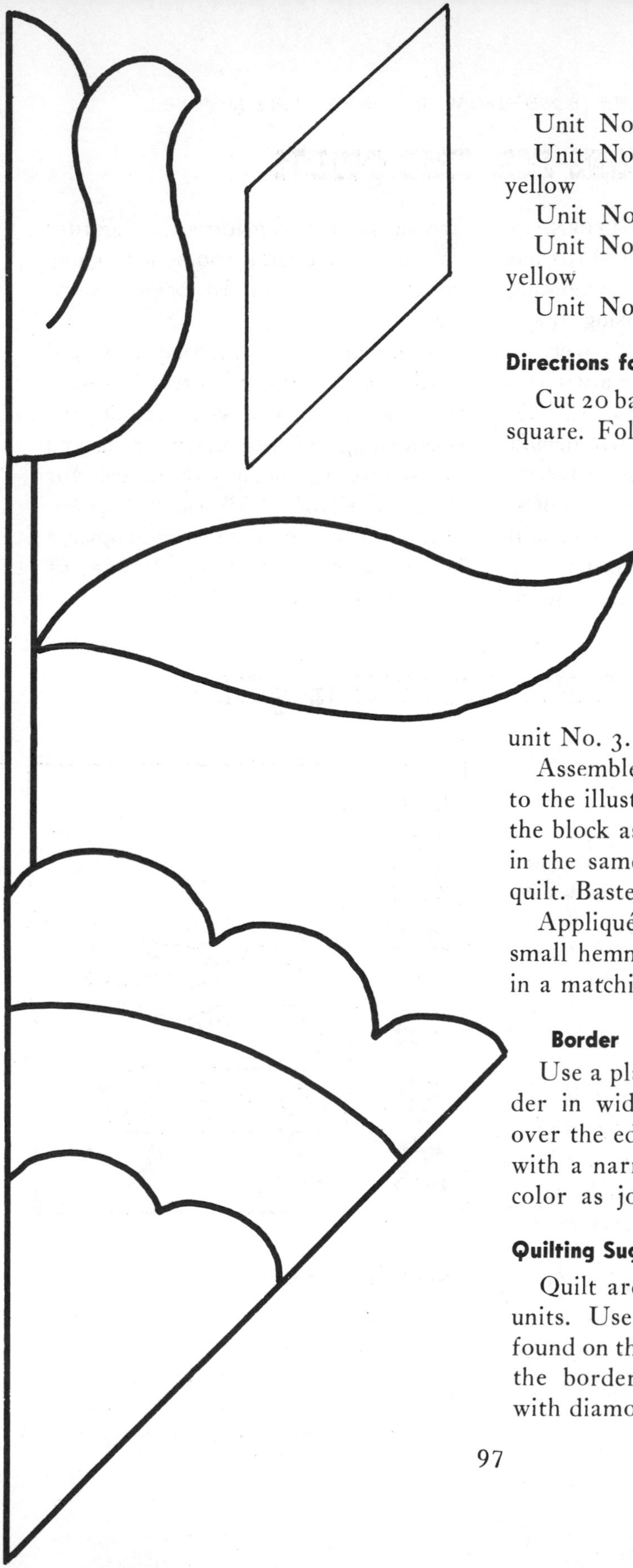

Unit No. 2 . . . 1 white

Unit No. 3 . . . 1 light rose or yellow

Unit No. 4 . . . 8 plain green

Unit No. 5 . . . 8 deep rose or yellow

Unit No. 6 . . . 16 green

Directions for Sewing

Cut 20 background blocks 14 inches square. Fold them diagonally across each way and then across the center in both directions. Press in the creases with a warm iron.

Cut out units for each block, turn in the edges and baste in place. Appliqué unit No. 1 to unit No. 2 then unit No. 2 to unit No. 3.

Assemble units on block according to the illustration. Use the creases in the block as a guide for placing them in the same position throughout the quilt. Baste them in place for sewing.

Appliqué to background block with small hemming stitches, using thread in a matching color.

Border

Use a plain white strip for the border in width needed to hang down over the edge of the bed. Bind edges with a narrow bias strip in the same color as joining strips.

Quilting Suggestions

Quilt around the outline of design units. Use the corner tulip design found on the block at intervals around the border. Fill in the background with diamonds or squares.

97

DESIGNS FOR CRIB QUILTS

ALMOST ANY QUILT PATTERN IN the book may be adapted for use on a crib or child-sized bed by making the designs smaller and using fewer blocks to complete the quilt cover.

Fine textured fabrics are always to be preferred for use on the smaller beds, and fast colors which will permit frequent launderings are advised. Materials used should be plain but if figured fabrics are chosen these should have very small units of design.

In the modern nursery pastel colors are no longer considered obligatory for use in a child's room, for young children react well to bright, vivid shades.

More and more antique cribs and cradles in the dark rich woods—walnut, mahogany and well waxed pine—are being rediscovered in attics and barns and are being put to use for children of today. Pieced and appliquéd quilts make the most appropriate bed coverings for these old bits of nursery furniture.

PENNSYLVANIA DUTCH CRIB QUILT

THESE CHARMING PENNSYLVANIA Dutch designs are combined as a suggestion for a cradle quilt. The design may be applied to any size you need for a particular crib or bed. You may make it as long as you like by adding additional groups of six leaves on the side border or, you may add another tulip in the center.

Suggestions for Materials

Since the material needed is less than ½ yard of each color, you may find what you need in your rag bag. However, we suggest these colors:

Unit No. 1 . . . old-fashioned yellow print calico
Unit No. 2 . . . brown or tan
Unit No. 3 . . . light blue
Unit No. 4 . . . green
Unit No. 5 . . . green
Unit No. 6 . . . red
Unit No. 7 . . . yellow

Sewing Instructions

Cut out white background any size you wish to make the quilt. Fold the material across the center each way and press in creases with a warm iron.

Cut out design units, turn in the

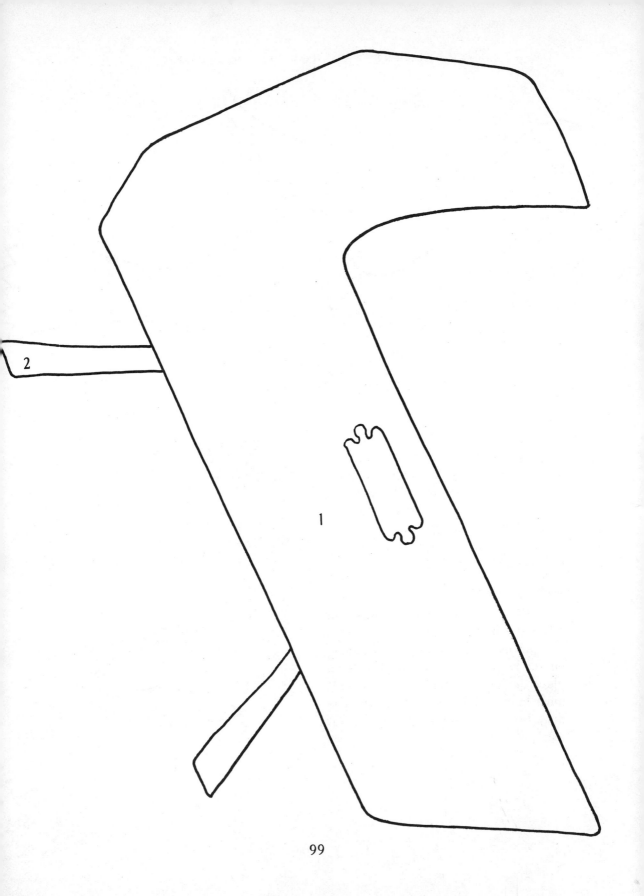

99

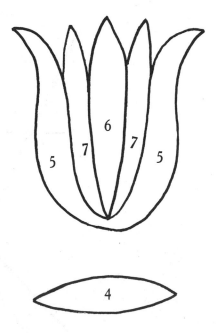

edges and baste ready for sewing. Assemble units on quilt, using the center creases as a guide for placing them. Baste in place ready for sewing.

Appliqué to background with small hemming stitches using thread in a matching color.

Quilting Suggestions

Quilt around the design units and fill in the background with diamonds or squares. The quilting stitches must be fairly close to hold the cotton in place during the many times the quilt must be washed. Use a large embroidery hoop for holding the quilt taut for quilting.

THE TULIP QUILT FOR A CRIB

THE ILLUSTRATED TULIP PATTERN is one that can be used effectively on the child's bed in smaller dimensions but can be applied to a full sized matching quilt for use in the parents' room. If the child's room opens out of the main bedroom the corresponding pattern will tie the decorations of the two rooms together.

The pattern is very simple to appliqué as the units are large and the outlines smooth and straight. The novice will find this quilt design one to use in making an easy and successful start in appliqué work.

The color of the tulip is optional —red, pink, yellow and even purple. If you think the design is too large or bold, the design can be reduced in size and repeated on six small blocks with a narrow white border around the edge.

Materials Needed

White material for background (measure crib or bed for amount needed)

1 yard plain green percale
½ yard color for tulip

Units in Each Block

Unit No. 1 . . . 8 green
Unit No. 2 . . . 8 green
Unit No. 3 . . . 4 tulip color

Cut green bias strips ¾ inch wide for center stems.

Sewing Instructions

Cut 4 white background blocks according to the size you wish to make the quilt. Fold each block diagonally through the center each way and press in creases with a warm iron.

Cut the design units, turn in the edges and baste in place. Cut bias green strips ¾ inch wide and turn in both edges for the center stem.

Assemble units on background block using the diagonal creases as a guide for placing them. Baste in place and appliqué to block with short hemming stitches.

TULIP CRIB QUILT

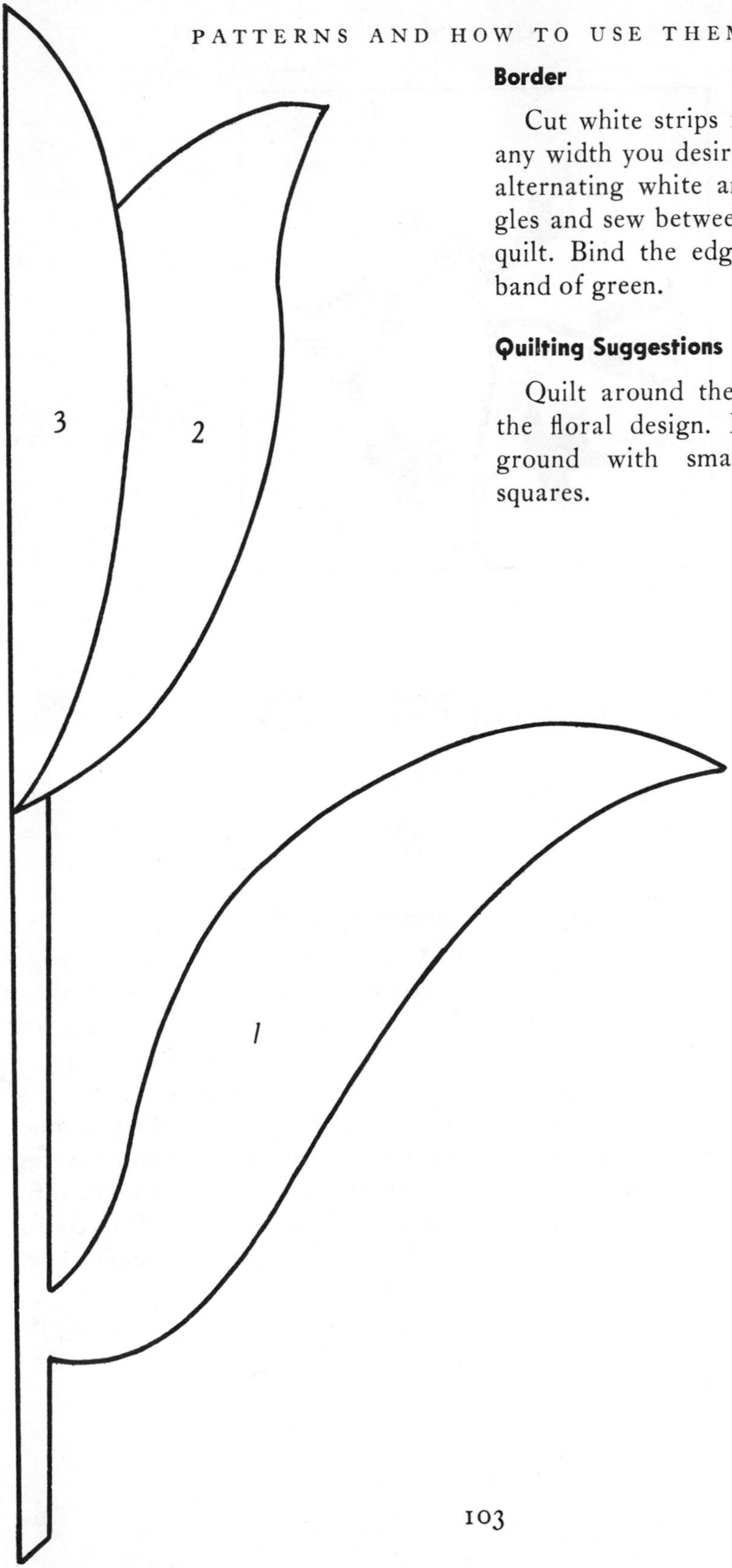

Border

Cut white strips for the border in any width you desire. Piece a row of alternating white and colored triangles and sew between the border and quilt. Bind the edge with a narrow band of green.

Quilting Suggestions

Quilt around the outside edge of the floral design. Fill in the background with small diamonds or squares.

3

2

1

PENNSYLVANIA DUTCH DESIGN

THIS QUAINT DESIGN IS TAKEN from a decoration on an old Pennsylvania Dutch chest. We have added it to our quilt patterns, as it may be used as a central block in a period quilt, or used as a hanging in a room with antique furniture. It may also be used as a cushion top.

It combines three favorite motifs used in the early nineteenth century —tulips, tulip leaves and a bird. Since the Pennsylvania Dutch usually combined vivid primary colors, this is a typical design of the period.

Units in the Block

Unit No. 1 . . . 1 blue
Unit No. 2 . . . 2 green
Unit No. 3 . . . 1 red
Unit No. 4 . . . 4 yellow
Unit No. 5 . . . 4 green

Sewing Instructions

Cut out all units and turn in edges ready for sewing. Cut the wing of the bird separate, turn in the edges and baste in proper place on the body.

Appliqué all units to background block (pattern is drafted for a block 14 inches square). Appliqué a tiny yellow diamond cut from percale for the bird's beak and a small circle for the eye. Do not use embroidery thread.

Use scrap material for cutting the patches.

OAK LEAF QUILT

OAK LEAF QUILT

THIS IS A VERY OLD DESIGN MADE of old-fashioned red and green printed calico. There are a number of patterns similar to this one—for instance, the Reel. The center motif is the same, but instead of oak leaves being placed at the corners there are four oblong handles. There is also an old pattern called the Hickory Leaf

in which the units of the design are exactly the same shape only wider at the centers. The Reel is usually made of dark blue figured material and the Hickory Leaf of figured green calico.

The design of green oak leaves and red circle and square is appliquéd to a white block. Each block may be decorated or alternated with plain white blocks.

There are a number of ways in

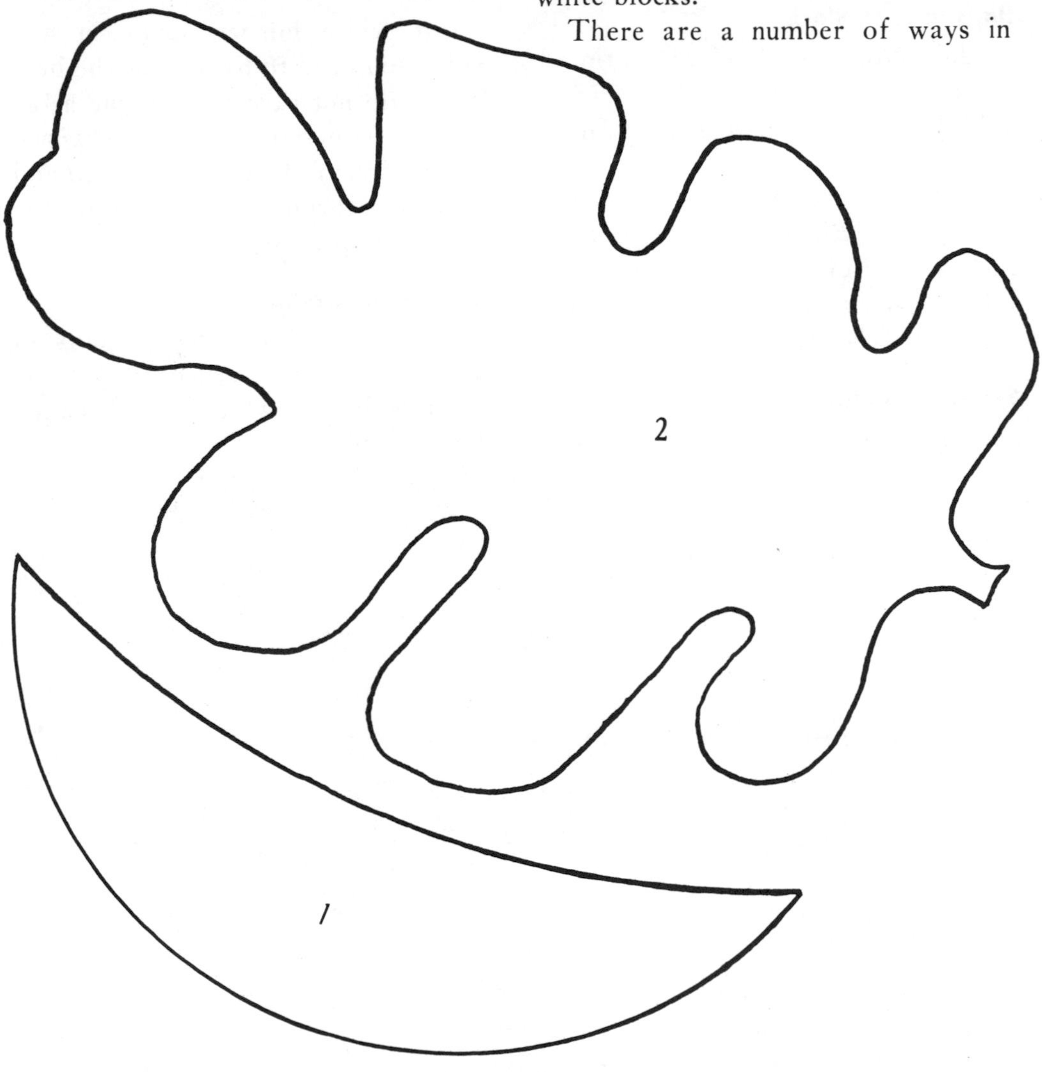

2

1

which the border may be planned. If you want to include one or more of the design motifs in the border, you can either use scattered oak leaves along the outside edge, or make a row of scallops using the pattern of one of the arcs in the circle.

Materials Needed

9 yards white background material
3 yards green figured calico
3 yards red figured calico

Units in Each Block

Unit No. 1 . . . 4 red printed calico
Unit No. 2 . . . 4 green printed calico

Note: Draw center square by forming first a circle with unit No. 1 on each side. Reverse the curve on inside of circle to get pattern for center unit. Cut from red printed calico.

Sewing Directions

Cut 20 white background blocks 14 inches square. Fold each diagonally across the center both ways and press in creases with a warm iron.

Cut design units, turn in the edges and baste them ready for sewing.

Assemble units on white block using the creased lines as a guide for placing them. Baste in place and appliqué to background with short hemming stitches.

Border

Cut white border strips in any width you need to hang over the bed. If you do not care to appliqué a design as suggested before, cut 2-inch bands of the red and green calico and sew them through the center of the border strips.

Quilting Suggestions

Quilt around the design units in each block. Quilt stitch wreath of feathers in the white area between the designs.

TULIP DESIGN QUILT

THIS BEAUTIFUL OLD TULIP PAT-tern with a cactus-like center motif will fit into any bedroom. The design can be made lacy in effect by using pale shades of percale, or it can be bold and striking with red and yellow calicos.

While the design looks intricate to make, it presents no more difficult problems than any other appliqué quilt. Once you have learned the trick of turning in edges around curved and acute angles, you can easily master the center motifs which require more detail than do the tulips in each corner.

The original colors pictured in this block were two shades of yellow surrounded with green leaves. However, you may substitute two shades of any other color you may wish to use.

This quilt may be of solid decorated blocks without a separate border, or you may use a border decorated in an appliquéd design. You might consider the Tulip border illustrated in the Chapter on Borders. Another suggestion is to use yellow and green bands running through the center of a plain white border.

Units in Each Block

Unit No. 1 . . . 8 light yellow
Unit No. 2 . . . 8 green
Unit No. 3 . . . 8 green
Unit No. 4 . . . 8 green
Unit No. 5 . . . 8 light yellow
Unit No. 6 . . . 4 deep yellow
Unit No. 7 . . . 1 deep yellow or green
Unit No. 8 . . . 1 light yellow

Materials Needed

 • 9 yards white background material
 5 yards green percale
 4 yards light yellow percale
 1 yard deep yellow percale

Sewing Instructions

Cut 20 white background blocks 14 inches square. Fold them diagonally through the center each way and then make center folds. Press in creases with a warm iron.

Cut out design units and turn in the edges ready for sewing. You will

TULIP DESIGN QUILT

have to make ⅛-inch cuts frequently along the outside edges of center units in order to turn in material around the curves.

Assemble units on block according to the illustration. Use the creases in the block as a guide for placing them. Baste all units in place and appliqué to background with small hemming stitches.

Quilting Suggestions

Since the Tulip design is very decorative, you do not need an elaborate quilting design. Quilt around the edges of the design units and fill in the background with small diamonds.

THE PRAIRIE FLOWER QUILT

THIS ILLUSTRATED QUILT WHICH uses the long stemmed, tulip-like prairie flower as the basis of its design reveals the interesting quality of the half-wreath so challenging to balance of the over-all pattern.

The color tones can be two shades of rose or pink, the deeper shade being chosen for use at the apex of the motifs with yellow employed as an accent and green for the accompanying foliage. In this original quilt, the large motif-filled blocks are alternated with others bearing smaller and more delicate designs using balancing and harmonious colors.

Most of the quilts made in the nineteenth century were designed for use on wide, commodious beds and were apt to be square or nearly square in shape. This Prairie Flower Quilt shows one almost entirely square with the half-wreath designs facing each other on opposite sides of the background.

When making a modern adaptation with emphasis on a narrower bed and the long lines to cover pillows, the half wreaths may be balanced in a vertical pattern to increase the interest in the longer, narrower quilt.

For a border on this quilt, none being shown on the illustrated one, choice may be made from the numerous border designs which can be found in this book in the Chapter on Borders.

Materials Needed

9 yards white for background
1 yard plain rose or pink
¾ yard figured pink
4 yards green

Units in Each Block

Unit No. 1 . . . 19
Unit No. 2 . . . 1
Unit No. 3 . . . 1
Unit No. 4 . . . 1
Unit No. 5 . . . 2
Unit No. 6 . . . 2
Unit No. 7 . . . 2
Unit No. 8 . . . 1

Sewing Instructions

Cut 20 background blocks 14 inches square.

Next cut out units for each block,

THE PRAIRIE FLOWER QUILT

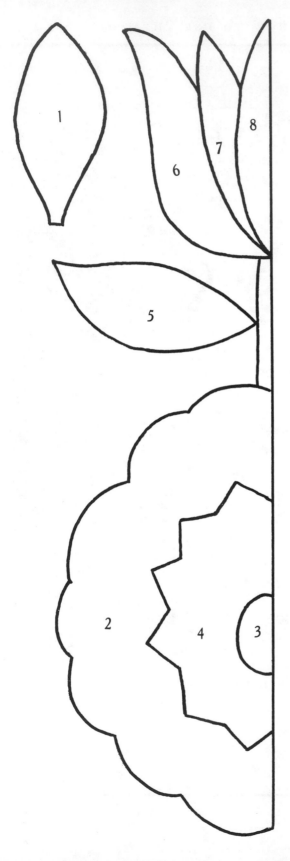

turn in the edges and baste ready for sewing.

Divide the block into 4 equal squares by folding across the center each way and pressing crease with warm iron.

Appliqué yellow center to larger figured pink center and then appliqué the figured center to the large pink flower.

Cut ¾-inch green bias strips for stem and half-wreath. Fold in the usual edges and baste in place.

Assemble units on block by first placing large flower in the center according to the creases. Baste a green bias strip to form a half circle and attach the leaves as shown in the illustration. Arrange units of tulip at top of flower according to center crease and add green bias stem. Attach all units in place ready to be appliquéd.

Border

Cut the remaining background material into any width border you wish. (If you wish, you may piece extra squares and eliminate a border as in the quilt illustrated.) However, a border with a continuous trailing vine would be most attractive and add to the interest of the quilt.

Quilting Suggestions

The quilt will be just as effective if the small center flower motif is eliminated and a special quilting design used in this area. Use a wreath design in feathers or leaves. Quilt around the units in the design and fill in the background with small diamonds or shells.

LOBSTER QUILT

THIS RATHER UNIQUE QUILT PAT-tern derives its traditional name from the resemblance to the shape of the lobster and its decorative claws. The central motif is a single design, cut in one piece of a solid colored material and appliquéd to a solid background block.

The colors for the central motif or large cut-out are chosen to make a bold contrast to the white or cream background. The bright scarlet red of the lobster after it is boiled may be chosen, or the duller but distinctive blue-green of the shellfish may be used instead. Provided one would im-prove on nature and, incidentally, make the quilt in colors matching other room decorations, a shade of bright, deep marine blue may be chosen with excellent effect.

This quilt is one which is designed to be made as illustrated in strips of appliquéd blocks. The effect can be lightened and brought more into bal-ance with modern furnishings by using one decorated block with an alternating plain background square.

Though not shown here a border is advisable for use on this quilt. One can be effectively designed using a narrow strip of the same tone as the large central cut-outs. This narrow strip edges the central panels on all four sides of the quilt with a regular sized plain border and a binding also

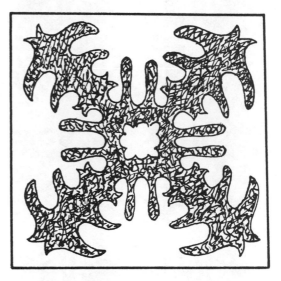

in the same tone as the dominant color of the cut-outs.

Materials Needed

9 yards white background material
5 yards lobster color material
2 yards lobster color for border strips

Units in Each Block

Unit No. 1 . . . 1

Sewing Instructions

Cut 20 white background blocks 14 inches square. Next, cut twenty lob-sters from colored material being sure the design is cut in one piece (doubling pattern shown here).

Turn in all outside edges and baste in place ready for sewing. You will

LOBSTER QUILT

have to make tiny cuts along the edge in order to turn the curves and acute angles successfully.

Fold the block diagonally and then across the center each way and crease with a warm iron. Lay on the center design according to the creases ready to be appliquéd.

Border

If you do not wish to make an extra row of decorated blocks for each side as shown in the illustration, there are a number of borders suggested in this book that may be applied. However, since the center designs are very decorative, a plain border with a colored band to match the center design can be used. Also, two bands can be used by placing one at the top and the other at the bottom of the border.

Quilting Suggestions

This quilt does not call for elaborate quilting designs. Quilt around edges of design unit and use any of the narrow designs illustrated in the Quilting Chapter for space between the blocks.

THE BRIDAL WREATH QUILT

THIS QUILT IN THE WELL KNOWN wreath design is an example of the many bridal quilts which were designed in America and sewed at the quilting parties held to announce the engagements of happy pairs.

The hearts which form the central figures of each block, bounded by wreaths, are to be found in most of the quilts which commemorated weddings in the early days. They are also to be found in kindred patterns throughout the Middle West and South during the heyday of quilting in the America of the nineteenth century.

The illustration shows a quilt made for a wide bed, probably a feather bed, and should be adapted if it is to be used in a room of modern furniture. The border shown is well chosen in that it employs the same leaf design which is found in the central wreath but the proportion of this border for a quilt being made today, should be wider than that shown in the illustration.

The colors of the original quilt are red hearts contrasting with green leaves and appliquéd on blocks 14 inches square. The design which is very pleasing, can be made more appropriate to the modern decor with rose, pink or even mauve colored hearts surrounded by delicately toned green leaves in the wreath.

This pattern is one of the least demanding on the skill of a novice

quilter, as it can be easily pieced and sewed having smooth edges of all parts of the design.

Materials Needed

9 yards white background material
2 yards plain red calico
6 yards green percale

Units in Each Block

Unit No. 1 . . . 30 green
Unit No. 2 . . . 8 red

Sewing Instructions

Cut 20 white background blocks 14 inches square.

Cut number of units required in each design. Turn in the edges ¼ inch and baste in place ready for sewing.

Fold the block diagonally each way and crease by pressing with a

THE BRIDAL WREATH QUILT

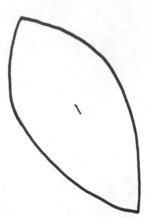

warm iron. Place the four center hearts on the diagonal lines so that the bottom points meet in the exact center of the block. Next place a heart in each corner as shown in the illustration.

Cut a bias strip ¾ inch wide of green material for center stem of wreath; turn in edges on each side and baste in place. Draw a circle half way between the center and corner hearts and baste the bias strip around the line. To make the strip lie flat, baste the *inside* edge *first* and then stretch the outside edge to place. Arrange the leaves around both sides of the circle to form a wreath.

Appliqué design to each block using a thread matching color of material.

Border

The border can be decorated in the same design but the border strips should be cut much wider. Decide how far the border should hang over your bed and cut the strips accordingly. Appliqué the continuous row of leaves along the center line of the strip. You should make special arrangements at the corner so that the decoration lines are not broken.

Quilting Suggestions

Since the decoration covers most of the quilt area, there is no need for elaborate quilting designs. Quilt around the outside edges of the design and fill in the background with small diamonds or straight lines. We might suggest that the hearts in the corner of each block be eliminated and the outlines be quilted instead.

THE ROSE OF SHARON QUILT

THIS IS A PATTERN WHICH IS FOUND with more variations than any other American design. One of the favorite flowers found in almost every Colonial and early American garden was the rose of Sharon. In many sections of the country the quilters adapted the familiar but decorative flower for use as the central motif of their quilt design. Many of the early quilters were original in their approach, which accounts for the numerous variations in the pink and white quilts of that era—all of which are labeled "Rose of Sharon."

In the pictured quilt the blocks have a large central flower conventionally balanced with buds and leaves and the border shown is composed of large flowers alternating with a balanced bud and leaf design.

The quilt shown is made in two shades of rose in the central flowers with the darker of these two shades repeated in the buds. The stamens of the real flowers are represented in the design with a yellow central eye in the conventionalized rose. Usually figured calico was employed for the patches and by its variation of tone represented the lights and shadows of the real flower.

The leaves and stems are cut from green fabric and, like the flower, this too was usually figured calico. The motifs repeated in the border follow the colors as well as the design of the central blocks.

Materials Needed

9 yards white background material
3 yards plain rose
2½ yards figured rose
½ yard yellow
5 yards green

Units in Each Block

Unit No. 1 . . . 1 yellow
Unit No. 2 . . . 1 figured pink
Unit No. 3 . . . 1 plain rose or pink
Unit No. 4 . . . 4 green
Unit No. 5 . . . 4 figured pink
Unit No. 6 . . . 4 green
Unit No. 7 . . . 4 figured pink
Unit No. 8 . . . 4 green
Unit No. 9 . . . 4 figured pink

Sewing Directions

Cut 20 background blocks 14 inches square.

Cut the correct number of units for each block, turn in the edges ready for sewing. Appliqué yellow center to pink figured center and then the figured center to large flower.

Fold block diagonally each way and then across center and press in creases with a warm iron. Assemble the unit pieces according to the illustration, following the creased lines as a guide for placing them. Baste in place ready for sewing.

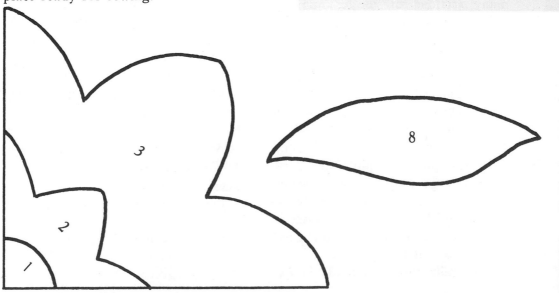

Appliqué in place with small hemming stitches, using thread in a matching color.

Border

Since the decoration on the quilt blocks is most elaborate, we suggest you simplify the border design. The rose shown in the corner of the border suggests a large flower on a diagonal stem with two buds on either side. A repetition of this motif at

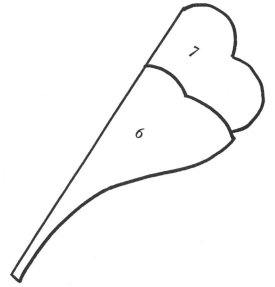

regular intervals around the outer edge would be pleasing. A leaf motif would be equally effective. Cut the border strips in the width you need to hang over the bed and add the decoration.

Quilting Suggestions

This quilt does not call for elaborate quilting designs. Quilt around the edges of the design units and fill in the background with small diamonds or squares.

THE MELON PATCH QUILT

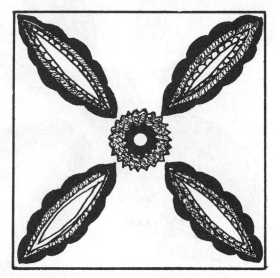

THIS KENTUCKY QUILT MADE IN solid color cottons on a homespun background, uses wide conventionalized oval melon-like forms in an interlacing design not a little reminiscent of the spreading melon vines and their fruit. The blocks are appliquéd with the designs using plain colored fabrics for the materials.

In color the outer rims of the melon-like segments can be executed in a pleasing green, shading into a deep yellow with the innermost sections being in pink or rose tones. The same three colors are repeated in the suggestion of the bud, the round center of the block, the colors being concentrically arranged with the green outside.

For an adaptation for use today, the designer may prefer to use the green outside with orange-yellow and deep yellow centers. Or she may elect to discard the yellow tones and use instead two tones of rose or pink.

Another variation of this pattern may be made for modern use by disregarding the interlacing possibilities and instead, placing each motif on a separate block and alternating the decorated blocks with ones made of background material.

As no borders are shown on the pictured quilt, three types of border may be suggested. Stripes of the three color tones of the central quilt can be run horizontally around the outer quilt edge. Variation of this may be the use of wider stripes of color at the outer edge of the border narrowing as they reach the edge of the quilt proper. Another border can be attractively made by using one of the melon segments as a scallop and repeated as often as necessary around the edge of the quilt.

Materials Needed

9 yards white background material
2 yards plain green
2 yards plain rose
1 yard figured rose
½ yard plain yellow

> or orange yellow

Units in Each Block

Unit No. 1 . . . 1 yellow
Unit No. 2 . . . 1 green
Unit No. 3 . . . 1 figured rose
Unit No. 4 . . . 4 green
Unit No. 5 . . . 4 rose (plain)
Unit No. 6 . . . 4 rose (figured)
Unit No. 7 . . . 4 yellow

Sewing Instructions

Cut 20 background blocks 14 inches square. Cut the different units for each block and turn in all edges excepting those on units 5 and 6. On these units turn in the inside edge only and baste in place. Appliqué the yellow center (unit 1) to green center (unit 2) and then to the large center unit of figured rose.

Fold the block diagonally across each way and press in creases with a warm iron. Assemble the units according to the illustration by placing unit 3 first in the center of the block. Next place the corner units according to the diagonal lines. Lay the yellow unit first and then the turned-in edge of the rose on the unturned edge of the yellow. Now place the green unit along the unturned edge of the rose (unit 5). Baste all units in place and appliqué to block with thread in matching colors.

Border

Cut border strips in any width you need to hang down over the bed. Decorate them according to taste—there are a number of suggestions in the introduction to this quilt.

Quilting Suggestions

The quilting design in this quilt follows the outlines of the design units. Quilt around the outer edge of the unit and make parallel quilting lines a $\frac{1}{4}$ inch apart until the lines meet in the center of the block. Quilt the area between in small squares.

127

HEARTS AND FLOWERS QUILT

THIS PATTERN CAN BE VARIED many ways by using different combinations of colors and materials. To make a dainty design, use pink hearts and a deep shade of rose for the buds with the green leaves. Another variation is to use a deep shade of rose for the heart and superimpose a smaller one cut from light rose material on the top.

If you have a room furnished in Pennsylvania Dutch type of furniture, you may use the red, yellow and green colors in this quilt to blend with the room. Make the hearts of figured yellow calico, the center and buds plain red calico and the leaves and stems green.

There are a number of ways to set the quilt together. If shades of pink are used in the design, the lighter shade can be used for 3-inch strips between the block. Add a plain white border separating it from the quilt with a green band an inch wide. Make large scallops around the outside edge and appliqué a heart and bud in each scallop (see Chapter on Borders).

If you use the Pennsylvania Dutch colors, set the blocks together without the colored strips between. Use a plain border without the scallops.

Materials Needed

9 yards white background material

3 yards green percale

5 yards light rose (includes material for strips)

1 yard deep rose percale

½ yard yellow percale

Units in Each Block

Unit No. 1 . . . 4 pink

Unit No. 2 . . . 4 green

Unit No. 3 . . . 1 yellow

Unit No. 4 . . . 4 deep rose

Sewing Instructions

Cut 20 white background blocks 16 inches square. Fold diagonally through the center each way and press in creases with a warm iron.

Cut the design units and turn in all edges for sewing. Assemble the units on the background block as shown in the illustration. Place the hearts and buds on the diagonal creases.

Appliqué the units to the blocks with small hemming stitches with thread in a matching color.

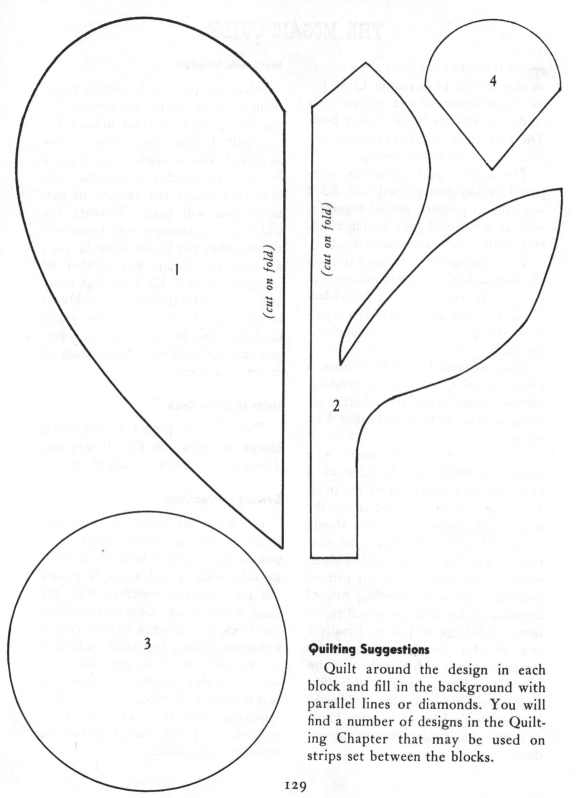

1 *(cut on fold)*

(cut on fold)

4

2

3

Quilting Suggestions

Quilt around the design in each block and fill in the background with parallel lines or diamonds. You will find a number of designs in the Quilting Chapter that may be used on strips set between the blocks.

THE MOSAIC QUILT

THIS ILLUSTRATED QUILT IS KNOWN also as the Honeycomb Quilt for its resemblance to the waxen cells made for storage by the honey bees. The pattern is an all-over design entirely of pieced workmanship.

The entire quilt cover is composed of hexagon shaped—six sided —pieces or patches, pieced together, with an occasional quilt having a central motif as in the one illustrated.

While the quilt appearance is of an all-over design, the pattern is made in blocks, the colors of the individual blocks being so arranged that a repetitive design is formed throughout the quilt.

This pattern has always been a great favorite, as it so successfully employs mixed materials and arranges them in true balance and color harmony.

For the modern designer who wishes to carry out the idea of a flower garden suggested by the overall impression of the quilt cover, the central hexagon of each block should be cut of yellow material, the next two rows of hexagons should be blues, pinks or yellows in different printed materials and a surrounding row of hexagons in tones of green will represent the foliage or leaves. Finally a row of white hexagons frames this central design and forms the path between the flower beds in this Old-Fashioned Flower Garden, or Martha Washington's Flower Garden Quilt, as it was sometimes called in colonial days.

Materials Needed

Since this pattern is usually made from scrap materials, we are not giving the amount of cloth needed for this quilt. If you want to place a row or two of plain hexagons in each block in order to develop a pattern, it is easy to estimate the amount of material you will need. Measure the width of the hexagon and figure the number that can be cut from ½ yard of material. Count the number of hexagons in each block in that color and multiply by the number of blocks in the quilt. If you know how many hexagons can be cut from ½ yard, you can easily estimate the amount of material needed.

Units in Each Block

This quilt is pieced in individual blocks as shown in the illustration. There are 65 units in each block.

Sewing Instructions

Cut hexagons from any color material you choose. Select center hexagon first and sew a hexagon to each six sides with ¼ inch seam. Next sew the six hexagons together with the same width seam. Continue building the block by adding a row of twelve hexagons, sewing first to the edges of the second row of six and then sewing the twelve together. Continue in this manner until block is pieced. It is important that the units be cut accurately and the seams sewed as straight as possible.

MOSAIC QUILT

Border

This quilt does not require a border. When all the blocks are set together, there will be a naturally formed row of scallops around the edge.

Quilting Suggestions

All quilting lines should follow the seams between the patches. Do not quilt over the patch itself.

THE WHIG ROSE QUILT

A DISTINGUISHED QUILT PATTERN is pictured in the photograph of a quilt made by Mathilda Kramer Whistler in 1861. With a name reminiscent of early political days in this country, the pattern, though more intricate and involved for the quilter, has such beauty that the extra care needed for piecing and appliquéing, is well rewarded by the decorative value of the finished quilt.

The bold yet pleasing color combination in this pictured quilt brings red and pink, yellow and green, all into harmony in a design which uses plain color materials for the separate parts of the pattern.

Despite the striking colors, the design itself is delicate, its appearance graceful, and its balance so true that it forms a quiet harmonious note in a decorative scheme.

When adapting this pattern for modern use, the paler decorators' colors can be used but to be sure that the harmony and balance are retained, the designer must make certain that the deepest tones chosen are used as the central feature of each block.

The border as shown in the illustration is astonishingly modern in conception, with scallops cut from the dominant color tone of the quilt and appliquéd around the edges.

Materials Needed

9 yards white background material
2 yards light rose or blue
1 yard dark rose or blue
½ yard yellow

Units in Each Block

Unit No. 1 . . . 1 yellow
Unit No. 2 . . . 1 light blue or pink
Unit No. 3 . . . 1 dark blue or pink with white triangles
Unit No. 4 . . . 1 dark rose or blue
Unit No. 5 . . . 4 light rose or blue
Unit No. 6 . . . 20 plain green
Unit No. 7 . . . 4 light rose or blue
Unit No. 8 . . . 4 green
Unit No. 9 . . . 4 yellow

Directions for Sewing

Cut 20 white background blocks 14 inches square. Since the pattern is quite elaborate on each block, you may prefer to make them larger and have only 12 in the quilt. If so, cut the blocks 18 inches square.

Cut out units in design, turn in the edges and baste ready for sewing. Appliqué all the center units to middle flower including yellow center, second center unit and small white triangles. Also appliqué yellow center to small outside flower.

Fold block diagonally each way and crease with warm iron. Assemble units on block according to illustration. Lay center units on first and then add outside flower and leaves, using diagonal lines as a guide. Ap-

WHIG ROSE QUILT

pliqué units to background block, using thread in a matching color.

Border

Cut border strips from remaining background material in a width wide enough to hang over the side of the bed. The scalloped design illustrated in the picture may be cut from any color harmonizing with the quilt design.

Quilting Suggestions

The original quilt stitch design shows a row of stitches around the edge of each unit; and in the rest of the block, fill-in with small parallel lines. A continuous line of feathers are used between the blocks.

BIRDS IN AIR QUILT

THIS QUILT PATTERN IS ONE OF THE earliest patchwork types we know, and its great value lies in the opportunity it gives to the designer to use small pieces of assorted fabrics. This is a prime case where the Victorian "scrap bag" comes well to the fore as a source of materials.

The pieced patches are all cut out in the form of triangles of exactly the same size for the entire quilt cover. The many variations known of this quilt come from the different sizes used to make the design. The most effective quilt cover in this pattern is one made of small sized triangles with meticulous stitching of the patches.

The illustration shows just one block of the quilt. The block is 12 inches square, and small triangles are $\frac{1}{2}$ of 2-inch square. Here we see the triangular patches arranged hit-or-miss fashion in two diagonal lines which cross between triangular half blocks of background plain material. The quilt pictured uses alternating white and darker-toned plain triangular blocks but the quilt is equally effective and less confusing to the eye when all the triangular blocks are of the one color tone.

Another variation for this design can be the use of two-color triangular patches alternating light and dark tones in the set pattern of the diagonals.

This quilt can be made without a border with the design running to the edges of the quilt and then be bound with a narrow bias strip. Or a plain border may be used with 1 ½ inch colored band at the top and bottom separating the quilt center from the border at the top and binding the outer quilt edge at the bottom.

Materials Needed

8 yards white background material
Scrap calicos and ginghams for center diamonds

Sewing Instructions

While this is an all-over pattern, the quilt is pieced in blocks as shown in the illustration. When they are sewed together the pieced strips will run diagonally across the quilt. The triangles on each side of the block will form diagonal squares, 12 inches on a side.

The triangles must be cut exactly and all must be the same size. Be sure to press all scrap pieces before attempting to cut them. Piece the center cross first and then set in the side triangles.

Quilting Suggestions

You may use any quilting design you choose in the plain squares. The illustration shows a series of parallel lines. Quilt around the seams of the small triangles.

BIRDS IN AIR QUILT

BUD AND ROSE WREATH QUILT

THIS IS ONE OF THE DAINTIER PAT-
terns that will fit well into any
modern bedroom. The design is built
around a wreath on which there are
four roses in a light shade of rose or
yellow with a bud design in each corner made from a deeper tone of the
same color. The circle that forms the
wreath is made with a green bias
strip.

Since the design is of a delicate nature, the fabric in the quilt should be
of fine texture and the colors in pastel
shades. A fine sateen may be chosen
as a material for the quilt, as the
edges of the design units are fairly
straight thus eliminating problems in
turning edges.

This quilt may be set together with
three-inch strips cut from the light
shade used in the flowers between the
blocks. If this method is used, add a
plain white border and scallop the
edges.

Another suggestion is to have the
entire quilt made up entirely of
decorated blocks and eliminate the
border entirely. Bind the edges of the
quilt with a narrow green bias strip.

Materials Needed

9 yards white background material
4 yards green percale
2 yards light pink percale
1 yard deep pink or rose percale
½ yard yellow percale

Units in Each Block

Unit No. 1 . . . 4 yellow
Unit No. 2 . . . 4 light pink

Unit No. 3 . . . 12 green
Unit No. 4 . . . 4 green
Unit No. 5 . . . 4 green
Unit No. 6 . . . 4 deep pink or
rose

Sewing Instructions

Cut 20 white background blocks 14
inches square. Fold them diagonally
through the center each way and
press in creases with a warm iron.

Cut out design units and turn in
the edges ready for sewing. Cut a
green bias strip ¾ inch wide, turn in
edges on both sides and sew it in a
large circle on the block on which the
wreath is to be built.

Assemble units around the wreath
as shown in the illustration. The
creases in the block will be a guide
for placing the flowers and buds. Appliqué all units to the block with short
hemming stitches.

Quilting Suggestions

If colored strips are used between the squares, you will find a number of quilting designs in the Quilting Chapter that are used for this purpose. Quilt around the outside edge of the design units and fill in the background with parallel lines or diamonds.

1

2

3

4

5

6

HAWAIIAN GRAPE VINE QUILT

THERE ARE TWO DISTINCT DECORA-
tive qualities about the quilts made
in the Hawaiian Islands. The most
prominent feature is the large over-
all motif, repetitive in nature which
is cut out and appliquéd to the background. The other distinguishing feature of these quilts is the single color
tone of these cut-outs and the contrasting backgrounds upon which they
are appliquéd.

Native designers use the fruits,
vegetation and tropical surroundings
for the inspiration of their designs—
palms, pineapples, seaweed, coral,
and the lush tropic flowers—all are
used as motifs for design.

The techniques used by the Island-
ers for cutting out the large, quilt-
sized motifs, are first to fold the
fabric into segments leading to the
point which is the center of the quilt.
Then they cut with a sharp knife
pressed against a firm, stiff pattern
through all the layers, to produce the
over-all cut out motif.

To make these designs more fea-
sible for use in modern sewing rooms,
these methods must be adapted and
the cutting-out process scaled down
to $\frac{1}{4}$ of the over-all pattern. A pattern for $\frac{1}{4}$ of the quilt is made and
cut out and this is repeated in the
other three corners. This will make
the work of appliqué less difficult, because it can be held for sewing so
much more easily.

The illustrated quilt has a bright
red motif on a white background, but
even more brilliant color contrasts

will be found in old Hawaiian quilts.
Color contrasts both bold and harmonious can be found. One charming
quilt had graceful seaweed festooned
in designs of deep green over a pale
sea green background. The warm yel-
lowish green of pineapple fronds were
appliquéd on a deep cream or ivory
background. The natives used tropical colors—fuchsia, magenta, electric
green—against contrasting colors to
make gaudy but attractive quilts.

The Hawaiian quilt does not call
for a border as the motif itself makes
the decorative whole.

Materials Needed

9 yards white background material
6 yards green or red calico

Units in Each Block

Unit No. 1 . . . 13 red or green
Unit No. 2 . . . 4 red or green
Unit No. 3 . . . 1 red or green
Unit No. 4 . . . 1 red or green

Sewing Directions

Cut 4 blocks 1 yard square. Fold
them diagonally each way and then
across the center twice, and press in
creases with a warm iron. The creases
will be a guide for laying on design
units.

Cut out design units and center
stems according to the illustration.
Turn in all edges and baste in place
for sewing.

The 36-inch squares will not be
large enough to hold the complete design. Arrange the design that covers

HAWAIIAN GRAPE VINE QUILT

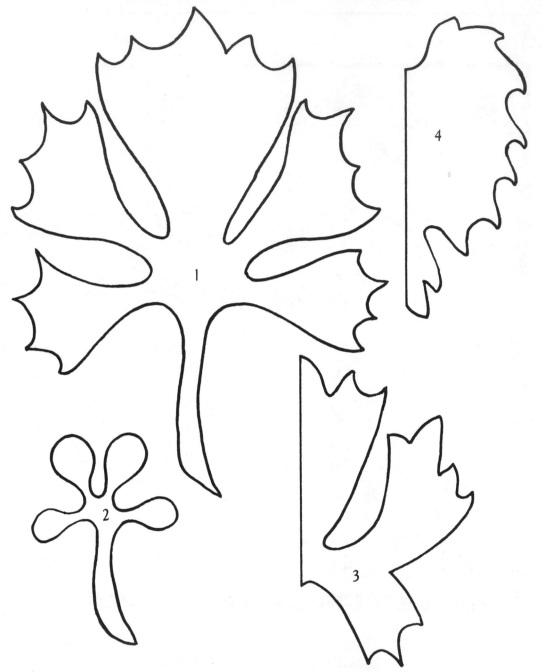

that area and appliqué in place, then cut border strips and sew around the edge of the blocks after they are set together. Extend the design over on the border and appliqué.

Quilting Suggestions

Quilt around the outlines of the grapevine design and fill in the background with diamonds to represent lattice work.

MEXICAN CROSS

THIS PATTERN DATES FROM 1840 when there was an awakening of interest in our neighbors to the South. It is made of bright warm colors such as continue to be associated with Mexico. The design is usually worked out by using two plain shades in different colors combined with a print material in a third color. Since the Zinnia flower is a native of that country, it would be safe to use the shades found in the flowers for a purely Mexican effect.

The design is too striking and colorful to fit into most bedrooms, but it can be used very effectively as a bed cover in a den, or as a covering for a couch on the porch. A single block may be used as a cushion top by enlarging the units in the design to the appropriate size. A patchwork tablecloth may be made by setting enough blocks together to fit your table to give a colorful background for Mexican pottery.

This pattern is entirely pieced with no alternating plain blocks used between the squares. Sew the patches together in each individual block and then set them together. The plain cross through the center of the block makes a series of crosses throughout the quilt.

Materials Needed

6½ yards of background material 4 yards light colored material (for cross)

5 yards darker material (for rays bordering cross)

Units in Each Block

Unit No. 1 . . . 4 light colored squares

Unit No. 2 . . . 5 squares background material

Unit No. 3 . . . 4 large triangles

Unit No. 4 . . . 8 small triangles

Unit No. 5 . . . 8 pointed strips

Unit No. 6 . . . 4 long pointed strips

Sewing Directions

Join the 9 squares in center block. Sew on the 4 prongs of the cross, and adjoining bars, then add on large and small triangles.

Border

Make border from plain or print material, cutting 2 strips 6½ inches by 61½ inches and 2 strips 6½ inches by 96½ inches. Join to ends and sides of the quilt, making a square for each corner using 2-inch squares.

Quilting Suggestions

Quilt units forming the cross and adjoining bars ⅛ inch away from seams. In triangle sections divide all sides in equal parts and quilt in diagonal lines.

MEXICAN CROSS QUILT

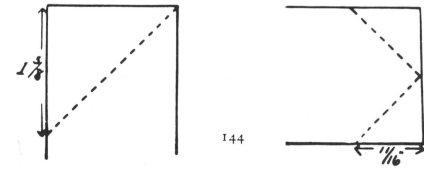

144

FLYING GEESE QUILT

THE FLYING GEESE QUILT

THIS IS ONE OF THE PATCHWORK patterns that is designed for parallel stripes running lengthwise on the bed. The colors in the patches and background can be varied to suit almost any room. The small triangles in the pieced strip are usually white, but the large triangles representing birds may be in mixed colors or in a single color in contrast to the background.

The illustration suggests large pieced triangles of a dark blue with small white triangles set on each side. The wide connecting strips are of light blue. For a more delicate design, use light rose triangles for the birds, white triangles on either side and light blue for the in-between strips.

This is an all-over pattern and no border is required. A single pieced strip in this pattern is often used as a border design on patchwork quilts.

Materials Needed

6 yards plain material for background

2 yards white material

3 yards for large triangles

Sewing Instructions

Cut out triangles for pieced strip and string the patches together according to color. Sew the patches in each strip together with a ¼ inch seam. After the strips are pieced, set them together with wide strips of plain material in any color you choose.

Quilting Suggestions

Quilt around the outside edges of the triangles in the pieced strips. Quilt in the background of plain material with small diamonds or squares.

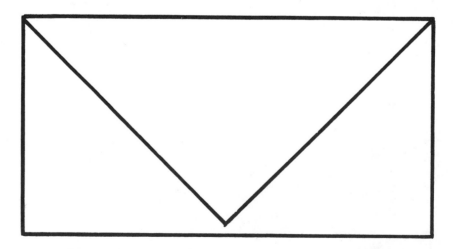

MOON OVER THE MOUNTAIN

IF YOU ARE PLANNING A QUILT FOR a mountain cabin, or for a guest room in your summer cottage, you will find this pattern amusing and easy to make. The background square is cut from figured blue calico to represent the Milky Way. The mountain is a triangle of dark blue and the moon, of course, is gold or yellow.

The two design units are appliquéd to the background square. The decorated blocks should be set together with plain blocks cut from unbleached muslin of equal size. Use a border of unbleached muslin with a narrow band of dark blue at the top and bottom.

Units in Each Block

Unit No. 1 . . . 1 dark blue
Unit No. 2 . . . 1 yellow or gold

Materials Needed

9 yards unbleached muslin
3 yards dark blue percale
3 yards yellow percale

Sewing Instructions

This quilt is a simple problem in

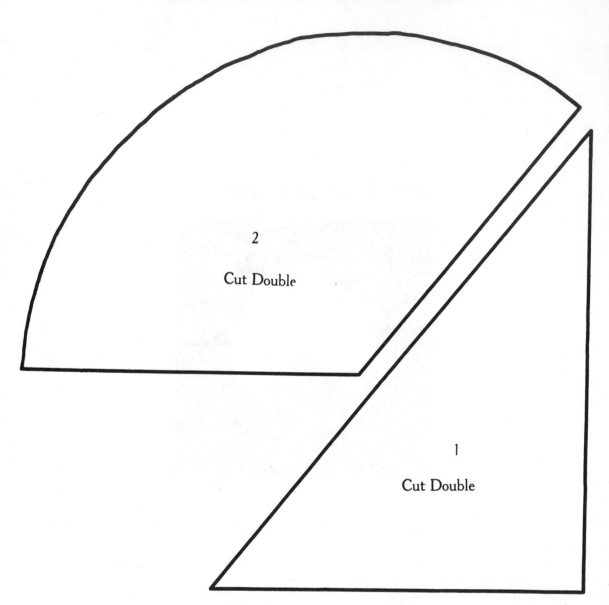

2

Cut Double

1

Cut Double

appliqué. Cut out design units, turn in edges and baste in place on figured background square. Sew in place with small hemming stitches.

Quilting Suggestions

Repeat "Moon Over The Mountain" pattern in the plain squares for the quilting design.

STORM AT SEA PATTERN

THIS IS AN INTERESTING PATTERN because the arrangement of the patches depict so vividly the name of the quilt—a Storm At Sea. It is a patchwork quilt pieced of patches of dark and light blue percale with intermittent patches of white for contrast and building the design.

To make the quilt, you should piece individual blocks (shown in illustration) and set them together after they are completed. Since the quilt is made up of hundreds of small patches, it is very important to cut them accurately and keep the seams an even ¼ inch throughout the quilt. Be sure the corners meet where the patches are joined.

Border

The quilt illustrated is pieced solidly throughout with no definite

STORM AT SEA PATTERN

border. However, it would be equally effective with the center part pieced to come to the edges of the bed and a plain border added, thus eliminating much of the piecing. Cut a white border the width you need and sew 2-inch bands of each shade of blue through the center. Bind the edge with a narrow bias strip of the dark blue color.

The quilting should be along the seams of the patches. If a plain border is used, you should include some of the outlines of the quilt design in your quilting pattern.

Materials Needed

6½ yards white material
3½ yards light blue
5 yards dark blue

Units in Each Block

Each 7-inch block is made up of 8 units. Patterns are given for units No. 1 and No. 2. Unit No. 3 is a 3½-inch square; unit No. 4 is half of unit No. 3; unit No. 5 is half of a 1⅝-inch square; unit No. 6 is a 1¼-inch square; unit No. 7 is half of unit No. 6; unit No. 8 is half of a ⅞-inch square.

Unit No. 1 . . . (diamond)—2 dark blue

Unit No. 2 . . . (triangle)—8 white

Unit No. 3 . . . (2½-inch square) —1 light blue

Unit No. 4 . . . (half unit No. 3) —4 light blue

Unit No. 5 . . . (half 1⅝-inch square)—4 white

Unit No. 6 . . . (1¼-inch square) —1 light blue

Unit No. 7—(half unit No. 6)— 4 dark blue

Unit No. 8 . . . (half of ⅞-inch square)—4 white

Sewing Instructions

To combine units to form a block, sew the long sides of No. 5 units to each side of No. 3 unit. Sew No. 4 units to No. 5 units to form a square. Sew the long sides of No. 2 units to each side of No. 1 unit to form a rectangle. Make another rectangle like this. Sew each rectangle to square as shown. Sew the long sides of No. 8 units to each side of No. 6 unit. Sew No. 7 units to each side of No. 8 units to form a small square. Sew small square in place, as shown, to complete a block. For double size, set 13 by 15 blocks. Complete as shown.

Quilting Suggestions

Quilt all units ⅛ inch away from all seams. Bind edges with dark blue.

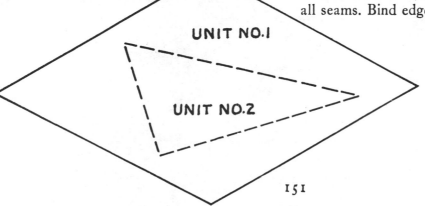

UNIT NO.1

UNIT NO.2

PEONY PATTERN

152

THE PEONY PATTERN

A NOVICE AT QUILT MAKING WILL make no mistake in choosing this pattern for a first attempt at the art. The result of the finished quilt will be very rewarding with a design so pleasing in simplicity and color.

This quilt is a combination of patchwork and appliqué. The flower is pieced from colored diamond-shaped patches with white triangles set around the edges and a small white square in each corner. The lower part of the block is made from a plain white rectangle to complete the square. The green leaves and stem are appliquéd to this area after the block is pieced together.

Since peonies come in almost any color, you may select the color you like for the flower. The old quilts were usually made of plain red and green calico. If you have an antique bed, you might use old-fashioned figured calico in red or yellow for the flower in keeping with the period. For a modern room, use rose, dark red or yellow for the flower and a harmonious shade of green for the leaves and stem.

Materials Needed

13½ yards of white material
2 yards red print
3 yards green print

Units in Each Block

Unit No. 1 . . . 6 red or yellow
Unit No. 2 . . . 4 white
Unit No. 3 . . . 1 green
Unit No. 4 . . . 2 white
Unit No. 5 . . . 1 white

Color of Border Units

Unit No. 6 . . . green
Unit No. 7 . . . green
Unit No. 8 . . . red or yellow
Unit No. 9 . . . red or yellow

Sewing Directions

Cut out all units and arrange patches according to color and size. Each block is made by combining appliqué and patchwork techniques. Sew the diamonds together first (unit No. 1) to form the Peony flower and then fill in the edges with the white units (Nos. 2, 4, and 5) to complete a square.

Turn in edges of unit No. 3 and baste in place to form stem of flower. Appliqué with small hemming stitches with thread in matching color.

Border

The quilt illustrated shows an appliquéd border in quite a different design. If you are a beginning quilter and hesitate to attempt an elaborate border, you may use a plain one instead. Cut a plain white border in the width you need and set a narrow band of green and one of equal width of the color of the flower through the center. Bind the edge with a narrow bias strip of green.

Quilting Suggestions

Quilt around the outside edges and along the seams of the patches in the decorated block. Use the Peony Pattern for the quilting design in the plain blocks.

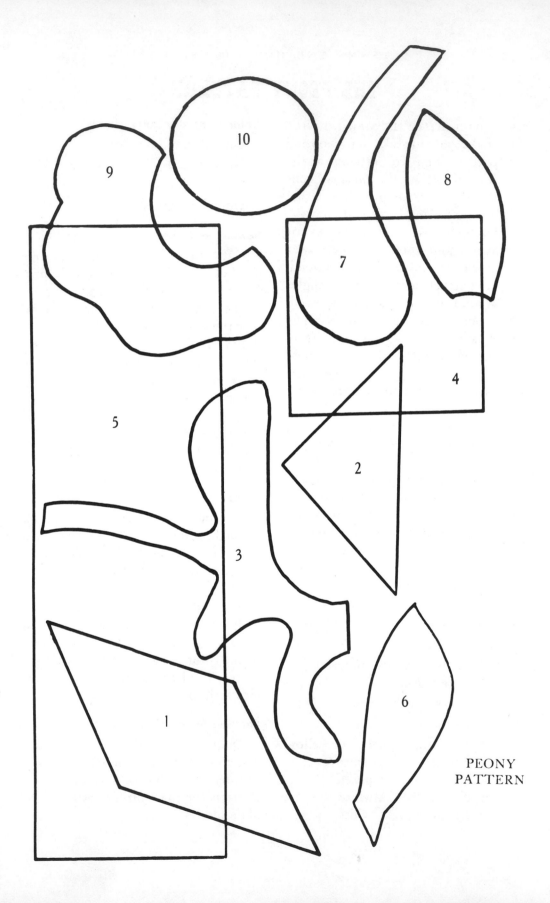

PEONY
PATTERN

5.

Borders

ABORDER, THE DICTIONARY TELLS us, is a boundary, or a margin or edge. It surrounds and hedges in, and also supports and protects what lies within the border. All these things are done for a quilt by its border. The border frames the pattern of the quilt as a picture is framed.

The rules which apply to picture framing are followed in selecting a border for the quilt. It must reflect and sustain the pattern, but not outshine it. A heavy ornate border on a dainty patterned quilt would be as unbalanced as a heavy carved gilt frame around a delicate pastel painting.

DESIGN OF THE BORDER

The central motif of the quilt should be echoed or repeated in the border. Sometimes the border offers a harmonious contrast to the motif. The strong and vigorous lines of the central pattern should find its repetition in the border, while the more fragile designs should have only light overtones. A delicate pattern is ideally framed by a border of ribbon streamers and bows, but you can imagine how absurd the same border would look around the edge of a **Log Cabin** or the rugged Saw Tooth Pattern.

WIDTH OF BORDER

In size as well as pictorial quality, the border must harmonize with the central theme. Most of the patterns discussed in this book are based on the 14-inch block. For a quilt composed of these squares, the border is well proportioned when it is a little wider than each of the center blocks —say, 18 inches. A border that is too narrow makes the central part of the quilt overly conspicuous, and on the other hand, a frame which is too wide will dwarf the significance of the central pattern.

Turning Corners

There is an old saying that the proof of the quilting ability lies in

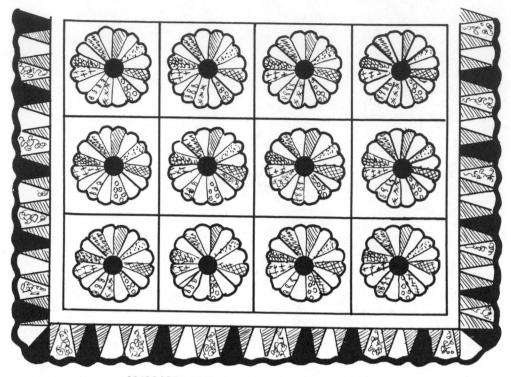

SCALLOPED BORDER OF PATCHWORK AND STRIP

the border. The turning of the corner tests the skill of both the designer and the quilt maker, and a neat and well turned corner is proof of the proficiency of both. The eye must follow the design easily as it makes its way clearly and in perfect balance. Ask a quilt connoisseur which part of the quilt receives her keenest attention, and she will surely tell you—*the corners!* Superstitions developed in the old days over the broken lines and stray ends of the corners, when carelessly designed or quilted, and they were taken as a foreboding of disaster to come.

The decoration of the border, generally speaking, should include at least one motif from the central area of the quilt, and one or two of the col-

ors. The material must match the body of the quilt, regardless of the design used, and if a figured material makes up the design, it must also appear in the border. Then too, the border must be wide enough to carry a motif equal in size to the central motif, although the outline may be simplified. The proportions must remain the same. However, if you decorate your border in a design altogether foreign to the quilt top, such as a trailing vine, the width is immaterial.

The borders offered in this chapter should be regarded as "types," not as designs for particular quilts. For instance, any quilt decorated in floral wreaths or designs would look well with a border of ribbons or small scallops, Leaves or vines seem suitable

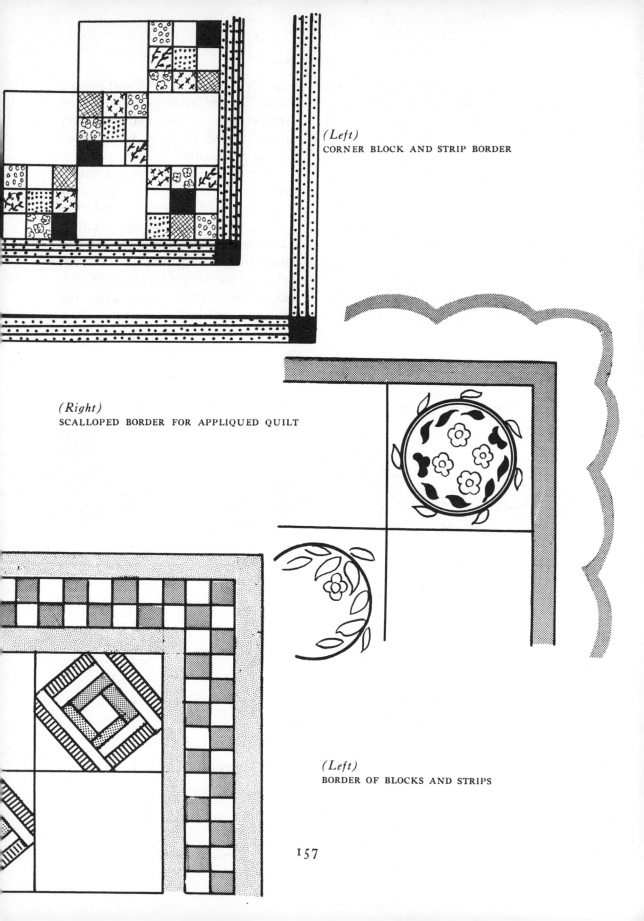

(Left)
CORNER BLOCK AND STRIP BORDER

(Right)
SCALLOPED BORDER FOR APPLIQUED QUILT

(Left)
BORDER OF BLOCKS AND STRIPS

157

with any theme drawn from nature. Likewise any rose design suggests the use of a floral and stem arrangement in the border.

APPLIQUÉD BORDERS

The center squares should be sewed and set together before the border strips are cut, and must be equal in measurement on the two sides and on top and bottom. Cut the border strips first for the top and bottom of the quilt. Next, cut strips for the sides long enough to equal the quilt's length with the added top and bottom strips. Do not attempt to miter the corners, for you will find that they will stretch out of shape when pulled tight in the frame.

After the border strips are cut to size, arrange the different parts of the design in place and appliqué. Sew it to the quilt cover. If the design is a continuous one and must turn the corner in some fashion, leave several inches of the design free at each end, and complete the appliqué after the border is attached.

APPLIQUÉD BORDERS

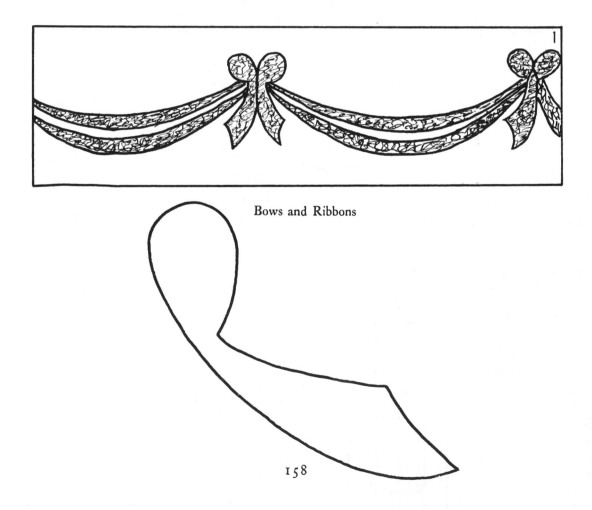

Bows and Ribbons

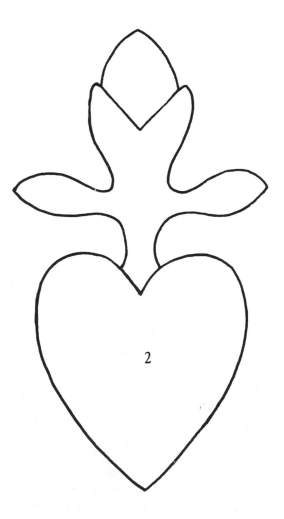

Strawberry Border

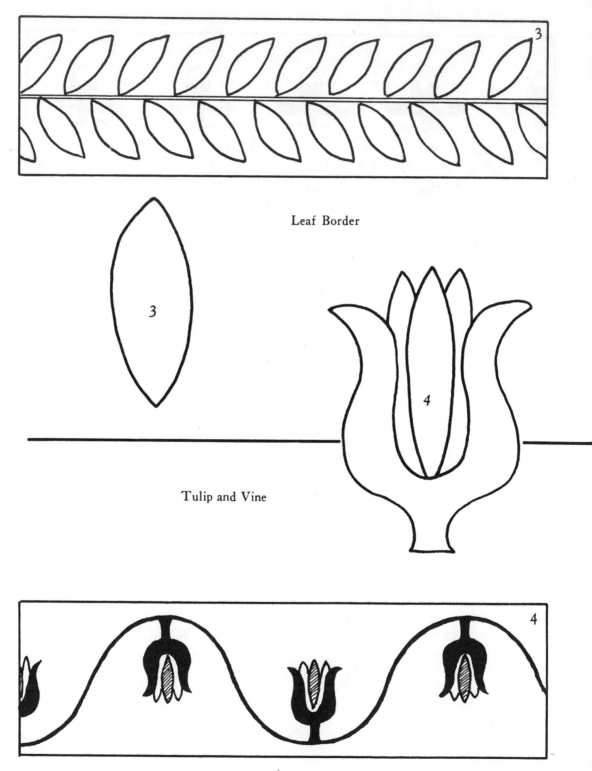

Leaf Border

3

Tulip and Vine

4

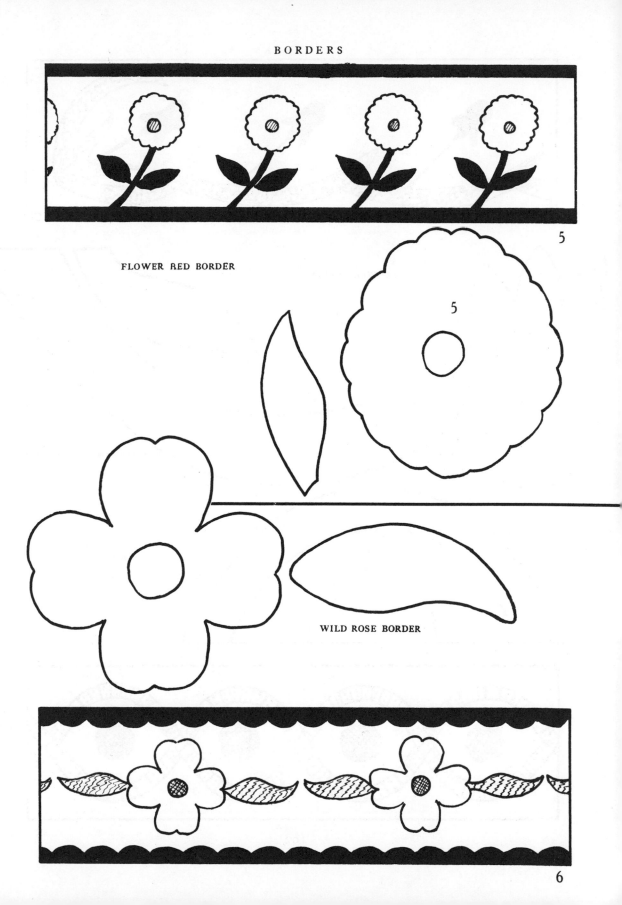

5

FLOWER RED BORDER

5

WILD ROSE BORDER

6

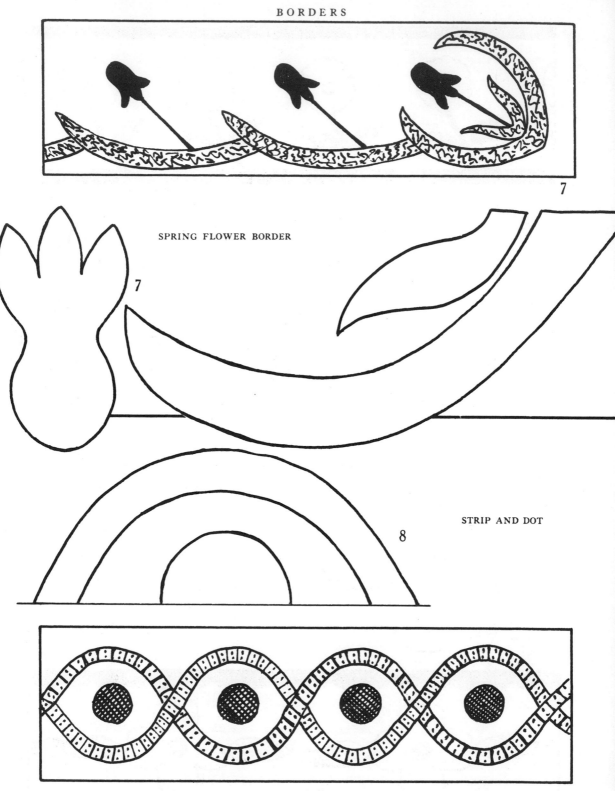

BORDERS

7

SPRING FLOWER BORDER

7

STRIP AND DOT

8

8

PATCHWORK BORDERS

The borders illustrated on these pages are designed primarily for patchwork quilts. They are made up of squares, rectangles, diamonds and triangles cut from matching materials of the quilt, and sewed into long rows one or two patches wide. They are usually used as a decorative row running through the center of the border strips, but they may also be placed at the top of the border as a dividing line between it and the quilt top. Of course, if you are ambitious enough to sew two rows, you can place them parallel to each other through the

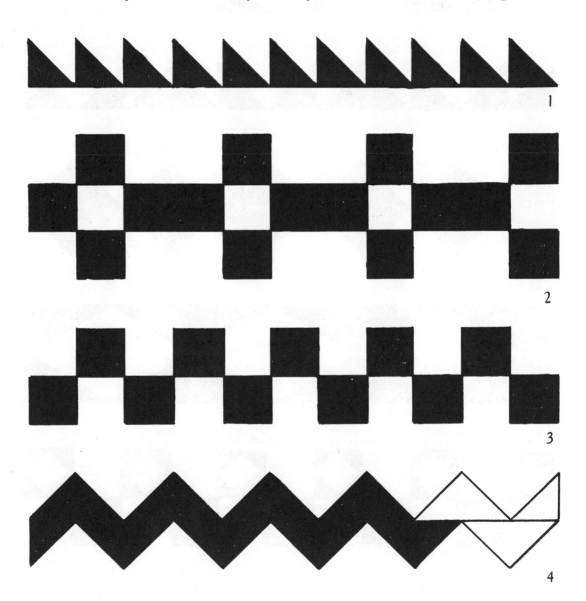

1

2

3

4

5

6

7

8

9

10

11

12

13

14

15

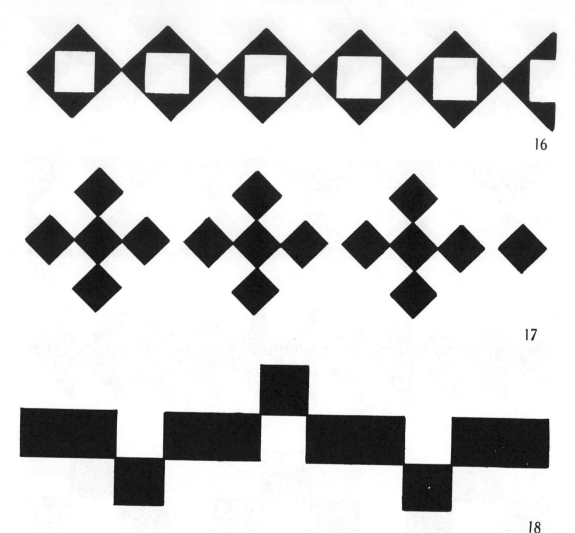

16

17

18

center, or one at the top and the other at the bottom of the border.

To make the border, cut patches according to shape shown in the design and from the same material as used in the quilt. Sew together in long rows the length of the border strip. If the corners must be turned by making some special arrangement of the patches—either add an extra one, or cut one in different shape or size. Sew these extra corner pieces in place after the border has been attached to the quilt top.

6.

Quilting

THE PURPOSE OF THE QUILTING stitch is to firmly lock the top of the quilt to both its back and the lining in between. In primitive times, the three layers of bed covering and clothing were held together by stitches at only a few main points, called the counter points or quilt points.

Next came interlacing diagonal lines, forming squares and diamonds, and the decorative quilt stitching gradually developed into more elaborate designs having a central motif and a border with a "fill-in" space between.

Alternating Blocks

Quilt stitching is used in all kinds of quilts—comforter, appliquéd and patchwork. When the quilt is composed of squares, the quilting stitches cover the plain squares which alternate with the decorated ones, and this gives the effect of throwing the decorated part into more pronounced relief. These quilting stitches in the plain squares are sometimes in straight or diagonal lines and are usually planned to form a contrast to the appliquéd or pieced blocks. Thus, straight lines are chosen to contrast with a curving design, and curves and whirls are chosen when the main pattern is straight or geometrical.

Two Variations of Quilting

It is interesting to point out that there are two variations in quilting the plain quilt or comforter. They are the Italian stitch and the padded or "bas-relief" design.

The Italian stitch is popular in the South, probably because it is associated with quilt making which requires no interlining and is therefore suited to a milder climate. The design of the quilt is outlined by two parallel lines about 1/4 inch apart, and when the quilting is finished, a small opening is made in the quilted back and a cord is pulled through between the parallel lines. This cord raises the outline of the design and makes it more ornamental.

QUILTED SATIN COVERLET

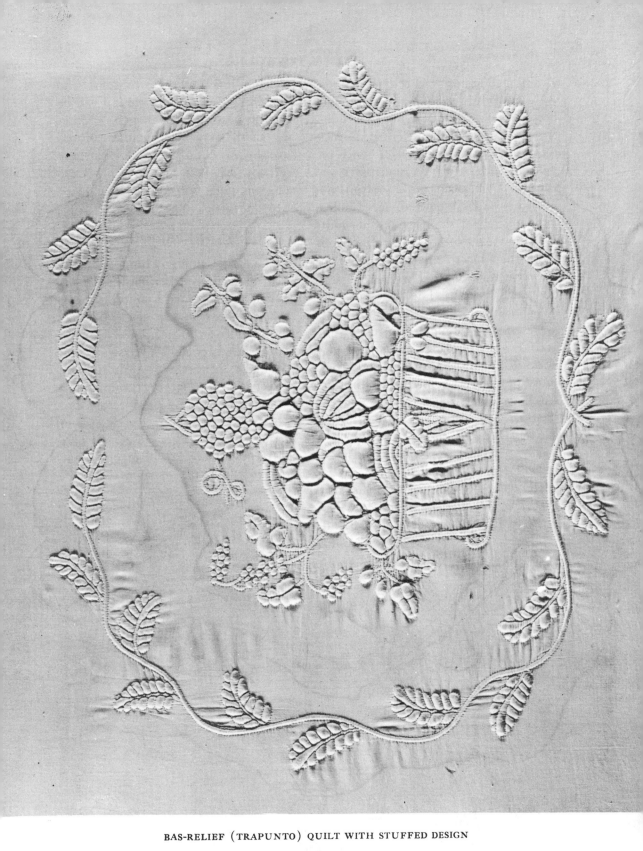

BAS-RELIEF (TRAPUNTO) QUILT WITH STUFFED DESIGN

The padded or "bas-relief" designs were developed in England, and have become very well known in this country. The design usually has a distinctive central motif, such as a bunch of grapes, horn of plenty, pineapples, or even an American eagle. After the design is entirely quilted, small holes are punched in the back of the quilt and tiny tufts of cotton are inserted from the rear to raise the design in appropriate spots. This forms the quilted bas-relief. The hole for the insertion of the cotton should be just large enough to admit the tiny wisps, and if not too large, will pass unnoticed on the back of the quilt. Because of the precision required in this stitching, a bas-relief quilt is considered an ultimate goal for the skilled needlewoman.

The quilted coverlet is often made of white material, and sometimes in pastel colors. White thread is usually preferred for this quilt stitching because of its strength. It is also found to have less tendency to twist and knot in sewing. White thread can be used on pastel material if the stitches are small and even, while colored threads are effective on white. Many times a sub-pattern can be worked out, combining both white and colored stitching in the same design.

QUILTING DIRECTIONS

The actual quilt stitching will probably be a new experience to many women today. It is a simple process for any one who can sew, and, like any other form of needlework, it is a matter of practice. The first attempt should be in stitching straight lines, with curves and feathers coming later. It is helpful to use a practice piece of two squares of material with a layer of cotton in between. Try stitching the pieces together with a plain running stitch. You will soon learn the

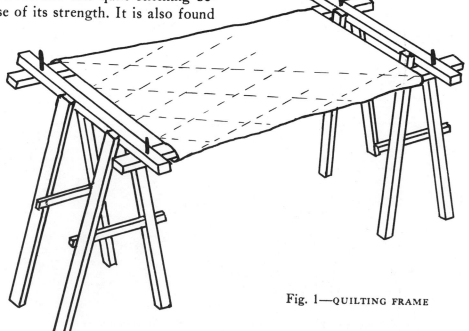

Fig. 1—QUILTING FRAME

ALL WHITE REVERSIBLE COUNTERPANE

171

best method of pushing the needle in and out, and also the direction in which to sew. You will be sure to find that it is easier to sew *toward* you.

Sending Out to Be Quilted

It is an interesting fact that many busy women who enjoy piecing blocks, but who do not care for the final quilting of the three layers, procure the services of professional quilters. There are church organizations and women who enjoy sewing at home who accept quilting, usually at the rate of $1.25 per spool of 125 yards.

QUILTING FRAME

The work of quilt stitching is greatly simplified by putting the quilt into a frame. A frame can easily be constructed so that it can be taken apart when not in use and stored away. The illustration shows a typical frame—rectangular in shape, with two long side bars the width of the quilt (Fig. 1). They are held in place by two shorter pieces on each end, thus keeping the quilt taut in the frame. The width between the two side bars should be two arm-lengths, as the frame must be narrow enough for the quilter to reach to the center to do the quilting on one side, and then move to the other side to complete the quilting before the frame is taken apart and rolled again. The rolling process is necessary because the average quilt is 108 inches long, much longer than the frame's long bars. This means the top and bottom ends of the quilt go on the side bars and as the quilting progresses, the pegs are loosened and the side bars rolled over.

The frame must be supported by legs at the four corners. It can rest on the backs of four chairs if they are the correct height. The two wooden horses are easily constructed and they can be put to many useful purposes around the house when not being used for quilting. The height of the legs is important to the quilt maker, for the frame should be high enough to allow the knees to go underneath it, and also the right height to allow the arms to reach out straight over the quilt in doing the quilt stitching. You may be able to judge the measurement by testing the height of your dining room table or other stands about the house. You will also want to take into consideration the height of the chair in which you will sit for the sewing.

The bars of the frame should be made of hard wood with a smooth finish. You may make it smooth by sanding it and giving it a coat or two of shellac to fill in the grains of wood. There should be a hole ½ inch in diameter in the end of each bar and when the bars are assembled, they are held in place with four wooden pegs which fit the holes. The corners of the bars overlap (Fig. 2). The two long bars have tape or strips of material on which the quilt is basted when it is ready for the frame.

PREPARING THE QUILT FOR FRAME

The perfection of the quilt stitching depends on the careful preparation of the quilt for the frame, and the directions for this important step should be read with utmost care and followed in every detail.

QUILTING DESIGNS FOR NARROW STRIPS AND BORDERS

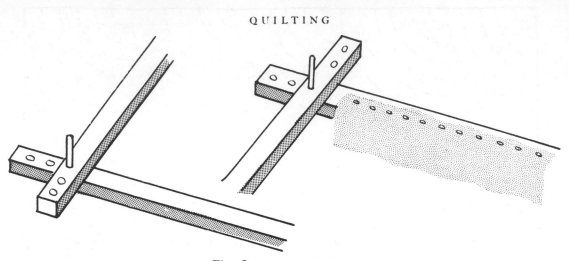

Fig. 2—CORNERS OF FRAME

Marking the Pattern

First the quilt must have the quilting lines marked or "laid out." This is usually done before it is put in the frame. However, some quilt makers prefer to do it later on the frame by marking in the design as they go along with the quilting. To mark the quilt top, lay it out on a large flat surface and trace around the outline of the pattern with a hard lead pencil. If the material is dark, use chalk or a piece of white soap with the edge trimmed to a thin point (Fig. 3). The pattern is usually in the form of a template or a piece of cardboard in one shape such as a circle, a feather, or a diamond, which is to be repeated many times throughout the quilt stitching. You should sew *on* the pencil lines and

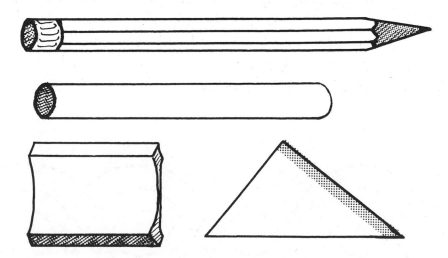

Fig. 3—TOOLS FOR MARKING PATTERN
(Top) Pencil and Chalk; *(Bottom)* Soap, cut in two ways.

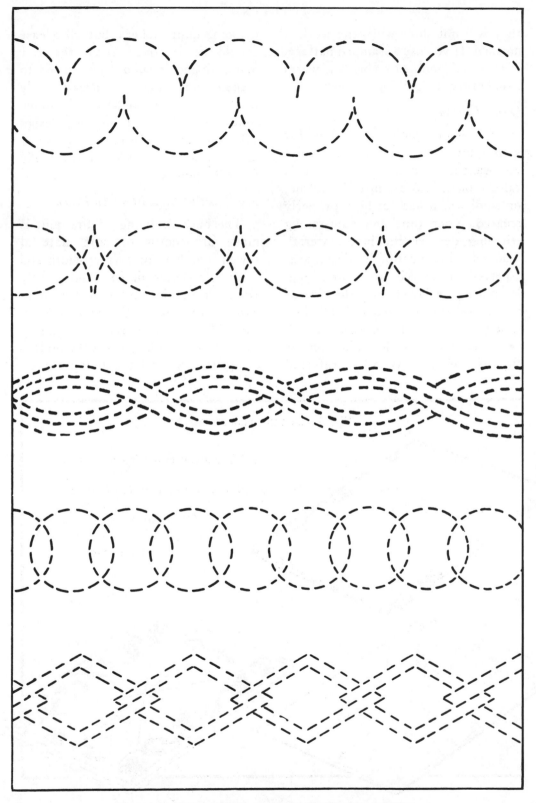

QUILTING DESIGNS FOR NARROW STRIPS AND BORDERS

they will not show when the work is finished. If you use a stamped pattern, it must be stamped on with a warm iron before the quilting begins.

Quilt Filling

You should choose the filling for your quilt with the greatest care if you want it to endure for years. It is false economy to use inferior cotton, or wool which has not been properly treated. Your time and painstaking stitching deserve the best material. You may obtain cotton batting that is especially prepared for quilt filling. It comes in a large sheet the size of a quilt, carefully folded and rolled into a large package. Perhaps you will need two packages, depending on the size of the quilt. Wool is preferred

by some quilt makers, but all grease should be removed from the raw material and it should be carded to make it fluffy enough to spread evenly in the quilt. Cotton flannel is sometimes used, but the quilting design will not stand out in relief because of its thinness. It is recommended chiefly for silk quilts.

How to Put the Filling In Place

The back or lining of the quilt is made of lengths of soft material sewed together for correct width and length. It should be soft and loosely woven to make the quilt stitching easier. The over-all measurements should be 2 inches longer on each side to allow for binding when the quilt is completed. Spread the lining out on

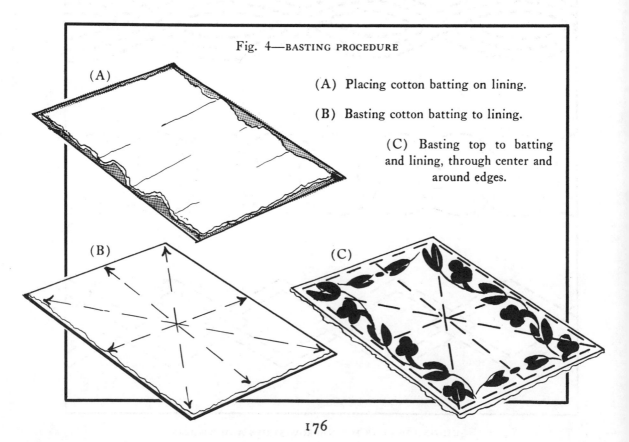

Fig. 4—BASTING PROCEDURE

(A) Placing cotton batting on lining.

(B) Basting cotton batting to lining.

(C) Basting top to batting and lining, through center and around edges.

DECORATIVE DESIGNS
FOR QUILTING PLAIN BLOCKS

the floor, arrange carefully, with the corners fastened to the carpet with thumb tacks. Unroll the cotton and spread it out evenly on the lining, making sure there are no lumps or thin places that will make the quilting uneven.

Basting

Next, you fasten the cotton securely to the lining with long basting stitches. Start in the center of the quilt, and sew toward the edge until you have a number of diagonal lines as shown in Fig. 4. All wrinkles and creases must be removed from the top of the quilt with a warm iron. You are now ready to lay the top in place over the lining and the cotton filling. Smooth it out and see that the edges correspond on all four sides. The three layers are now basted together just as you basted the first two together—in diagonal lines from the center to the edges of the quilt.

Fastening the Quilt to the Frame

After the three layers are basted together and the quilt is still on the floor, lay one of the long bars of the frame parallel with the top edge of the quilt, and the other bar parallel with the bottom edge. These bars have strips of material tacked to the sides and the quilt must be attached by sewing the top and bottom edges of lining securely to the strips. You must use heavy thread and stitch across several times so that the quilt will hold when it is stretched tightly in the frame. Roll the quilt up tightly on to one bar, leaving enough free at one end to stretch across the width of the frame. Carry the quilt rolled on the two bars to the frame, and begin with the free end bar to adjust it to the frame. Attach the corners of the free bar first and insert the pegs in the two holes at that end. Then unroll the quilt until the other end bar is in its place, and insert its pegs. Now the quilt should be stretched in the frame —straight and taut ready for quilt stitching.

Sewing

The quilt stitch is a very fine running stitch, as we have explained. The thickness of the layers and puffiness of the filling make it difficult for the beginner to make short, even stitches. We have suggested a practice piece, and for this practice, you may use an embroidery hoop. You will find that the needle should be held at an *acute angle*, pushing it up and down, rather than diagonally as in ordinary sewing. Push the needle down and then bring it back up near the point of entry. This is aided by holding the material down with the thumb of the opposite hand. Soon an experienced quilter can take several stitches of the needle before drawing it away from the quilt. The thumb should be protected by adhesive tape or commercial finger tip —otherwise the pricks of the needle will make it sore.

"Up and Down Method"

There is another method of quilting which is much slower but is unfailingly accurate. This is done with each stitch made in two separate movements—*downward* and *upward,* and not in one movement as in the first

ALL-OVER QUILTING DESIGNS

THE PINEAPPLE QUILTING DESIGN

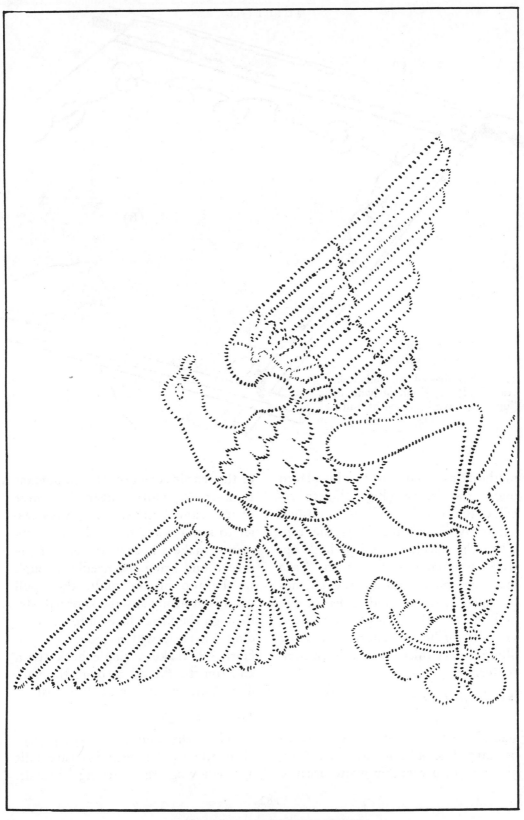

AMERICAN EAGLE QUILTING DESIGN

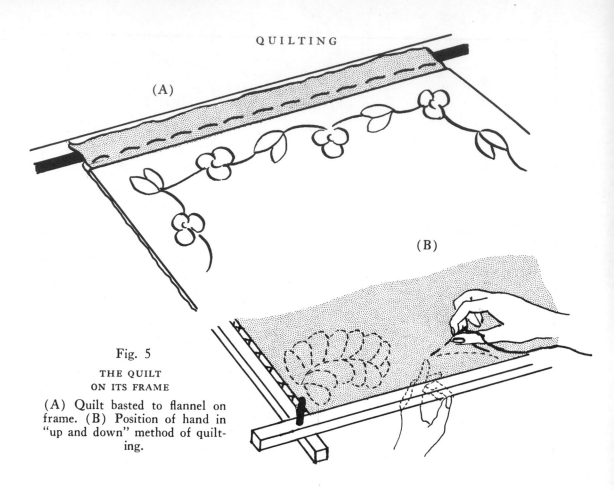

(A)

(B)

Fig. 5

THE QUILT
ON ITS FRAME

(A) Quilt basted to flannel on frame. (B) Position of hand in "up and down" method of quilting.

method described. One hand is placed under the frame (Fig. 5B) to receive the needle and it is pushed vertically downward from the top. Then the needle is pushed back upward to complete the stitch. Care must be taken to keep the stitches of equal space on both sides of the quilt. This method is usually employed on quilts of heavy material, or if the filling is very thick, as in a down comforter.

Needle and Thread

You will need a *short* sharp needle size No. 8-9 for quilting. The choice of thread should be between Nos. 50 and 70, preferably white because

of the tensile strength. It is important to start the quilting near the center of the frame because it is always easier to sew *toward* the body. To commence, make a knot at the end of the thread and bring the needle through to the top of the quilt, then pull gently but firmly and the knot will slip through the lower layer into the padding where it will not be seen. To finish off, make a single back stitch and run the thread through the padding. Cut, and the end will be lost.

Binding the Quilt

When the quilting is completed, dismantle the frame and release quilt by removing the tacking threads.

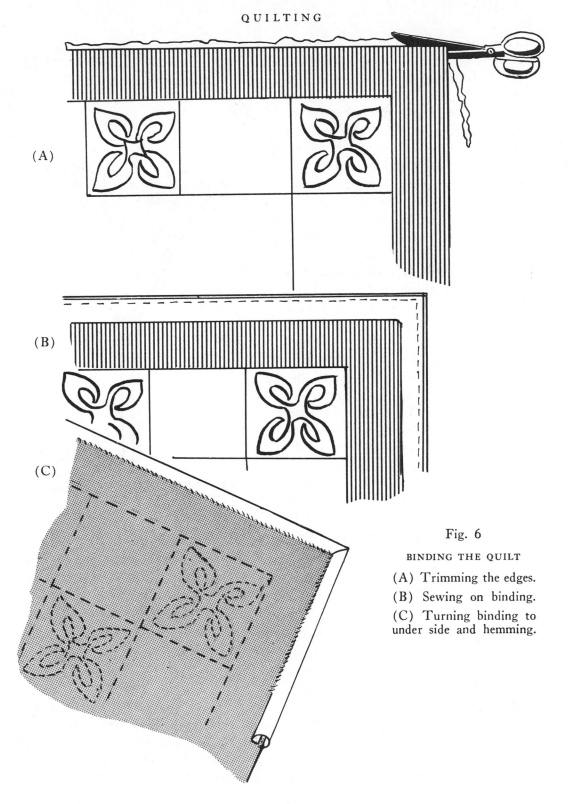

(A)

(B)

(C)

Fig. 6

BINDING THE QUILT

(A) Trimming the edges.
(B) Sewing on binding.
(C) Turning binding to under side and hemming.

Trim the edges (except the lining extension if used for binding) on all four sides in an even line, being sure to remove any cotton that extends outside the quilt's top (Fig. 6A). There are two methods for binding the edges: (1) Make use of the 2-inch extension of the back lining which was left on during the quilting process. Even it off all around, turn up edge for a seam, and fold up over the top of the quilt. Sew in place with small hemming stitches in matching color thread. (2) Bind the edges with bias strips, if you are going to use a binding of different color or a scalloped border (Fig. 6B). Cut the bias strips 1 inch wide and sew them together. The binding is done by laying the bias strip along the outside edge of the quilt, and fitting the edges together so they match exactly. Sew the bias strip and all three layers together with a ¼-inch seam, using a running stitch. After the sewing is done, turn the quilt over and turn down the edges of the bias strip ¼ inch. Fold this over the back of the quilt and sew securely to the bottom layer with small hemming stitches (Fig. 6C).

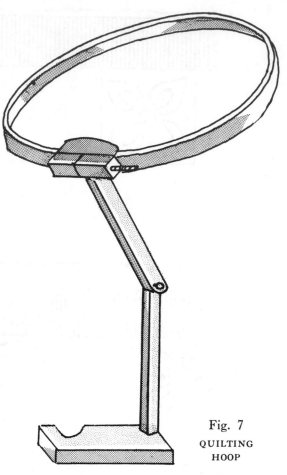

Fig. 7
QUILTING
HOOP

QUILTING HOOP

If you have no quilting frame, you may use the quilting hoop. This is obtainable in department stores, and although experienced quilt makers prefer a quilting frame, the hoop has its advantages, too. It is easily handled and can be moved around (Fig. 7).

In using the hoop, more care must be taken in basting the three layers of the quilt together. Basting stitches should be closer so that they will hold in place as you change its place in the hoop. Begin the quilting in the center of the quilt and sew toward outer edge, taking particular care to work smoothly.

COVERING A DOWN PUFF

To cover a down puff, first cut the covering material in strips 10 inches longer than the puff and allow five inches on each side for over-lapping. The extra amount is to allow for the

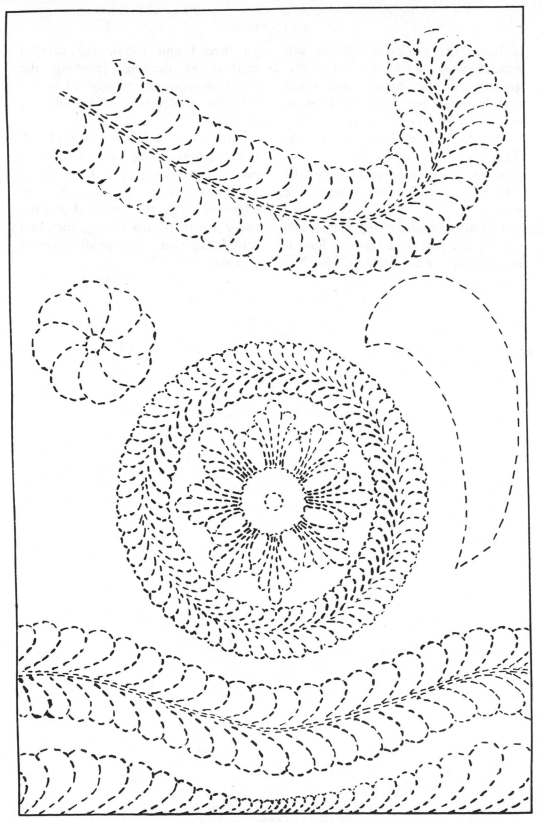

FEATHER DESIGNS IN QUILTING

quilting; the thick inner-lining will require deep sewing lines for the quilting and the pattern will stand high in relief. Sew covering strips together, mark out the pattern on top layer, then baste them to the puff. This is done by basting in long diagonal lines, beginning each one in the center and leading out toward the edge.

If you have no quilting frame, you can lay the puff on a table or hold it in your lap while stitching. Use No. 50 thread and follow the vertical method of quilting (pushing the needle downward and upward in two different movements to complete a stitch).

After the quilting is completed, trim the outside edges of the covering material, allowing ½ inch to extend beyond the edge of the puff. The edges of both the top and bottom cover are then turned in ¼ inch and sewed together with small overcast stitches.

7.

Tufting

TUFTING IS THE ART OF DECORAT-ing material with small puffs of cotton yarn, known as candlewicking. The yarn is obtainable in hanks, the same as knitting wool. Tufted bed spreads are seen everywhere. They blend so nicely with various woods and styles of furniture that they are widely used in both conventional and modern rooms.

Today most tufted spreads are used in color rather than white as in pioneer days. While many are still being made by hand, the craft has gone into factory production. Machine tufting usually appears in continuous rows, rather than in the separate dots or tufts found in handmade designs. The machine tufted ones are also called chenille spreads.

MAKING TUFTED BEDSPREADS

Those who enjoy handwork find tufting a fascinating and speedy art and also an inexpensive means of producing attractive spreads, with color schemes planned to fit one's personal needs.

Curtains, pillows, and scarfs, may also be decorated with tufting, of course avoiding too much of it in a room as it would prove to be monotonous.

Materials

Unshrunken material—natural or pastel colors. Look for sheeting and lighter weight cotton fabrics, wide enough for seamless spreads.

Needles—either short darning needles or notched tufting needle for the usual tufts or double needle for large, thick tufts.

Candlewicking—in desired colors.

Size

Use a generous size, as skimpiness can spoil an otherwise beautiful effect. Most beds today are equipped with inner spring mattresses, which are thicker than the other type. The spread should cover bedding, mattress and springs at sides and foot and tuck

TUFTED BEDSPREAD

White candlewick on homespun foundation tufted in design of grapes and leaves.

in well over the pillows. Also, some shrinkage occurs in laundering. The following sizes are suggested:

Double bed . . . 90 inches by 116 inches or 97 by 116. (It will be smaller after washing.)

Three-quarter bed . . . 80 inches by 116 inches or 84 by 116

Single bed . . . 72 inches by 116 inches

Colors

Every room needs a dominant color. If the bedroom now has several colors, but none dominant, select one of those present and repeat it on the spread, thus establishing it as dominant. In other schemes, a note of contrast may be needed on the spread. However, when a new color is introduced, on the spread, repeat it elsewhere at least once, perhaps in a pillow, a piece of pottery, a wastebasket, or a scarf for the dresser, or in rugs (preferably in a darker form). Even in the spread itself a dominant color is desirable, so do not use colors in equal amounts.

Avoid harsh colors, such as intense pink or yellow and strong yellow-greens.

For backgrounds use cream, tan, light blue-green, peach, soft yellow, and natural, as well as deep rich jewel tones, such as emerald green, royal blue, dubonnet.

DESIGNS

Stamped designs may be purchased, but there are many which can be composed by the worker. In many of the early spreads the tufts were closely and evenly distributed over the entire surface, but most people prefer a pattern of some sort.

Spotty patterns are not as attractive as all-over effects. Many are block units, which are repeated over the entire surface. There are beautiful designs in squares and plaids, some of which are diagonal. One advantage of these abstract patterns is that they may be used with either plain or patterned walls, and another is the ease of working them out at home.

Straight Line Patterns

By folding and creasing, one can get the main units, after which each crease is marked in pencil. Marking beside a yardstick, other lines are then drawn parallel with the first to develop whatever spacing is desired. The larger the plaid, the further apart these lines may be. (Caution: Be very sure that the yardstick used is straight. Those of thin, unfinished wood are inclined to warp badly.)

Cardboard Cut-Outs

A simple, geometric pattern, or one with a conventional flower design may be drawn or adapted from quilt patterns. It may then be drawn on cardboard, cut out with a razor blade, and marked on muslin. A firm cardboard is needed which will not rough up too much with repeated tracing.

Tracing with Carbon

Another method is to mark off design for one-fourth of spread on plain paper and transfer with large sheets of carbon paper. This plan might be desirable when part of the pattern fits the top of the bed and a wide border drops on the sides and ends as this type involves designing a corner.

Tracing Objects

Patterns may be worked out from saucers, cups, plates or other household articles. A rhythmic repetition of some one form assures unity.

MAKING

Thread needle and use candle-wicking double. If large ball-like tufts are wanted, thread two strands of wicking through the special double needle. The first method gives four short ends in a place, the second, eight.

The single tufting needle is notched so that stitches are automatically spaced. If one wishes to make a large tuft, but has no double needle, a second stitch may be made directly across the first one. To avoid getting this second stitch too long insert needle between muslin and wicking of first stitch.

Take a running stitch about ½ inch long, then a short one, picking up only a few threads, or about ⅛ inch. Several stitches are taken at once, as in gathering. When the design is complete, clip each long stitch in the center.

Edge

Use a narrow hem held down by a row of tufts or by a fringe of wicking. To make this, bring needle through to right side, take a ⅛-inch stitch, putting needle back to wrong side. Cut off ends to desired length. Knot the fringe, if desired.

WASHING

The spread is washed in warm, soapy water. If it is done in a machine, continue 20 to 30 minutes; if by hand, let it remain in the water 3 or 4 hours, then rub thoroughly by hand or on the board. Shake out, but do not squeeze or wring. Hang right side out where it will get the sun and a stiff breeze, if possible. When about half dry, rub tufts thoroughly with a stiff brush, and beat vigorously with a light peeled switch. This helps in fluffing up the tufts.

MARKING PATTERNS

The first step toward stamping the spread is seeing that the corners are even when it is folded. If not, stretch fabric thoroughly to straighten it.

Plaids are easy to design. They may be either straight or diagonal. In placing a straight plaid on the bed, especially a large scale plaid, one should be sure the design runs entirely parallel with the edge of the mattress. Slight variation in this respect is less evident with a diagonal plaid.

1. To begin a design composed of diagonal squares, lay one end of the spread along the side, seeing that edges are even. Crease a true bias fold exactly to the corner.

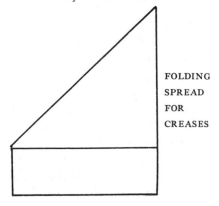

FOLDING
SPREAD
FOR
CREASES

2. Open spread, then crease a true bias fold to the other corner of the same end. The intersection of these two diagonal creases falls along the center of the spread. Starting the pattern there insures the same spacing out to both edges.

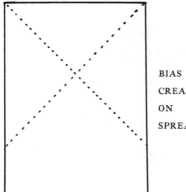

BIAS
CREASES
ON
SPREAD

3. Decide upon the size of the unit. If, for example, it is to be 8 inches, measure out 4 inches from the crease and mark several dots by which to determine a line parallel with the crease. In the same way locate a line 4 inches to the other side of the crease. These two become the sides of an even row of diagonal squares.

4. If a diagonal plaid is desired instead of the single line square, creasing is again the first step, but the crease then becomes the center of the band. For a 3-, 5-, or 7-line plaid, crease becomes the middle line. In a 2-line plaid, it is half way between the lines.

5. Having worked out the spacing of the individual band and the width desired between it and the next, proceed by marking necessary lines toward the opposite corners.

6. Now, starting with the diagonal crease going in the opposite direction, use the same procedure to get the cross lines.

7. Plaids may be regular or irregular as to spacing and color arrangement. Diagram No. 6 is an example of the irregular.

SOME SUGGESTIVE DESIGNS

No. 1. Brown and rust on tan background. Large 7-line diagonal plaid. All lines 1⅛ inch apart. (Width of

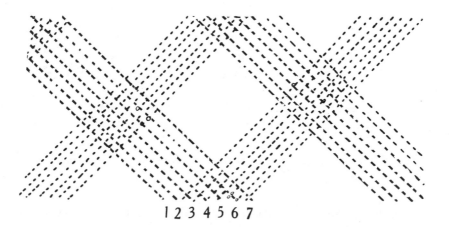

1 2 3 4 5 6 7

No. 1

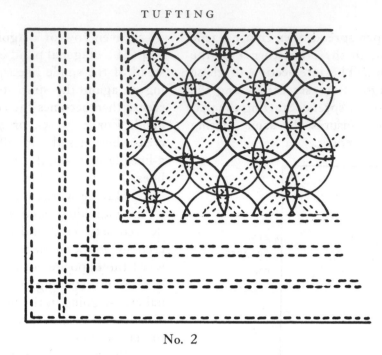

No. 2

the yardstick used.) Distance from center to center of tufted bands 13 inches. Center line rust (4). Lines on sides of it (3) and (5) dark brown. All others (1), (2), (6), and (7) rust. Nine dots—double tufts of dark brown in center. Amount of wicking needed: 2¼ lb. rust, 1¼ lb. brown.

No. 2. Corner of design combining circular and diagonal lines, made to fit top of bed and with an 18-inch border. Double lines ½ inch apart. 7½ inches diagonal. Medium blue-green on natural. Amount of wicking needed: 12 oz. thread.

No. 3. Peach and brown on peach background. 3-line plaid, 8 inch diagonal square (from one center to center of tufting bands). Center row brown, outer rows peach. Large circle 3½ inches in diameter, smaller circle 2 inches. Dot in center. Amount of wicking needed: 10 oz. brown, 2½ lb. peach.

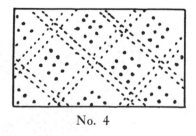

No. 3

No. 4

No. 4. 4-inch diagonals with two lines ½ inch apart. Peach lines and cream colored dots on peach background. Amount of wicking needed: 2¼ lb. peach, 1¼ lb. cream.

No. 5. 4-inch diagonals. Central

lines dark brown, others rust. Design small enough in scale to be suited to a pillow. For tufting both sides of it, 2 oz. rust and 1⅓ oz. brown needed. For spread, use approximately: 2 lb. rust; 1¼ lb. brown.

No. 6. Irregular plaid in yellow, cream, and orange on yellow background. Space between inside lines of

square 7 inches. (All other diagrams shown give measurement from center to center of tufting bands.)

No. 7. Interlacing circles. Medium blue on natural. 1 pound thread. This would also be attractive in a two-tone effect, using the darker blue for (a) outer border, (b) center line of the three parallel rows, and (3) all dots.

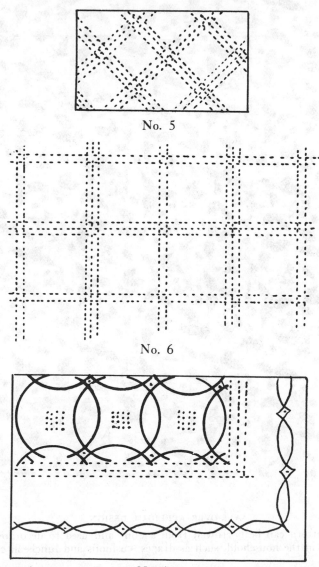

No. 5

No. 6

No. 7

ALL-OVER APPLIQUÉ DESIGN

An appliqué pattern can be borrowed from a quilt and used to decorate other useful articles in the household, such as drapes, cushions and luncheon cloths.

8.

Other Uses For Quilting

APPLIQUÉ IS POPULAR TODAY NOT only in making quilts but in decorating other attractive articles used in our homes. The art of applying one material atop another brings into play a contrast of colors and materials, and shows off the skill and precision of the needlework.

The same intricate and graceful patterns which served to beautify our appliquéd quilts may be brought to use in decorating the draperies of the bedroom, the dresser scarf, or cushion tops. The colors and patterns may reflect the motif of the bed covering or bring a note of contrast to the room.

The other rooms in the home, too, may be enlivened by attractive appliqué work. In fact, every room—from the living room to the kitchen may be made more interesting and attractive with many artistic uses of our patterns. Bright colored fruits or animals are favorite motifs for the kitchen, making jolly-looking curtains or tray cloths of the ordinary un-

bleached muslin or checked gingham. We may need dignified drapes for a stately dining room, and thus make use of a conventional border design of flowers appliquéd on heavy material. If our furnishings are modern, we find that an occasional use of patchwork is suitable and extremely handsome for the purpose.

In fact, the use of appliqué and patchwork is unlimited in its possibilities for beautifying the home. Your imagination may suggest many uses for your favorite patchwork patterns, as well as appliqué, and we offer some specific suggestions for use in both kinds of quilting.

LUNCHEON SETS

Patchwork

Luncheon cloths made of patchwork patterns for quilts are both attractive and practical for informal use in a dinette or summer cottages. The patterns must be reduced in size so that the finished block is not over

6 inches square and they are set together with plain blocks of unbleached muslin in the same size. Since the size is limited, you must choose a design with a minimum number of patches. You may use only one color in the design, or alternate patches cut from scrap materials with ones in a plain color, placing them in the same position on each block.

The number of blocks you will need depends on the size of the cloth you wish to make. Cut the patches and sew them together in a block as you would for a quilt, then set the plain muslin squares between, using a ¼-inch seam. Add a plain muslin border in any width you choose and bind the edges with bias tape in a color matching the design. The border design can be varied by using a colored strip ½ to 2 inches wide at the top and bottom. In this case, roll the edges under and sew in place with small hemming stitches. It is not necessary to line the cloth. When it is laundered, iron on the wrong side and press the seams flat.

TABLE MAT AND NAPKIN
The leaf pattern is appliquéd in colors which harmonize with the china and table setting, and may be made of linen or muslin.

Appliqué

Luncheon cloths decorated in appliquéd designs of colored materials can be used for either formal or informal settings, according to the material used. Formal cloths are made of fine, closely woven linen with designs cut from varicolored handkerchief linen or other cloth of the same texture. If the background material is heavy, do not attempt to use the same weight for the decoration; the extra turn in at the edges will make them bulky and hard to sew.

Informal cloths can be made from muslin or any material that comes in a 54-inch width. It is possible to use a narrower width by joining two sides together with a narrow center strip, using the same width strip around the outer edges for a border. The design should include a center and border decoration, leaving a plain area between, where dishes are set on the table. Napkins decorated in the same motif can be placed at each plate.

Leaf Design

A simple leaf pattern is suitable for luncheon cloths, napkins, or table mats. The leaves are cut from contrasting shades of the same color and tied together in a spray with stems embroidered in an outline stitch. If green leaves will not harmonize with the color of your dishes, use two tones of blue, pink, or any other color; you need not be realistic when planning a design for appliqué. You may even use 2 different colors that are complimentary to each other such as yellow and brown.

The border around the napkin and mat consists of 2 narrow bands cut from the same material as the leaves. Be sure to place the light colored band on the inside as shown in the illustration, as you need the heavier color on the outside to act as a frame. The material may be linen or muslin and percale, depending on the type of setting you wish to use.

Appliqué and Embroidery

The luncheon set illustrated shows a design in which both appliqué and embroidery are employed to carry out the decoration. If the cloth is to be used on a small square table the design shown in the illustration will be ample if repeated in each corner. However, if it is to be used on a long table and is rectangular in shape, you should add an extra spray on each side.

The center of the cloth is cut to the exact size of the table top and a double hem is added for a border. You will note that the design includes calla lilies with leaves and a conventional flower in appliqué; the stems, tendrils and veins in leaves are embroidered in green cotton thread. This particular design can be used equally well on a white or pastel background. If the cloth is to be white, use yellow lilies with a deeper yellow in the center; on a pastel background, the lilies should be white with a yellow center. The conventional flower can be in any color you choose.

After the decoration is completed, turn up a large hem for the border. Sew in place with small hemming stitches. On the right side of the cloth

COMBINING APPLIQUÉ AND EMBROIDERY

Cloth of linen is dec-orated with calla lily appliqué pattern and embroidered leaves and stems.

Courtesy of Woman's Day

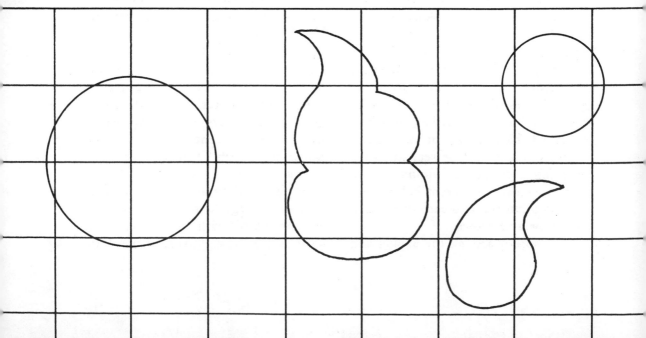

APPLIQUED COCKTAIL CLOTH

A gay design of roosters is appliquéd on the striped cloth. The tail feathers are feather stitched and feet are embroidered.

Courtesy of Woman's Day

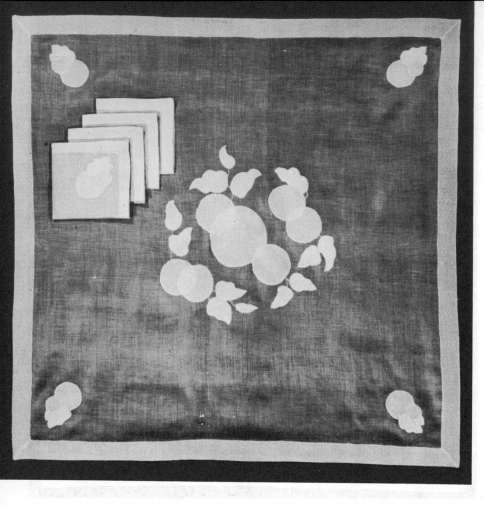

APPLIQUÉD
ORGANDY
CLOTH

White apples and
leaves of dotted Swiss
are appliquéd on this
fine organdy luncheon
cloth. It is delicate
enough for formal
table settings.

Courtesy of Woman's Day

make a single row of outline stitches
at the top of the hem, using the same
embroidery cotton as used in the design. The napkins are hemmed in the
same manner.

The cloth and napkins should be
made of closely woven linen with a
smooth texture. Use handkerchief
linen or a fine quality of percale for
the appliqued patches.

Cocktail Cloth

This attractive cloth is made from
cotton material with wide stripes on
the background. If you do not care for
the stripes, you may use a plain colored material instead. Cut the bodies
of the roosters from white muslin

and use plain red calico for the
combs. If you want a gay cloth use
the same red calico for the border
strip, if not, use the color of one of
the background stripes.

Cut out the bodies of the roosters,
turn in edges and baste in place ready
for sewing. Next, cut the combs, turn
in edges all around and attach to the
heads of the roosters. Lay them on
the cloth and stitch in place ready to
be appliquéd. Sew the edges down
with small hemming stitches and em-
broider the tails with feather stitches
as shown in the illustration. The legs
and feet are embroidered also—the
eyes are made from a small circle of
red calico.

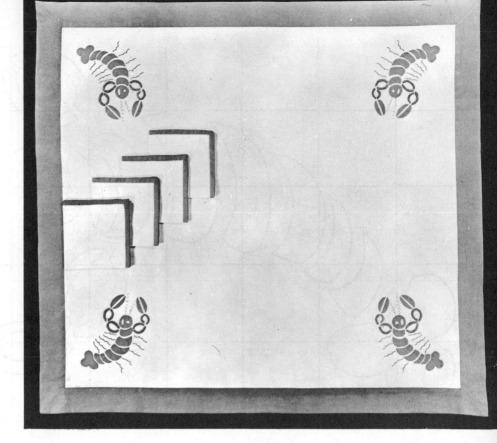

COLORFUL
LOBSTER
PATTERN

Made of linen or muslin, this pattern is unusual and effective. The plain band of the border matches the appliquéd lobsters in each corner. (See pattern on next page.)

Courtesy of Woman's Day

If you want to make cocktail napkins to match the cloth, cut 7-inch squares from plain material in a color matching one of the stripes. Draft a pattern of a smaller rooster by using reducing squares and place one in a corner on each napkin. Draw threads on each side to make ½ inch fringe and sew a row of machine stitches along the top to prevent further raveling.

Organdy Luncheon Set

Organdy is one of the most satisfactory materials one can use for table cloths or individual mats. It is easily laundered and the natural stiffness remains after washing, if the material is ironed while it is still quite wet. The transparent background is ideal for applique and the patches cut either from white or colored materials show up equally well.

To make a luncheon mat and napkins from organdy, it is very important to pull a thread to use as a guide for cutting. After the napkins and mats are cut, you may find it is impossible to pull them straight and, if this is the case, you should dampen them first, stretch into shape and press with a warm iron.

The decoration is applied by following the methods used in appliqué. Since organdy suggests delicacy and fragility, the design should be entirely in white—a red apple with green leaves would be too forceful in

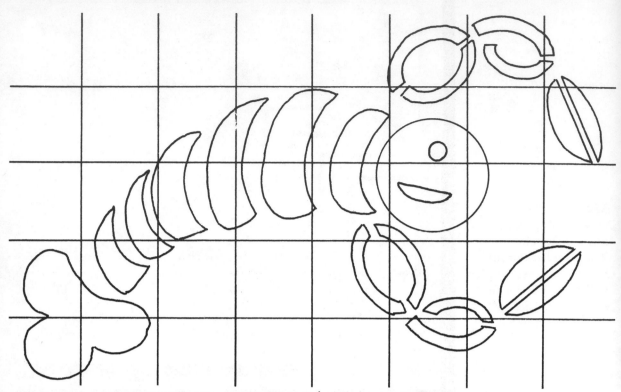

PATTERN FOR LOBSTER APPLIQUÉ. (Picture on preceding page.)

size and color for such a delicate background. You should choose a design of flowers or small fruits if color is to be added. Use white handkerchief linen or a fine quality of lawn for the design and the same material as a border.

This pattern may also be used on informal luncheon sets by substituting heavier material for the foundation and making the apples of red and green calico. The border around the table mat and napkins may be a narrow strip of red or green as used in the design, or you may bind the edges with bias tape. A fringed border can also be used.

Lobster Design

This novel luncheon set should appeal to seafood lovers, or those who have cottages along the shore. The cloth can be more or less elegant made of linen, or very informal made of muslin or cambric, depending on the way you usually serve your lobster. If the cloth is to be formal, an effort should be made to find material for the design in a lobster color if possible. The design need not be so realistic on a muslin cloth—a lobster made from red cambric muslin will give the needed effect. Use plain bands as a border on the cloth and napkins as shown in the illustration.

Oilcloth or Plastic Mat

Table mats made of oilcloth are gay, colorful and easy to make. No other material is as practical for children's mats, and if they are decorated in whimsical designs cut from bright colors they will delight any child. Cut the background mat first and make deep scallops around the edge as shown in the illustration. The second mat should be about 1½ inches smaller on all sides to allow the scallops to extend beyond the edge. Seal the two mats together with rubber cement.

The next step is to cut out the decorations. Use any colors you choose but if there is a choice in tone use the darkest one for the seal. Rubber cement is also used for holding the designs in place. Waterproof ink is used for the name "Johnny," as well as the markings on the seal.

OILCLOTH TABLE MAT

Bright colored oilcloth is practical for children's table mats. The lower mat is topped with a rectangle, and designs are secured with rubber cement.

Courtesy of Woman's Day

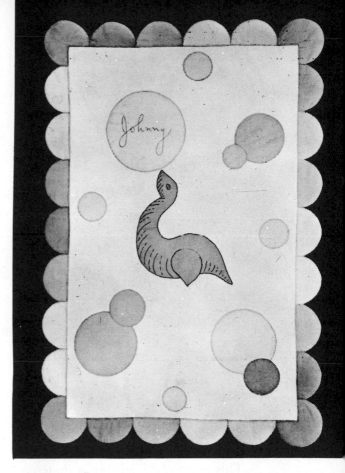

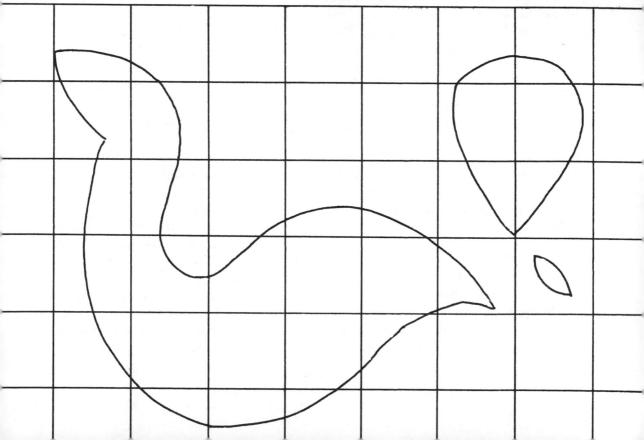

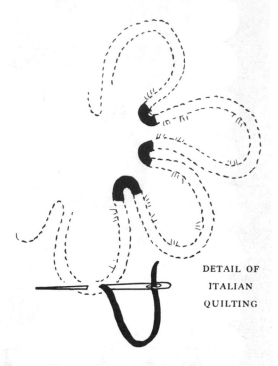

DETAIL OF
ITALIAN
QUILTING

ITALIAN QUILTING

This method of quilting is done on two layers of material, the inner layer of cotton being omitted. As explained in the Quilting Chapter the design is made by making two parallel lines of stitching about ¼ inch apart through both layers of material. The two lines form a narrow channel through which a thick cord or heavy wool is pulled with a needle working from the back. A quilt decorated with Italian quilting is for decoration only, as it lacks the warmth of the inner lining.

Working Methods

Draw your design on the material to be used for the lining or back of the quilt. Draw a second line a ¼ inch from outside edge of design forming a parallel line completely

around it. Lay this lining carefully over the back of the surface to be used for the top of the quilt and baste securely together.

The work is now ready for quilting. Sew along all the lines in the design with small running stitches and remember to keep the stitches even on the underside as you work, for it will be the right side of the quilt when it is finished. Be sure to stitch along the line of the design, keeping the width of the channel always the same in order to receive the heavy cord.

The cord or padding is put in from the wrong side. Use a soft cotton cord such as candlewicking or cotton yarn for padding cotton material, or it may also be used for a silk top if you want the design to stand high in relief. Use a blunt needle with a large eye for pulling the cord through the double outline.

The needle is first forced through the quilt lining between the two layers of material and threaded through the channel or double outline of the pattern. At any pronounced curve or turn, you must force the needle up through the lining, pull the extra cord through to the surface and insert the needle again through the same hole or a little farther along and continue with the threading.

If the design is small and has sharp turns, leave a small loop of the cord between the holes on the underside to prevent the design from "pulling" when washed. You may push your needle in and out as often as you wish on the underside as it will not show in the finished design.

ITALIAN QUILTING
ON PURSE
AND CUSHION

Other Uses of Italian Quilting

You will find many uses for this type of quilting other than the making of bed spreads. It is a useful decoration for wearing apparel such as bed-jackets, dress trimmings, and handbags. For household furnishings, it can be applied to cushion tops, couch covers, flounces for the dressing table, draperies and many other articles too numerous to mention. The choice of material is not limited —you may use any fabric that can be stitched with a needle and thread.

QUILTED HANDBAG

Cut a paper pattern of the size and shape handbag you wish to make. If you plan to use a plastic or wooden handle such as are sold at the department stores, you should secure the handle first and cut the pattern for the bag accordingly.

If you are making a bag for summer use, linen or rayon would be a good choice of material. For a winter bag, you may use satin, woolen fabrics, soft leather, or suede—if it is thin enough for stitching.

Use a thin muslin or cambric for the lining. Draw the design on the background and baste it to the material you have chosen for the top of the bag. To quilt the design, follow instructions given under "Working Methods." Attach the finished bag to the frame or handles and add an inner lining to cover back of design.

QUILTED CUSHION TOP

The same procedure is used for decorating the top of a cushion in Italian Quilting. Cut a paper pattern the size and shape of cushion you wish to make. Draw on the design and then transfer it to a piece of thin muslin to be used as a lining for the top. You may transfer the design with carbon paper as the dark lines will be on the wrong side.

Sew around the edges of the parallel lines of the design and thread the heavy cord through from the under side. Use any plain material for the top of the cushion—a figured material will confuse the design. Use a heavy covered cord for binding the edges of the cushion to tie in with the design.

9.

Unusual Quilts

THE OLD SAYING THAT "VARIETY is the spice of life" might well be applied to quilts! Among the choice collections and heirlooms there can be found quilts of every variety and form. Some seem to speak in soft voices and reveal decorous manners, while others are bold in design depicting the rigors of pioneer days, of war between the states, or vigorously fought out political campaigns. Important events that take place in every household are the inspiration for making many of the so-called "variety" quilts. Among these are the special ones for weddings, winter and summer use, expression of friendship, and many others too numerous to mention. Of these, the Friendship and Presentation Quilts were the most elaborate. The blocks were exchanged or given away, and each individual maker strove to contribute a masterpiece in design and needlecraft.

The purpose of this chapter is to describe a few of these quilts which are quite different, both in purpose and technique, from others described in the book.

ALBUM OR PRESENTATION QUILTS

The Album or Presentation Quilts are made up of elaborately designed blocks, each created and carefully stitched by a different woman. As the name indicated, they expressed friendship or admiration for a particular person. Usually the minister or a notable leader in the community was chosen to receive the gift quilt. The presentation usually took place at a public gathering where each block was given in person by the donor, then assembled and stitched together as a whole, as shown on page 208. Many of the blocks were signed with names cross-stitched, embroidered or written in indelible ink in one corner.

Album Quilts have no set pattern, except that they are made in blocks or squares; each block has a different design created from materials chosen

207

PRESENTATION QUILT

Quilts like these of the nineteenth century were "presented" to persons of renown with ceremonies at public gatherings. Each block was made by a different needlewoman. The sixteen blocks of this quilt are all designed with wreaths except the corner eagles, and show an interesting variety of flowers, grapes and leaves. They are appliqued in red, figured green and yellow calico on an unbleached cotton background. Eagles were favored patriotic symbols of pre-Civil War era.

by the woman who made it. Such motifs as flowers, ferns, birds, trees, fruit, or hearts might appear on individual blocks, yet were pleasing in design when assembled and sewed together. They might be called an example of primitive art. Because the designs were elaborate in effect, the quilts were seldom put to utility use and many were carefully wrapped and stored away, only to be gotten out occasionally to recall old friend-

ELABORATE CHINTZ PATTERNS

This quilt of light tan background is appliquéd with intricate floral patterns cut from chintz (glazed calico). It is an example of skilled workmanship.

ships and the women who made them. For this reason, there are many Album Quilts in existence today and, since the owners find it difficult to adapt them to a modern setting, many of the best examples find their way to museums and permanent collections.

CHINTZ QUILTS

It is probable that the first quilts in America were made of glazed calico, or better known as chintz. Since the material was decorated in designs of great beauty, there was no need to add color or additional decorations

STAR QUILT

Chintz patches form the huge central star pattern, and decorative chintz flowers
are appliquéd. The wide border is also small-figured chintz.

to the quilt. The background colors
were usually tan or brown and the designs were many and varied, ranging
from sweeping floral motifs to tiny
dots or figures.

In the late 18th and early 19th
centuries, cotton prints depicting early
historical scenes, such as "Penn's
Treaty with the Indians," "Lafa-
yette," and the "Louisiana Purchase,"
were brought over from France and
England to attract American trade.
The pictorial designs were usually
printed in green or rose on a light
background and were used also as
decorative panels for the wall. The
most favored pattern was the "Tree
of Life" which was later adapted to
appliqué and patchwork. These panels
were often placed in the center of a

WINTER QUILT OF SILK PATCHWORK

Hexagon blocks of light and dark colored silks are pieced together in diamond formation. The richness of the material and the deep coloring make this Winter Quilt unusually beautiful.

quilt surrounded by a border of the same material but printed in a small design.

Later, when chintz was plentiful and the women were able to get scraps and remnants, they were fashioned into patchwork designs such as the one illustrated. However, the results were not always rewarding because the varied motifs had a tendency to interrupt the design. Chintz was often combined with other material as used in borders or decorative strips through the center of the quilt.

The next step was to cut out flowers and other designs printed on chintz, turn in the edges, and appliqué to a white or tan background. Quilts decorated in this manner were really quite beautiful.

SILK QUILTS

Among our most cherished and beautiful quilts are the silk ones, with designs fashioned from silks, satins, velvets and brocades and embroidered in elaborate stitches that gave elegance and charm to the finished quilt. It is not unusual to find a hundred different embroidery stitches worked and blended into the design of a single quilt! The exquisite loveliness of these quilts should inspire many women to make one to add to their collection, using the soft, blended colors we have in our silks today.

The silk quilts are usually made by combining a number of different materials such as silk, velvet, wool and satin into the design, so the planning must be quite different from a cotton quilt where the appliqué or patchwork decoration is from the same type or quality. Silk is delicate in texture so the block must have an inner lining of thin muslin or cambric; the design is stitched to the silk and lining at the same time. A different technique is also used for turning in edges, for appliqué. Silk frays easily and the edges cannot be basted down, as the holes made by the needle would remain after the threads are removed.

Silk quilts can be divided into two general groups—the appliquéd type with designs applied to a neutral background, and the crazy patterns arranged in an all-over design resembling patchwork. We suggest you read the following directions carefully if you decide to make a quilt of either type.

Silk Quilt in Appliqué

We have chosen a beautiful example of a silk quilt in appliqué made in Baltimore, Md., in 1845 by Mrs. Mary Jane Green Maran, shown here. It is a basket design in varicolored silks and velvets, appliquéd to a background of plain white silk. The flower baskets are filled with fruit and flower sprays and strawberry vines. A running vine is used to separate the blocks.

To make the quilt, you will have to cut the following background pieces: 13 squares white silk, 17 inches square; 13 squares thin muslin, 17 inches square; 12 triangles white silk (cut 17-inch square diagonally across); 12 squares thin muslin, 17 inches square; 20 strips white silk, 3 inches by 17 inches (to set between blocks); 20 strips thin muslin, 3 inches by 17 inches; 2 strips each muslin and silk, 3 inches by 57 inches; 2 strips each muslin and silk, 3 inches by 97 inches.

Cut border material, both muslin and silk, 7 inches wide.

After the entire background is cut —match the silk and muslin pieces according to size and baste together. You are now ready to cut and assemble the designs on the block. You must take the following steps in preparing the quilt for stitching:

1. Draft a pattern of the flower basket, being sure the height is not over $\frac{1}{4}$ the width of the block. The designer of this quilt made each basket different, but making them all alike will not make the quilt less interesting or less decorative. The lat-

SILK BASKET QUILT

This luxurious quilt was made in Baltimore in 1845. On a white silk background the appliquéd baskets have silk and velvet fruit and flower sprays. A strawberry vine decorates the block seams and an appliquéd running vine frames the quilt.

tice work in the body of the basket is made with ·¼ inch bias strips and we suggest you get bias silk tape at the department store. The top and base are made of plain silk in a matching color.

2. The flower sprays and vines should be in an original design. They are cut from silk scraps and the color and shape of the pieces will suggest varieties and shapes. A seed catalogue is an excellent source for designs as well as your own flower garden. The flowers can be more interesting and colorful by cutting them from different types of material such as velvet,

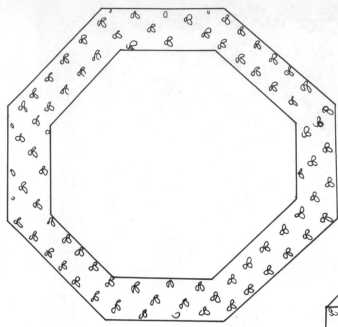

Fig. 1A—TURNING EDGES

(*Left*) To avoid basting silk pieces, heavy wrapping paper is placed on material for turning edges.

Fig. 1B—BASTING STITCHES

(*Below*) Diagonal stitches hold edges in place over paper while patch is pressed. Threads and paper are removed before appliquéing patch.

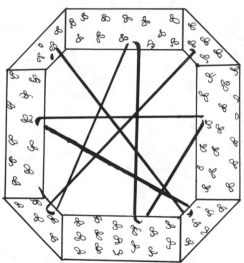

satin, or brocade, and garnishing with embroidery stitches.

The edges of the flowers and leaves must be turned in before laying them on the block for stitching. To do this, cut a pattern the exact size and shape of the flower from heavy wrapping paper. Lay this on the material and cut around the outline ¼ inch *away* from the pattern to allow for the turning in of the edges (Fig. 1-A). After the piece is cut, place paper pattern in center on reverse side and turn edges down over pattern. Hold in place by taking diagonal stitches across from side to side (Fig. 1-B). Press with warm iron and remove paper just before sewing to the background.

3. Assemble the design on the block and fasten in place with one or two tiny stitches. Baste the basket in place *first* and then arrange the flowers according to taste; be sure the heaviest part of the design is at the top of the basket with equal bal-

ance on either side. The trailing vines between the blocks and around the border can be in either embroidery or appliqué.

4. After the pieces are arranged on the block, they must be stitched to the background with small hemming stitches. Care must be taken that the needle goes all the way through the muslin lining. Use silk thread in a matching color for the stitching. The flowers can be enhanced by adding yellow centers in embroidery floss— tendrils and veins can also be added to the leaves.

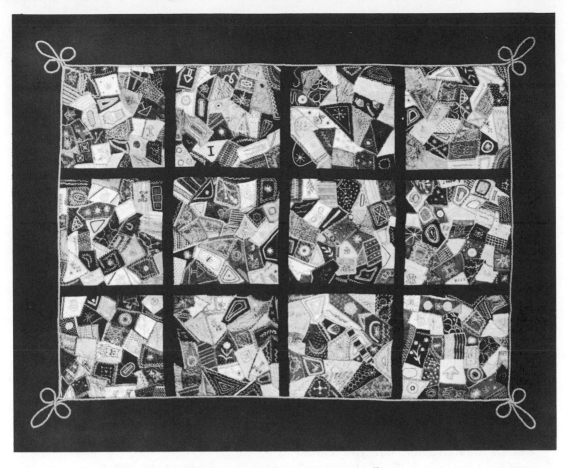

CRAZY QUILT "SLUMBER THROW"

Silk and velvet pieces of many colors are patched into twelve blocks in an irregular way which makes use of the smallest scraps of material. A variety of feather-stitches cover the seams, and each patch is adorned with fanciful embroidery. The joining strips and border are of deep red velvet, and the gold silk cord is matched by a lining of gold sateen.

5. Set the quilt together by arranging the blocks in diagonal lines, sew the 3-inch strips between and then add border. Make the lining of the quilt either of silk or fine muslin. The quilt is prepared for the frame as described in Chapter 6.

CRAZY QUILTS

Crazy quilts, born of necessity, were made in an all-over design consisting of pieces of material, regardless of size or color. With the scarcity of materials in the early days of our country, women cut from worn and discarded woolen clothing any parts that were intact or considered useful. They were sewed together in crazy fashion, usually on an inner lining as it helped to hold the pieces in place while they were being sewed. On the better quilts, yarn was sometimes employed to join the pieces in simple embroidery stitches.

In 1870 the lowly crazy pattern was elevated to the parlor by substituting scraps of silks and velvet for the worn woolen pieces. It was used as a throw for the couch or as a slumber robe. The pieces were fastened together with fancy stitches, silk floss was used instead of yarn, and even the centers of the patches were decorated in flowers, fruits, and hearts, in hand-painted designs. Certainly a quilt of this type was a challenge to any needlewoman—the keener her sense of the artistic the more intricate her embroidery stitches!

It is not difficult to make a crazy quilt if you enjoy combining colors and have some knowledge of embroidery. If you are a novice at the art, you will find illustrations and directions for making several embroidery stitches most commonly used at the end of this chapter, but you should study a few "fancier" stitches if you want to imitate the old quilts. The following steps must be taken in making a crazy quilt or slumber robe:

1. Collect scraps of silks, satins, velvets and brocades (ribbons and men's ties are excellent) and press out wrinkles and creases with a warm iron. Separate the pieces into light and dark tones and again sort them into piles of the different colors.

2. Cut a foundation block 16 inches square of muslin or cambric—use twenty blocks for a full size quilt. If you want to add warmth to the quilt, get wadding or cotton that comes in sheets with a glazed surface on either side and cut it to the size of the block. Do not use regular cotton batting as it will not stay in place and interferes

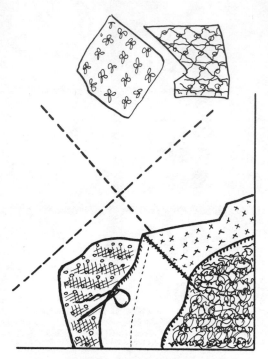

Fig. 2—PLACING PATCHES
IN CRAZY QUILT

Beginning in corner of block, work to the left. Stitch left sides of patches *after* the next patch has been laid in place under seam.

with the sewing. Place the wadding on top of foundation block and baste together.

3. The next step is to place the silk pieces in place on the block. They must be cut and placed one at a time, as each piece will be a different shape and the second patch must fit around one side of the first. Begin by placing the first patch in one corner on the *padded side* of the block and baste in place. Trim the two outside edges to fit corners of block and leave the inside edge free for setting next patch.

Now cut two more patches and arrange them on the block so one side extends ¼ inch *under* free side of the corner patch (Fig. 2). Turn in edges of first patch and sew in place with hemming stitches. Continue placing the patches in the same manner until the block is completely covered. Cut away any silk edges that extend beyond the foundation block.

4. Cover seams with embroidery stitches and decorate the center patches in any manner you wish. Set blocks together to form an all-over pattern, or use velvet strips between the blocks as shown in illustration.

5. After the quilt is set, a lining must be added to the back. If you have wadding in the blocks, it is not necessary to add a middle layer of cotton. Baste the lining to the quilt top and fasten together with knots placed at 3-inch intervals throughout the quilt. After the knotting is done, trim the edges straight and turn them in ¼ inch all around. Sew the edges together with overcast stitches.

6. *To make a knot*—thread a darning needle with yarn and pull the ends even to make a double thread. Push the needle up from the back of the quilt at a point where it will come out on top between a seam—not in the middle of a patch. Pull the yarn through but not all the way, leave 2 inches on the underside for tying the knot. Now place the point of the needle ⅛ inch from point of entry and push it through to underside. Cut the yarn 2 inches away from the background. Tie the four strands together to form a square knot, and cut ends ½ inch away from the knot.

YO YO QUILT

This novelty quilt is decorative but, lacking an inner lining, has no utility purpose. It is made of varicolored material with connected circular patches which have been gathered into small, wheel-like shapes.

YO YO QUILT

This novel pattern is used to make a decorative bedspread but lacking warmth, has no utility value as a quilt. It is an all-over design, usually made of varicolored materials scattered throughout the quilt in no set pattern. The patches must be of the same general type of material throughout the quilt; that is, the pieces must be entirely of silk or all cut from cotton materials such as calico, gingham or percale—also, the texture and quality must be the same. The spread has no inner layer of cotton and the foundation lining is sometimes omitted, so the planning is quite

EMBROIDERY STITCHES

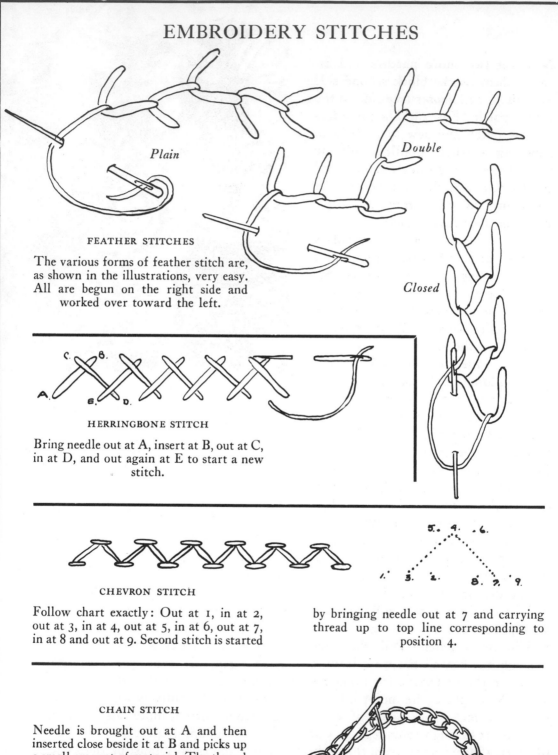

Plain

Double

Closed

FEATHER STITCHES

The various forms of feather stitch are, as shown in the illustrations, very easy. All are begun on the right side and worked over toward the left.

HERRINGBONE STITCH

Bring needle out at A, insert at B, out at C, in at D, and out again at E to start a new stitch.

CHEVRON STITCH

Follow chart exactly: Out at 1, in at 2, out at 3, in at 4, out at 5, in at 6, out at 7, in at 8 and out at 9. Second stitch is started by bringing needle out at 7 and carrying thread up to top line corresponding to position 4.

CHAIN STITCH

Needle is brought out at A and then inserted close beside it at B and picks up a small amount of material. The thread is swung around under tip before drawing needle through.

different from an ordinary quilt. If you decide to make a spread, look at the illustration carefully so that you have a general idea of the design and proceed as follows:

1. Draw a circle on a piece of cardboard according to the size of patch you wish to make (3 inches in diameter will make a dainty design). Cut out circular patches and sort them according to shade and color.

2. To prepare the patches for sewing, turn in the edge ¼ inch all around, being sure the edge goes down on wrong side of material. Sew the edges down with short running stitches ⅛ inch from edge of circle, holding the right side of the material toward you. The sewing must be in straight, even stitching, with *no back-stitches* as the patch is made by pulling the thread until the edges of the circle are gathered to form a small hole in the center. The thread must be strong as the strength of the quilt depends on the quality of the thread;

we suggest you use a double thread No. 50 or 60. A heavier thread would require a needle too large for comfortable sewing.

Begin the sewing by pushing the needle up to top of patch so the knot will remain on the underside. Pull gently but firmly on the thread until all edges are gathered to the center as shown in the illustration. Secure in place by taking several back stitches. Spread the gathers evenly around the center hole, flatten the patch by covering with a damp cloth and pressing with warm iron.

3. After the patches are made, arrange the colors according to taste for sewing together. They are attached by placing the right side of 2 patches together and sewing the edges with small over stitches. Sew only about ¾ of the width of the patch as ¼ inch must be left free at each end for turning corners. Continue in this manner until all patches are connected.

10.

Collecting Quilts As a Hobby

Standing in front of a case in a great eastern art museum, was a slender, alert young woman. She examined keenly and attentively the beautiful patterned quilt displayed behind the glass. Twice she turned away and returned to feast her eyes on the exquisite handwork. Finally she looked toward me and spoke.

"You like it too, don't you? I see you're sketching that quilt," she spoke in a soft southern voice, meantime looking about the well-filled museum walls. "This is a wonderful collection, isn't it? The woman who made it must have started collecting years ago."

I agreed. It was a well known and authentic collection, gathered over the years and now on a loan exhibition.

"It's just too bad I wasn't born years ago," she continued. "That's what I would most like to do—collect quilts. I love old handwork. I like quilts better than furniture or glass or china. Of course I have my

family things, but there aren't any quilts—at least none like these."

"These" were a fine collection of very old Ohio Valley bed coverings and I could well understand anyone liking them. So I nodded and put a few more strokes on my sketch.

Never Too Late

"But now it's too late," sighed my new acquaintance, "All such quilts that were really good must have been picked up ages ago. I'll only be able to find them in somebody else's collection!"

"Not at all," I answered her, folding up my pad and putting it in my handbag, "You just haven't looked hard enough. Or maybe not in the right places. To find old quilts you have to really *hunt* for them, like a detective. But you must hunt in the most likely places."

Surprised, the girl looked at me sharply. "Go on, please. I want to know. I've been trying to find some handmade quilts to dress up my old

220

beds. There aren't any. At least, none I can afford to buy."

I replied, "I know from your charming accent that you're from the South. And if it's quilts you are seeking, my advice to you is to turn around and go right back home. I told you you'd find them in the likeliest places."

"But where will that be?"

WHERE TO FIND THEM

"If you have a car and can drive it, go out into the country districts and up into the mountains. There'll be quilts in both places, old ones and new ones. The farm wives and mountain women make them in the traditional patterns their families have had for years. Or if you live in a town or city, your happy hunting grounds will be the second hand stores. Often old quilts are discarded or forgotten in chests and bureau drawers. Second hand dealers find them and will be glad to show them to you if you ask for them.

"The second hand stores are your best bets in towns if you are persistent and want to acquire quilts at reasonable prices. Don't forget to inquire for any made-up covers they may have—patterned blocks sewed together but not quilted. And sometimes you can find batches of cut out pieces that sell for very little and there have been wonderful finds of rare patterns unearthed in antique and second hand stores."

The Quilting Question

"Wonderful! But what about getting them quilted?"

"That will take more hunting about in likely places. Some inquiries will locate a church sewing group or a charitable organization to do it. Then you may run across an old time quilter who likes to quilt at home, and who still has her frame. She will finish your quilts for you. And maybe some day you'll want to do it yourself!"

She thanked me and started to move away but I called her back.

"There are some other suggestions you may find helpful. Watch for all the country fairs. They always have a display of homemade quilts. All over the country you will find quilts being shown at fairs—old ones and new ones made today in famous patterns. I never miss the fairs myself. Be sure to make plenty of friends everywhere you go. People you meet will tell you where to go for good prospects. That makes for friendships that help you trace down old patterns."

"It sounds fascinating—I want to start right now." The girl's voice was laughing now, and she said, "I just thought of something. I can't wait to get back home to ask Mandy—she's my cook and she used to be my Mammy—nurse, you know. I never thought to ask her but if there are any quilts in Culpeper County, I wager Mandy will know where they are!"

Good Hunting

And quilt hunting was just what my young southern friend undertook. She set up quite a correspondence with me, telling me of her adventures tracing down quilts, old and new. First she found one in a mountain cabin a few hours' drive from her home and happily installed it on her four-poster. She went to fairs for miles around, and saw the antique shows as far off as Atlanta and Charleston, until at last she finally found the quilts she needed for her home. As she heard of quilts with intriguing names she became interested in learning about many famous traditional designs and patterns.

Letters from her have followed her frequent trips to country fairs and sophisticated shows in neighboring towns and cities. These shows seem to be increasing in number in ratio to the growing scarcity of old furniture and household goods.

FAMOUS AMERICAN PATTERNS

In every fair or show she finds a pattern unfamiliar to her, and within a day or two comes her insistent question, "What is the Hen and Chickens Pattern? I think I found a pattern for it but I must make sure. How do I cut it and is it pieced or appliquéd?" Following in rapid succession have come her queries—requests for more information about other designs. "What is a Log Cabin Quilt? I've just heard of the Crown and Thorns Pattern—is that like the Queen Charlotte's Crown? Wasn't she the poor woman who had such a time being crowned? And are these two anything like the Cross and Crown design?"

Again she wrote, "Fans are so decorative. I've just been told of a quilt pattern they call Grandmother's Fan, and it intrigues me immensely. Do you know about it?"

And at another time, "I'm really confused. Can you help me again? There's the Sunflower Pattern, and I've just learned of one they call the Kansas Sunflower. To cap the climax, there's an advertisement in today's paper of a quilt named the Triple Sunflower. Are they all the same or are they three different patterns?"

I quite well understood her confusion. In my correspondence to her I had tried to answer all her questions and as she became more interested in recognizing the old designs, her enthusiasm stimulated me into writing reams to this ardent seeker after quilting lore. I recalled patterns I knew well, others I had known and half forgotten, and I even started tracking down still more which had only been names to me in the past.

So, because other enthusiasts may well feel the way my young southern friend does, I've assembled drawings of many of the most famous American patterns about which I wrote her through the past few years. In the next chapter are more than 140 of the best known designs originated in this country.

Just as my young friend asked for a clear visual idea of these patterns, so she also wanted to know how to copy them for her own use. My explanation is included with the drawings, and may enable you to copy from collectors' valuable quilts or from various pictures and thus be able to draft your own patterns.

11.

Famous American Quilts and How to Draft Their Patterns

WHEN YOU COME ACROSS A quilt design which you wish to copy for your own use, and you do not have a full-size pattern to trace (such as you find in Chapter 4), you will have to draft the pattern yourself. You may be looking at a famous quilt in a collection, and can easily get an idea of the size of each block and its individual units.

On the other hand, the pattern which you wish to copy may be a picture of smaller size, like the drawings in this chapter. It requires a little study to see how the block is divided. Are the divisions based on squares, circles or diagonal lines? Looking at the sides of the block, it is easy to tell how many sections there are and how they are formed. Using a square piece of paper as a block pattern, you will find that folding and creasing it will help you find the main sections into which the quilt design is divided.

For those who cannot work out the pattern by the folding method, there is the system of enlarging by squares.

It is a well recognized method of getting the approximate size of each piece, and is particularly useful for drafting designs which are to be appliquéd. A few suggestions on this method are included in the drafting plans given below.

STEPS IN DRAFTING

The size of your paper block should be the exact size of the quilt block. The 14-inch square is considered a good size, but there is no adamant rule about it. The size of the top of the bed is what you have to consider, so that the decorated part reaches to the edge and no further.

The first step in drafting the pattern is to divide the paper block into the sections. The size and number of the sections depend on the general design. The shapes of the units will be based on one of these seven basic forms: a circle, arc, triangle, diamond, square, rectangle, or parallelogram.

The first lines you draw will follow one of the plans which follow. Start with the basic lines and fill in the smaller units. Note the number of each unit and cut out one of each from paper for tracing on cardboard. Lay each different kind on the cardboard, allowing space between the pieces so that after they are traced you may draw a line around the outside edge ¼ inch from outline to give room for the seam.

Cut out the cardboard unit patterns and smooth edges with sandpaper. Note the number of times each shape is repeated in the quilt block and mark the number on the cardboard pattern. This will help you in cutting the exact number of pieces from the material without referring back to the design.

METHODS FOR FOLDING

Here are the plans for folding and drawing your lines as you proceed to draft different kinds of patterns:

Method 1—Center Square and Parallel Lines

Many of the patterns are based on a small center square with two parallel lines running from each corner to edge of block. These form four rectangles. Decide on size of square.

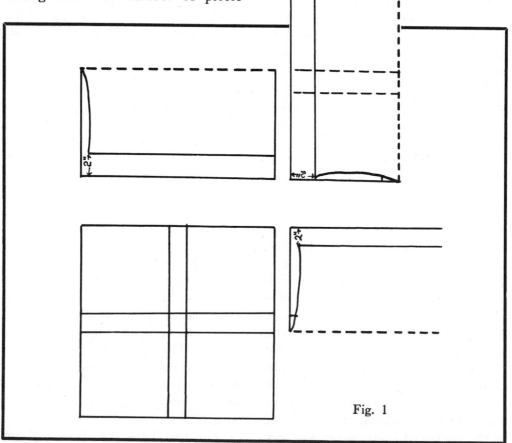

Fig. 1

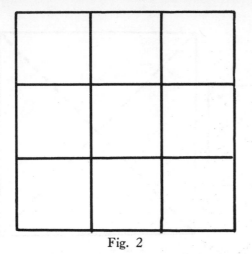

Fig. 2

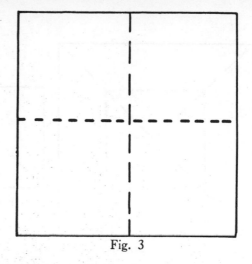

Fig. 3

Fold block (Fig. 1). The paper is folded so one side is some distance from opposite edge of block. The distance is determined by ½ of the width of center square. Repeat fold on all four sides.

Method 2—Nine Patch

Some of the patterns are based on dividing the block into 9 equal squares. Cut paper block and fold it over twice so that each fold represents ⅓ the width of the block. Unfold and again divide the block into thirds the other way. This will give you a Nine Patch (Fig. 2).

Method 3—Squares

A few of the patterns are based on folding the block into 4 equal squares. To do this, simply fold the block

through the center each way and crease (Fig. 3). To get 16 squares, fold block in half and then over again into fourths and crease. Unfold and repeat the same folds the other way (Fig. 4).

Sometimes you have a large center square. Draw two diagonal lines across center of block (Fig. 5). Measure points of square on each diagonal line. Use a ruler and draw a line from each point to form the square (Fig. 6).

Method 4—Diagonals

Many of the patchwork designs are based on diagonal folds. They may also include squares as well as diagonal lines, so you will have to refer to both methods.

To divide block into 4 equal tri-

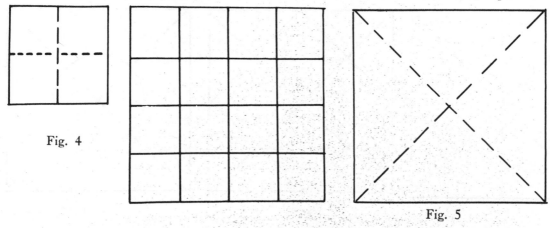

Fig. 4

Fig. 5

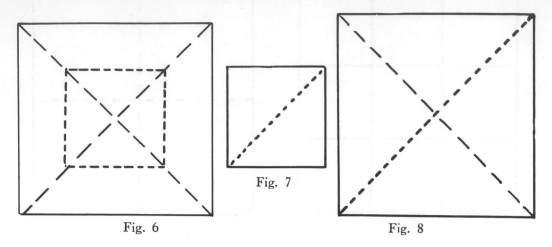

Fig. 6

Fig. 7

Fig. 8

angles—place opposite corners of square together and crease middle line (Fig. 7). Repeat fold with other corners (Fig. 8).

To divide block into 8 equal triangles—repeat folds as in Fig. 8. Unfold and fold block in half each way to get center creases (Fig. 9).

To divide block into 4 squares and 8 triangles—fold square diagonally through the center by bringing opposite corners together. Crease and then bring the corners up to the center of middle fold and crease again. Unfold and proceed to fold the other side in the same way (Fig. 10).

Method 5—Circle

Draw two diagonal lines across square in order to find center of circle. Mark in circle with a compass. If

you do not have one, you might use a plate or saucer. If you use this method, be sure your circle is equal distance from all 4 edges (Fig. 11).

Method 6—Enlarging Squares

This is done by ruling squares of equal dimensions on pattern. Next, prepare a paper square the size you wish quilt block to be and rule in an equal number of squares, only larger. Assuming that the squares on the original pattern are ¼ inch and you wish to enlarge it to 4 times the size, the squares for the enlargement will measure 1 inch. To make the enlargement, point off on the larger squares, using the same comparative proportions, wherever the original crosses the lines of the smaller squares. Next, connect these points,

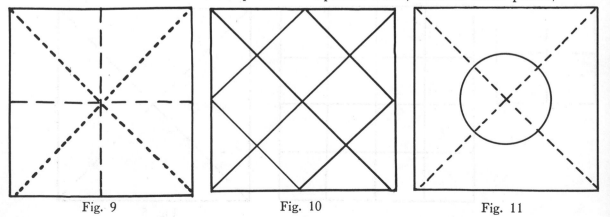

Fig. 9

Fig. 10

Fig. 11

taking care to follow the original drawing (Figs. 12 and 13).

How to Draft a Pattern

After you have cut a paper pattern the size of your quilt block, make a study of the design you wish to make. Is it based on diagonal lines, squares or circles? The first step in drafting the pattern is to divide the block into sections by folding as explained in the various preceding methods. The lines you draw will follow one of the plans given below. Start with the basic lines obtained by folding and fill in the smaller units, namely triangle, square, diamond, rectangle, parallelograms, or arc shown here.

(*Above*)

Fig. 12

(*Right*)

Fig. 13

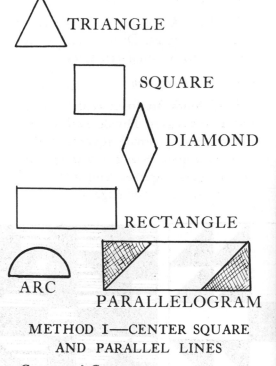

TRIANGLE

SQUARE

DIAMOND

RECTANGLE

ARC

PARALLELOGRAM

METHOD I—CENTER SQUARE AND PARALLEL LINES

Cross and Crown

Fold block to form center square and 4 rectangles. Divide each corner

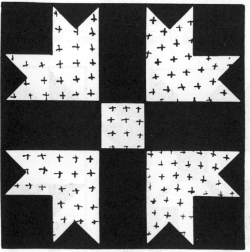

CROSS AND CROWN

GOOSE TRACKS   HEN AND CHICKENS   BEAR'S TRACK

square into one large triangle, 4 small triangles and 1 small square.

Goose Tracks

Same pattern as Cross and Crown. Light and dark spaces are in reverse.

Hen and Chickens

Fold block to form center square and 4 rectangles. Divide each corner square into 1 large square, surrounded by 10 equal triangles.

Bear's Track

First, fold block to form center square and 4 rectangles. Divide each corner square into 1 large square, 8 small triangles and 1 small square.

Peony

Draw a 2-inch square in center of block and then a 6-inch square around it. The flower in each corner square is made from 2 red diamonds, 2 red triangles, and 2 green triangles at the base for leaves. Fill in edges with 4 small white triangles and 2 small squares. Add a white rectangular piece between each square. Appliqué stems and center square after block is pieced.

Flying Geese

Fold block to form center square and 4 rectangles. Divide each corner square into 8 equal triangles.

Lincoln's Platform

Fold block to form center square and 4 rectangles. Divide each corner square into 5 small squares and 2 large triangles. Sew the 2 long sides of triangles together and add small squares along outer edge.

PEONY   FLYING GEESE   LINCOLN'S PLATFORM

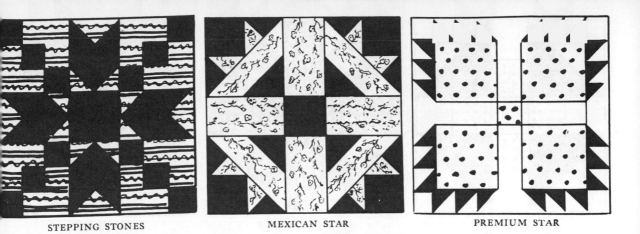

STEPPING STONES   MEXICAN STAR   PREMIUM STAR

Stepping Stones

Fold block to form a 4-inch square in center. Divide each corner square into 9 small squares. Divide each rectangle between squares into diamonds, 2 small triangles and 1 large triangle.

Mexican Star

Fold block to form a 3-inch block in center and 4 rectangles. Divide each corner square into 4 small triangles, 1 large triangle, 1 square and 1 parallelogram.

Premium Star

Fold block to form a 2-inch square in center and 4 rectangles. Divide each corner square into 1 large square with 6 triangles on 2 sides. A small square forms the corner.

Morning Star

Fold block to form 3-inch square in center. Now fold entire block diagonally both ways. Draw an oval in each corner using the block diagonal as the long dimension of the oval. Fold block crosswise both directions to find the top of the triangle. The center of the design is pieced together and appliquéd, together with the corner ovals, to the block.

King David's Crown

Fold block to form 2-inch square in center and 4 rectangles. Next divide each side of the block into half. This will give you the base of the dark triangle.

Duck Paddle

Fold block to form a 3-inch square in center and 4 rectangles. Divide

MORNING STAR   KING DAVID'S CROWN   DUCK PADDLE

CHURN DASH   JACK-IN-THE-BOX   JOSEPH'S COAT

each corner square into 4 diamonds, 3 triangles and 1 small square.

Churn Dash

Fold block to form a 3-inch square in center and 4 rectangles. Divide each rectangle into 2 squares. Divide each corner square into 2 triangles.

Jack-in-the-Box

Fold block to form a 3-inch square in the center and 4 rectangles. Divide ½ of each corner square into one large triangle and 2 small ones. The other half is divided into 1 parallelogram and 2 triangles.

Joseph's Coat

Fold block to form a 3-inch square in center and 4 rectangles. Divide each rectangle into 6 triangles and 1 square. Each corner square is divided into 1 square and 8 triangles.

Garden of Eden

Fold block to form a 3-inch square in center and 4 rectangles. Divide each corner square into 1 small square and 4 triangles.

Red Cross

Fold block to form a 4-inch square in center and 4 rectangles. Divide each corner square into 8 triangles.

Grandmother's Choice

Fold block to form a 3-inch square in center and 4 rectangles. Divide corner square diagonally across to form 2 triangles. Divide 1 triangle into 1 square and 2 triangles.

Swing-in-the-Center

Fold block diagonally to form a 3-inch square in center. Draw parallel lines from corners of square to edge of block. Divide into 1 square and 1

GARDEN OF EDEN   RED CROSS   GRANDMOTHER'S CHOICE

SWING-IN-THE-CENTER

MEXICAN ROSE

THE THREE CROSSES

parallelogram. Divide large triangle on each side into 2 diamonds, 2 small and 1 large triangle.

Mexican Rose

Fold block diagonally to form a 2-inch square in center. Divide each large triangle on sides into 5 triangles and 1 square.

The Three Crosses

Fold block to form a 3-inch square in center with parallel lines leading from each corner to edge of block. Fold block diagonally each way and draw in a 10-inch square. Divide this into the center square, 4 rectangles, 4 small triangles (top of rectangles) and 4 large triangles. The outer edge is made up of 4 parallelograms, and the corners have 4 triangles and 1 square.

Crown and Cross

Fold block diagonally to form a 2-inch block in center and parallel lines leading from each corner to edge of block. Draw in second cross by measuring equal distance on each side with a ruler. Draw in center triangles. Fill in edges with 4 large triangles and 4 small ones.

White House Steps

Draw a 4-inch square in center of block. Fold block diagonally and draw in other squares. Allow a 2-inch margin around each block.

METHOD 2—NINE PATCH

Jacob's Ladder (1)

Divide block into 9 equal squares. Divide 5 squares into 4 small squares or a Four Patch. Divide 4 other

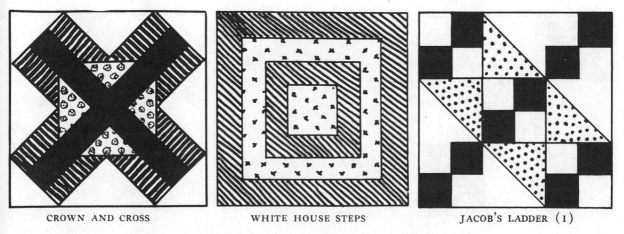

CROWN AND CROSS WHITE HOUSE STEPS JACOB'S LADDER (1)

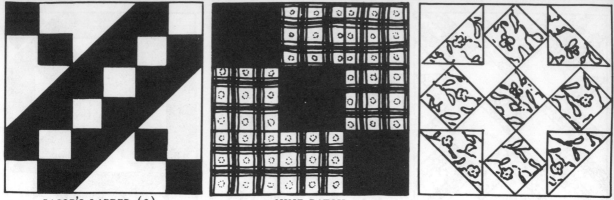

JACOB'S LADDER (2)   NINE PATCH   SAW TOOTH

squares into 2 triangles each. This is an all-over pattern.

Jacob's Ladder (2)

This design is the same as Jacob's Ladder (1). Dark triangles are used in the center instead of figured ones.

Nine Patch

This is an all-over pattern. When the blocks are set together, the dark squares run diagonally across the quilt.

Saw Tooth

Divide block into 9 equal squares. Draw a diagonal square in 5 of the squares, thus forming triangles in the 4 corners. Divide remaining 4 squares into 2 triangles.

Turkey Tracks

Divide block into a Nine Patch.

Five squares are plain. The corner squares are divided into 4 diamonds, 3 triangles and 1 small square.

Puss-in-the-Corner

Divide block into 9 equal squares. Five of the squares are then divided into 4 small squares, 1 larger one and 4 rectangles. This is an all-over pattern.

Flying Dutchman

This pattern is based on the Nine Patch. Divide block into 9 equal squares. Divide each of these squares again into 4 small squares. Divide each square into 2 triangles and darker ones shown in the design.

Greek Cross

Divide block into 9 squares. The 4 corner squares are divided into 2 triangles, the squares between into 2

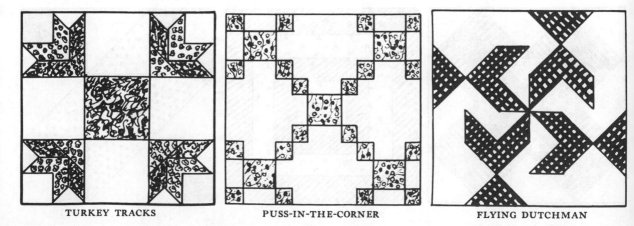

TURKEY TRACKS   PUSS-IN-THE-CORNER   FLYING DUTCHMAN

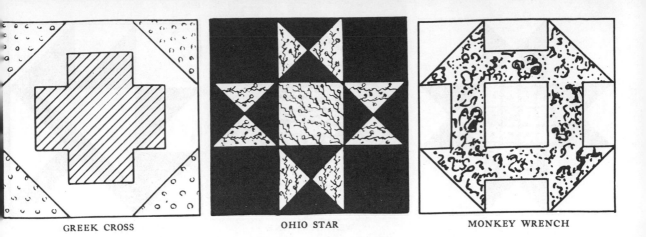

GREEK CROSS   OHIO STAR   MONKEY WRENCH

rectangles and the center square is plain.

Ohio Star

Divide block into 9 equal squares. Five squares are plain. The remaining 4 blocks are divided into 4 equal triangles.

Monkey Wrench

Fold block to form 9 squares. Divide corner squares into 2 triangles. The 4 middle squares are divided into 2 rectangles and the center block is plain.

Letter X

Divide block into 9 squares. Four blocks are plain and the remaining 5 are divided into 4 triangles. This is an all-over pattern.

Robbing Peter to Pay Paul

Fold the block to form 9 squares.

Divide each corner square into 6 triangles and 1 small square. The middle blocks are divided into 1 large triangle, 2 small ones and 1 rectangle. The center square is plain.

Combination Star

Fold block to form 9 equal squares. Divide each corner square into 1 square and 4 triangles. The middle blocks are divided into 4 triangles and the center block is plain.

Lone Star

Divide block into 9 squares. The corner squares are plain. Divide squares between into 4 triangles. Erase inner line of each of these squares and you will have the large center square.

Weather Vane

Fold block to form 9 equal squares.

LETTER X   ROBBING PETER TO PAY PAUL   COMBINATION STAR

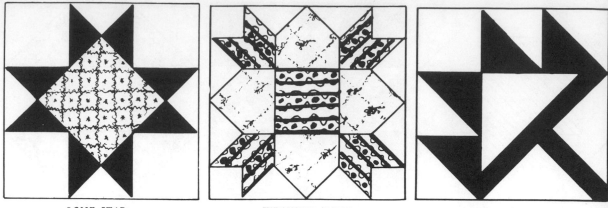

LONE STAR   WEATHER VANE   CACTUS FLOWER

Divide each corner square into 2 diamonds, 2 triangles and 1 small square. The middle squares are divided into 1 rectangle, 1 large triangle and 2 small ones. Erase the line between the large triangle and rectangle. The center square is plain.

Cactus Flower

Divide block into 9 squares. Divide 4 blocks forming flower into two triangles and make one corner square plain. Erase lines between other 4 squares to form 1 large square. Cut base of flower and stem separately. Appliqué to block after it is pieced.

Sweet Gum Leaf

Divide block into 9 squares. To draw flower, divide 3 of the squares into 4 triangles. Divide center square into 4 triangles. (The one on the bottom will be white.) Erase other 3 sides of center square to form flower. Erase lines between lower 3 squares to form a rectangle. Appliqué stem after block is pieced.

St. Louis Star

Fold block to form 9 equal squares. Divide the center outside squares into 9 small squares. This will give you the base and height of each triangle. Once you have this, you can easily draw the center square according to the pattern.

California Star

This pattern is drafted by first dividing the block into 9 equal squares. Each square is again divided into 9 small squares. This will form a graph. Divide the small squares into triangles according to the pattern.

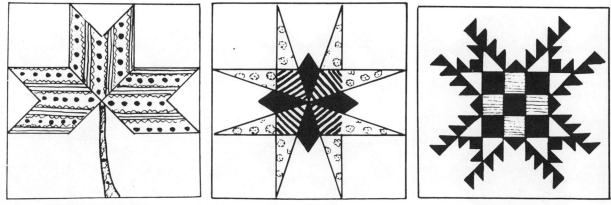

SWEET GUM LEAF   ST. LOUIS STAR   CALIFORNIA STAR

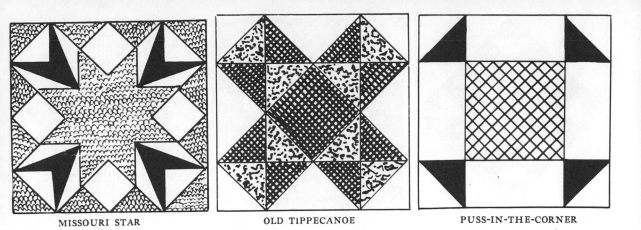

MISSOURI STAR   OLD TIPPECANOE   PUSS-IN-THE-CORNER

Missouri Star

Divide block into 9 equal squares. Draw a small square in each corner and divide it into triangles. Add 4 long triangles and 2 small ones to complete square. Draw a diagonal square in other outside squares as shown in the design.

METHOD 3—SQUARES

Old Tippecanoe

Fold block to form 16 squares. Divide each square into 2 triangles. This can be done with a ruler or bias folds.

Puss-in-the-Corner

Divide block into 16 squares. Divide corner squares into 2 triangles. Erase dividing lines between other outer squares to form 4 rectangles. Erase inner lines of 4 inside squares to form 1 large square.

Odd Fellow's Cross

Fold block into 16 squares. Divide 2 squares on each side into 2 triangles. The 4 corner squares are plain. Draw a diagonal square in center to complete design. Erase lines in center blocks.

Pierced Star

After block is folded to form 16 squares, divide each outside square into 2 triangles. The 4 center squares are also divided into 2 triangles. Arrange light and dark triangles according to design.

Octagonal Star

Fold block to form 16 squares. Divide 8 outside squares into 2 triangles, leaving the 4 corner squares plain. Divide the 4 inner squares into 4 triangles. 1 is colored and 3 are white.

ODD FELLOW'S CROSS   PIERCED STAR   OCTAGONAL STAR

GRANDMOTHER'S FAVORITE

PATIENCE CORNER

EIGHT HANDS ROUND

Grandmother's Favorite

Divide block into 16 squares. Divide each of the outer squares into 2 triangles. Draw in the small triangle on each side. Erase dividing lines of 4 inner squares to form a large square.

Patience Corner

Fold block to form 16 squares. Divide each square in half in order to draw in colored area.

Eight Hands Round

Fold block into 16 squares. Divide outer squares into 2 triangles. Erase dividing lines between center squares on outer edge to form large triangle. Divide each of the 4 center squares into 4 triangles and 2 small squares. Erase lines in center of block to form large square.

Tulip Lady Fingers

Divide block into 16 squares. Divide each corner square into 1 small square, 2 parallelograms and 2 triangles. Erase dividing lines between other outside squares to form 4 rectangles. Erase lines in center of block to form large square.

Crazy Ann

Fold block to form 16 squares. The 4 corner squares are plain. Divide all other squares in half to form a graph for putting in the design.

Rising Star

Divide block into 16 squares. Divide the 2 middle squares along the outer edge into 1 large triangle and 2 small ones. Divide each of the middle 4 squares into 4 triangles and 2

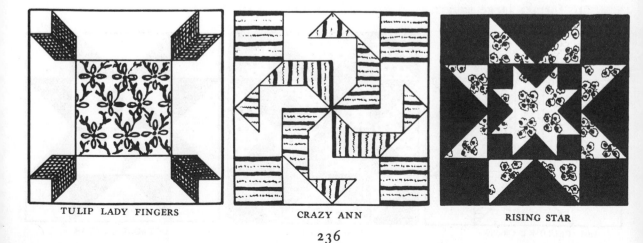

TULIP LADY FINGERS   CRAZY ANN   RISING STAR

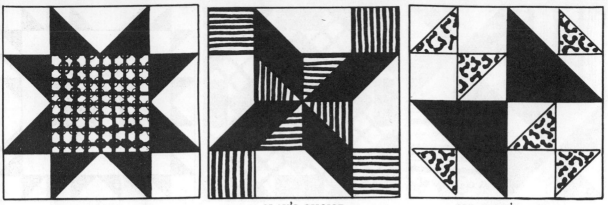

SAW TOOTH   CLAY'S CHOICE   OLD MAID'S PUZZLE

small squares. Erase center lines to form small square in center.

Saw Tooth

Fold block into 16 squares. Divide 2 center squares along edge into 1 large triangle and 2 small ones. The corner squares are plain. Erase lines in center to form the large square.

Clay's Choice

Fold block into 16 squares. There are 3 plain squares on each side and 1 that is divided into 2 triangles. The center 4 squares are divided into 8 equal triangles.

Old Maid's Puzzle

Divide block into 16 squares. Divide corner squares into 2 triangles. One square on each side is also di-

vided into 2 triangles. Leave two squares in the center plain and divide the other 2 into 2 triangles. Erase outside edges of 2 center squares to form the large triangles.

Dutchman's Puzzle

Fold block first into 16 squares. Divide each square into 2 triangles. Erase 1 line from each square to form large triangle.

Crosses and Losses

Divide block into 16 squares. Divide 4 squares in 1 corner into 4 triangles and 2 squares. The next 4 squares are divided into 2 large triangles.

King's Crown

Fold block into 16 squares. Divide 8 squares along outer edge into 2

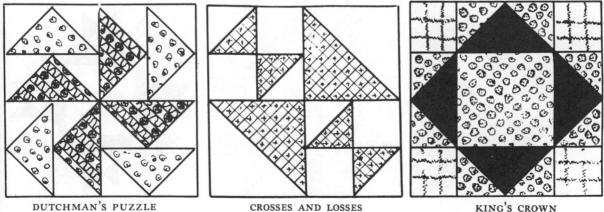

DUTCHMAN'S PUZZLE   CROSSES AND LOSSES   KING'S CROWN

DOUBLE T   DEVIL'S CLAWS   JAGGED EDGE

triangles. The corner squares are plain. Erase lines in center of block to form large central square.

Double T

Divide block into 4 equal squares. Divide 2 of the squares into 4 squares and then into 8 triangles.

Devil's Claws

Fold block into 16 squares. Divide each of these squares into 4 small squares. This will make a graph which you can follow in putting in the squares and triangles.

Jagged Edge

Divide block into 16 squares. Divide all squares along outer edge into 4 small squares. Divide all small squares along edge into 2 triangles excepting the 4 corner squares. Di-

vide each of the 4 center squares into 2 small squares and 4 triangles.

PATTERNS BASED ON 25 SQUARES

Greek Cross

Divide block into 25 equal squares. Once you have this graph, it will be easy to fill in light and dark colors shown in the design.

Sister's Choice

Divide block into 25 squares. There are 9 figured squares in the design and 8 white squares. 8 squares are divided into 2 triangles, 1 white and the other figured.

King David's Crown

Divide block into 25 squares. Eight of the border squares are divided into

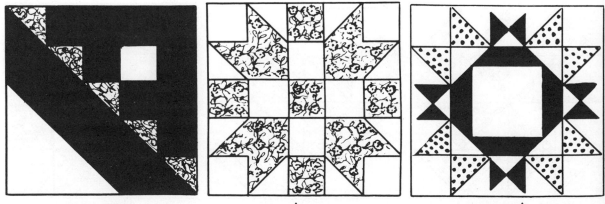

GREEK CROSS   SISTER'S CHOICE   KING DAVID'S CROWN

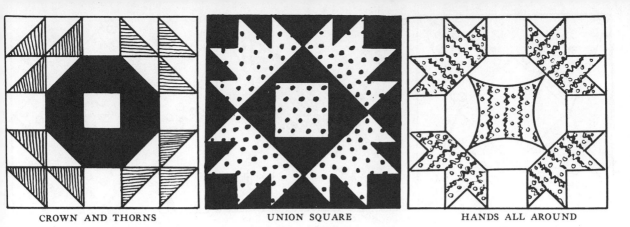

CROWN AND THORNS   UNION SQUARE   HANDS ALL AROUND

2 triangles and 4 into 4 small triangles. The corner squares are plain. Divide second row of squares in half to form white square in center. Divide space between center square and border into 4 parallelograms and 4 triangles.

Crown and Thorns

Fold block into 25 squares. Note there are 5 plain squares running each way through the center. Each corner is made up of 4 squares each divided into 2 triangles.

Union Square

Divide block into 25 squares. Divide all the border squares into 2 triangles, excepting the 4 corner squares which remain plain. Divide center squares to form 8 triangles and center square.

Hands All Around

Divide block into 25 squares. Every other square in the border is divided into 4 triangles. Erase dividing lines between lower 2 triangles and you will have figured pattern. Draw a triangle on each corner of inner square. Use compass to draw center design.

Handy Andy

Fold block into 25 squares. There are 9 plain squares in this design. 12 squares are divided into 2 triangles and the remaining 4 are divided into 4 triangles.

Queen Charlotte's Crown

This design can be drawn by dividing the block into 25 squares, or you may use a bias fold. Once you have drawn the squares, it is easy to fill in

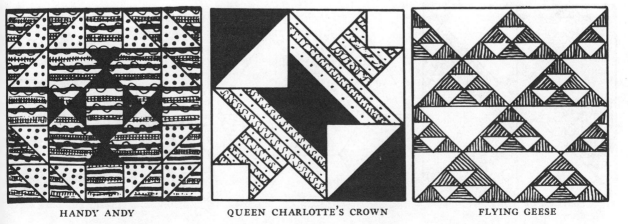

HANDY ANDY   QUEEN CHARLOTTE'S CROWN   FLYING GEESE

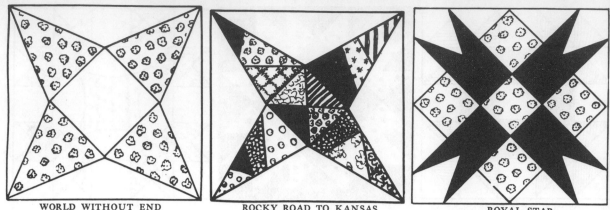

WORLD WITHOUT END   ROCKY ROAD TO KANSAS   ROYAL STAR

the outline of the design by following lines of squares.

METHOD 4—DIAGONAL LINES

Flying Geese

Fold block diagonally and then into 16 squares. The diagonal lines will give you the sides of the triangles and the squares the base. Divide every other triangle into 9 small triangles.

World Without End

Fold block diagonally through center each way. Next make a center crease each way by folding edges together. Mark corner points of diagonal center square on cross creases. Draw base of triangles to form center square. Complete triangles by drawing 2 diagonal lines to each corner of block.

Rocky Road To Kansas

Proceed as in *World Without End*, only make center square smaller. Divide center square into 4 triangles. The 4 large triangles are made from scrap material in various shapes.

Royal Star

Fold block diagonally and then into 16 squares. Draw in diagonal square in center first and divide it into 9 small squares. Draw in the 2 dark triangles in each corner and your design is complete.

Wheel Of Fortune

Fold block diagonally each way through the center. Next make a center crease each way by folding edges together. Mark in the 8 large triangles by following creases. Draw

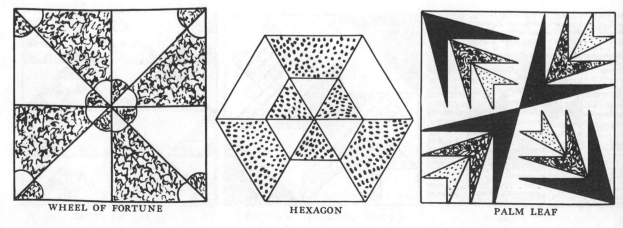

WHEEL OF FORTUNE   HEXAGON   PALM LEAF

WATER WHEEL   COWBOY'S STAR   BLAZING STAR

circle in center and quarter circles at each corner. Divide circles into small triangles as shown in design.

Hexagon

This pattern is drafted by folding the block diagonally and then across the center once. Draw in the 6 triangles first and add center hexagon. Cut corners from 4 sides on outside edge.

Palm Leaf

Consider 1 leaf only in drafting this pattern. Divide ¼ of the block into 16 small squares. Draw a diagonal line through the center of large square. The squares will guide you in drawing in the triangles to the diagonal line in center to form the leaf.

Water Wheel

This pattern is easily drafted by following diagonal folds.

Cowboy's Star

Fold block diagonally both ways through the center. Take a separate piece of paper ¼ size of block to cut pattern of diamond. Fold it through the center twice to form small square and cut diagonally across. When unfolded, it will be in shape of a diamond. Divide this pattern into 4 small diamonds.

Blazing Star

Fold block diagonally across center each way. Now fold it across each way to get center creases. Draw a 6-inch square in the center and from

MALTESE CROSS   CATS AND MICE   EIGHT-POINTED STAR

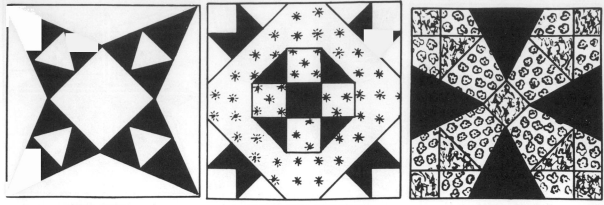

IOWA STAR   DAVID AND GOLIATH   DUTCH MILL

each corner draw a diagonal line to center of edge of block. This will give you the points of center star. Mark in triangles by following diagonal and cross creases in block. The base of the triangles of corner star should come 3 inches from tip of center star.

Maltese Cross

Draw in center square. Fold block through the center each way to find middle of block. Connect each point with a diagonal line to form square. Mark off a triangle in each corner of square. Now draw the triangles that form the Cross.

Cats and Mice

Fold block diagonally twice to get lines for the cross. Fold block through the center each way to get points for center square. The dark square forms the center of the cross and on each side is 1 plain square and 1 divided into 4 triangles. Cut 4 small triangles and 4 large ones to fill in the edges.

Eight-Pointed Star

Fold block each way through the center diagonally and then across twice to get center lines. It will be simple to mark in the 8 diamonds once you have these lines.

Iowa Star

Fold block diagonally each way through the center. Now fold block again to form 16 squares. This will give you the corner points of diagonal square in center. Draw in dark triangles and add the small white ones.

David and Goliath

Fold block diagonally each way through the center. Next divide block into 25 equal squares. This will give you a graph which can be easily followed in marking in the pattern.

Dutch Mill

Fold block diagonally each way through the center and then across each way to get center line. Draw in large center square, allowing about 3 inches for border. Draw a triangle in each corner of inside square and a small diagonal square in the center. Add a small square in each corner of block. Complete design by drawing diagonal lines from center square to edge of block.

Courthouse Square

Fold block diagonally several times each way and follow lines to mark out the squares. You can also start by

COURTHOUSE SQUARE

RISING STAR

LE MOYNE STAR (1)

marking out the block into 9 equal squares.

Rising Star

Fold block diagonally through the center each way and then across twice to get center creases. Mark in diamonds by following creases. Cut away corners to form hexagon.

Le Moyne Star (1)

Fold block across center each way to get center creases. Divide block into nine equal squares. The lines of the squares will give you the points of the triangles.

Le Moyne Star (2)

Same as Le Moyne Star (1). Figured material is substituted for plain white in star.

The Anvil

This pattern is easily drafted by folding block into diagonal lines. It can also be worked out by folding block into 16 squares.

Double X

This pattern can be drafted by folding block diagonally. However, it will be more accurate if the block is divided into 16 squares and then these divided into triangles as shown in design.

Double Z

Fold block diagonally. Mark off a triangle in each corner to form top of cross. Complete cross by following diagonal lines. The 2 light triangles in the center are appliquéd after block is pieced.

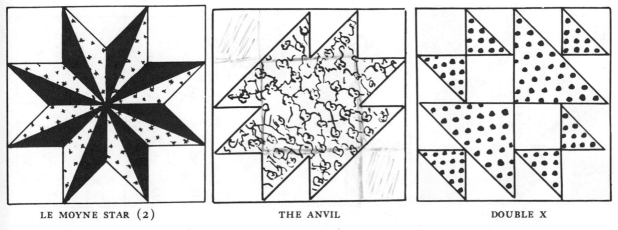

LE MOYNE STAR (2)   THE ANVIL   DOUBLE X

243

DOUBLE Z   IRISH PUZZLE   GEOMETRIC STAR

Irish Puzzle

Divide block into 4 equal squares. Next divide each square into 16 small ones. Eight squares in 1 corner are divided into 2 large triangles. The 3 small squares on 2 sides are divided into 2 triangles and the corner square is plain.

Geometric Star

Fold block diagonally each way through the center and then across twice to get center creases. Draw in diagonal square in center (corners at center creases) and add a triangle on each side according to diagonal lines. Draw in second square.

Aunt Sukey's Choice

Fold block to form a 4-inch square in center. Follow parallel lines on each side of square to form cross.

Each side is made up of 2 diamonds, 1 large triangle and 2 small ones. Draw a square in each corner.

METHOD 5—CIRCLES

Circular Saw

Draw a large circle on the block and then divide the block into 9 equal squares. Erase arc of circle passing through the central squares on each side of the block which will leave the base of a rounded triangle in each corner square. Draw in sides of each triangle and 11 small triangles along the curved side of each large triangle. Shape the central square as shown in design.

Country Cross Roads

Fold block to form small center square and draw in small triangles. Draw a quarter circle in each corner.

AUNT SUKEY'S CHOICE   CIRCULAR SAW   COUNTRY CROSS ROADS

HEARTS AND GIZZARDS

GRANDMOTHER'S FAN

CROSS ROADS

Hearts and Gizzards

A favorite all-over design usually made in red and white. Cut a small square of paper and fold it across center each way to form a square. Round the corners and you will have center design. Use ¼ of the pattern to mark design in corner.

Grandmother's Fan

Draw a large arc as indicated in the design and a small one in 1 corner of the block. Divide fan into 7 diagonal pieces.

Cross Roads

Fold block diagonally each way through the center. Mark off 1 inch on each side of diagonal line and put in center cross. Draw arcs the same width with a compass. This is an all-over pattern and is appliquéd.

Mill Wheel

Divide block into 4 equal squares. ¼ of a small circle serves as a pattern for this block. This is an all-over pattern and is pieced.

Chips and Whetstone

Draw a circle about 6 inches smaller in diameter than your block. Now draw a second circle about 3 inches smaller in diameter that will come at the base of the triangles. Draw in triangles and complete ¼ of the design. Fold block into a square and cut out 4 sides at once by following completed design.

Rolling Stone

This is really a Nine Patch so you do not need a compass. Divide block into 9 equal squares. Divide corner

MILL WHEEL   **CHIPS AND WHETSTONE**   **ROLLING STONE**

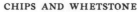

ROBBING PETER TO PAY PAUL (1)

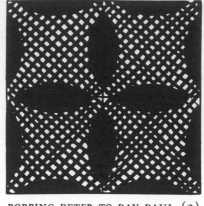

ROBBING PETER TO PAY PAUL (2)

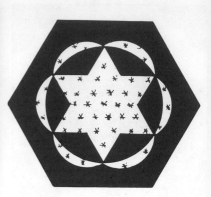

FLOWER STAR

squares into 1 square and 4 triangles. The squares between are divided into 2 rectangles. The center square in plain.

Robbing Peter to Pay Paul (1)

Divide block into 4 equal squares. Draw arcs with compass. This is an all-over pattern.

Robbing Peter to Pay Paul (2)

Same as Robbing Peter to Pay Paul (1), with different color arrangement.

Flower Star

Start with square block and cut away corners to form hexagon. Fold block first diagonally and then across, to get diagonal and center creases. Draw circle. Draw 6 diamonds to form star by following creased lines. Add arcs above circle.

The Reel (1)

Fold block diagonally each way through the center. Draw circle and add arcs by using a compass. The center of this design is pieced. Turn down outer edges and appliqué to block.

The Reel (2)

Same as The Reel (1). Shows effect of using figured material in design instead of plain.

King's Star

Fold block diagonally each way through the center and then across each way to form center creases. Draw a circle at point where diamonds meet. Draw in 8 diamonds according to creases in block. Appliqué an arc of plain material at center of every other diamond. Piece star and appliqué to block.

THE REEL (1)

THE REEL (2)

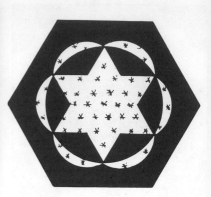

KING'S STAR

246

STAR FLOWER

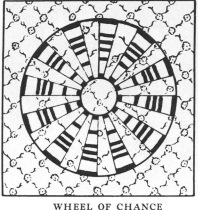

WHEEL OF CHANCE

ROLLING PIN WHEEL

Star Flower

Draw a small circle in center of block. The 8 flower petals are cut from the same pattern and overlapped when set on block. To cut petal—draw one side, then fold paper along center and cut both sides of petal at the same time to make it symmetrical. This design is appliquéd.

Wheel of Chance

Draw a large circle and then a smaller one, in the center of the block. Divide circle into 24 equal parts. Piece center of design and appliqué Wheel to block.

Rolling Pin Wheel

Draw three circles as indicated in the design. Fold block diagonally across the center each way and then fold it to form center creases. You easily can mark in the 6 large triangles and 6 small ones by following the creases. Draw hexagon in center.

Star and Planets

Draw large circle on block. Fold block diagonally each way across center and then make center folds. Draw 6 diamonds to form star by following folds. Add a small triangle at tip of each point of star.

Queen's Crown

Draw 2 circles as indicated in the design. Fold block diagonally each way across center to locate points for triangles. Sew triangles into circle and appliqué design to block.

Caesar's Crown

Fold block diagonally each way across center and then across to get

STAR AND PLANETS

QUEEN'S CROWN

CAESAR'S CROWN

FRENCH STAR   DRESDEN PLATE   THE COMPASS

center creases. Draw in 2 circles. Use compass to draw center block. The tops of the diamonds will come along the folds in the block. Piece design and appliqué to block.

French Star

This pattern is based on diagonal folds plus 2 center folds. Draw circle and divide it into 4 parts. Add triangles to form star. Draw an arc at base of each triangle. This design may be pieced.

Dresden Plate

Draw a large circle and smaller one in center. Divide into 20 equal parts. The design is made from mixed calicos or ginghams. Sew pieces together and appliqué to block.

The Compass

Divide the block into 4 equal squares and then fold it diagonally each way across the center. Draw a circle as indicated in the design. Draw in corner triangles.

Tennessee Star

Fold block diagonally across center twice and then make center folds. Draw 8 triangles to form star. Piece diamonds together and appliqué center design over seams.

METHOD 6—ENLARGING SQUARES

Star of the West

Draft pattern with enlarging squares. Piece design and appliqué to block.

Five-Pointed Star

Use enlarging squares to draft pattern. Make star of dark blue calico

TENNESSEE STAR

STAR OF THE WEST

FIVE-POINTED STAR

UNION STAR   VIRGINIA'S STAR   NORTH CAROLINA STAR

with small white figures, preferably stars if you can find it.

Union Star

Draw circle with compass and use enlarging squares to draw star. Make circle of dark blue and star of white material with small blue figures.

Virginia's Star

Use enlarging squares to draft pattern. This pattern is entirely pieced.

North Carolina Star

Draft pattern by using enlarging squares. This is an all-over pattern. The block is pieced.

Star of the Four Winds

Use enlarging squares to draft this pattern. Piece design and appliqué to block.

Star of Bethlehem

Enlarge pattern with enlarging squares. Piece star and appliqué center design. Appliqué star to block.

Winding Ways

If you are adept with a compass, you will want to use it when drafting this pattern. Otherwise use enlarging squares. This is an all-over pattern. Appliqué design on small squares and sew them together.

Double Hearts

Use enlarging squares to draft pattern. Another way is to fold a piece of paper in half and cut the heart design. Fold block diagonally each way through the center and follow creases for laying on design. Appliqué design to block.

STAR OF THE FOUR WINDS   STAR OF BETHLEHEM   WINDING WAYS

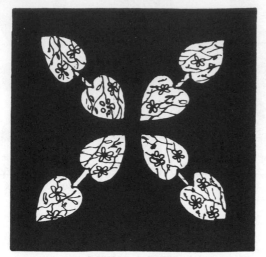

DOUBLE HEARTS

Castle Wall

Draft pattern with enlarging squares. It is important to contrast the light and dark material as shown in the design in order to have a 3-dimensional effect.

Secret Drawer

Use enlarging squares to draft pattern. This design is pieced.

The Snail's Trail

Enlarge pattern by using squares.

CASTLE WALL

THE SNAIL'S TRAIL

SECRET DRAWER

TURKEY TRACKS

This design is appliquéd and is an all-over pattern.

Turkey Tracks

Use either a compass or enlarging squares to draft this pattern. Appliqué design to block.

Royal Cross

Use enlarging squares to draft pattern. This design is pieced.

Children of Israel

Draft pattern by using enlarging squares. Piece the corners and appliqué dark design to block.

Job's Troubles

Draft pattern by using enlarging squares. Use contrasting dark and light materials for design. Piece small squares and sew them together.

Delectable Mountains

This pattern can be drafted by dividing block into 16 squares, or using enlarging squares. This design is pieced.

ROYAL CROSS

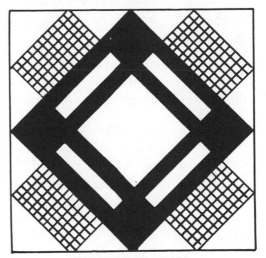

CHILDREN OF ISRAEL

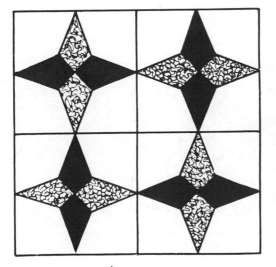

JOB'S TROUBLES

DELECTABLE MOUNTAINS

STAR UPON STAR BIRD OF PARADISE BLAZING SUN

Star Upon Star

Enlarge pattern with squares. Piece center of star and appliqué edges to block.

Bird of Paradise

Use enlarging squares to draft pattern. Use contrasting light and dark materials in design. Appliqué design to block.

Blazing Sun

This pattern can be drafted by using diagonal and cross folds Otherwise use enlarging squares. Draw circles with compass. This design is appliquéd.

Sunflower

Draft pattern by using enlarging squares. Use green for outer triangles and yellow figured material for flower. The center is orange surrounded by small green triangles. This design is appliquéd.

Kansas Sunflower

Draw circles on block with compass. Use enlarging squares for diamond pattern. Appliqué diamonds and center to large circle of figured material. Appliqué design to block.

The Little Giant

This pattern can be drafted by dividing the block into 16 squares and then dividing certain squares into 4 small squares. The circle is made with a compass. Use enlarging squares if you do not like this method. The design is pieced.

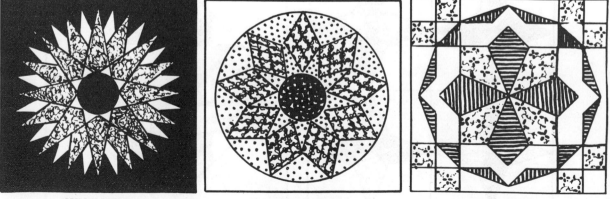

SUNFLOWER KANSAS SUNFLOWER THE LITTLE GIANT

12.

The Story of Quilt Making

QUILTING STANDS OUT PREEMI-
nently today among the fireside
crafts. In this machine age handmade quilts are recognized and valued
for the skillful artistry of their
needlework. There is both meaning
and memory in a fine quilt, and there
can be both history and heritage.

We may remember the cold frosty
mornings on the farm at Grandmother's when the gay homemade
quilt on her four-poster felt cozy and
warm, and was a prominent part of
the childhood scene. To the old-time
quilt makers the memory is more in-
timate. It seems "only yesterday"
that they pieced blocks for the well-
loved designs of the "Pine Tree,"
"Log Cabin," or "Twinkling Star
Quilt."

A Human Story

The famous quilt names may be
for many of us, only museum pieces,
but it remains a fact that a handmade
quilt still weaves a potent spell. Life
histories are tightly stitched within

the gay covers—tales of individuals
and communities filled with failures
and triumphs. The story of the quilt
is the record of the human family.

Sometimes decorated only with designs of the quilting needle, sometimes richly appliquéd with pieced
patterns of vivid chintz and calico, or
in crazy patchwork style, all quilts
are the products of a definite art-
craft that flourished at the firesides
of yesterday, and is still flourishing
today.

Quilts by Queen and Commoner

Through the centuries women of
all classes plied their needles at the
quilting frames in cottages, convents
and castles. Sir Samuel Pepys men-
tions in his celebrated diary that his
wife was at home busily quilting a
coverlet for his bed. Humble women
and ladies of the gentry did exquisite
quilting. There can be seen at Hard-
wicke Hall in England the quilts
wrought by the skillful fingers of
Mary Stuart, Queen of Scots, when

TRADITIONAL MAIDEN HAIR FERN QUILT

A well known pattern is shown in this quilt, which was made in 1845 in Ohio by the author's great-aunt for her own trousseau. The pattern is appliquéd in red and green on a white background. Quilt stitching is done in a plain diamond figure.

she was imprisoned there for so long.

There is no telling exactly when and where the craft of quilting began. All crafts grew out of the necessity to meet a basic human need. In the early civilizations along the Ganges, the Euphrates, and the Nile, where spinning and weaving brought forth the first fabrics, the way was opened for the allied crafts of sewing, embroidery, and quilting.

WHERE QUILTING BEGAN

Padded coverlets and padded clothing were needed for warmth, and the earliest form of quilting consisted of a few stitches to hold the three layers together at important points. These firm anchor stitches came to be known as counterpoints or quilt points. Hence come our words counterpane and quilting.

Whether the art began in India, Persia or Egypt, we know that the Crusaders discovered it in the Middle East and brought it back to Europe and the British Isles in the eleventh and twelfth centuries. Many of the knights, returning home, wore quilted material beneath their armor and thus was quilting introduced to the Western World.

In the time of the Roman Empire, the climate in Europe was mild. We may read in our Latin studies that when Roman soldiers fought the wars in Gaul and Britain, they wore long mailed shirts but no covering on the thighs. They were scornful of native Britons who wore woolen trousers in the winter time. But in the fourteenth century the Great Freeze changed all that.

Quilting Comes into its Own

A sudden early and extremely hard winter descended on all Europe. Rivers like the Rhine, Rhone and the Thames which had never iced over within the memory of man froze solidly and stayed frozen for a long, desperate winter. The Great Freeze kept up year after year. A shift in the ocean floor may have diverted warm water currents, but, whatever the geologic cause was, it brought a change in customs and costumes. A need for added warmth—both in day and night coverings—brought the art of quilting into its own. The women of Europe used it for both clothing and bed covering, especially the latter.

The quilting frame was devised and it soon became a common piece of the domestic equipment. At first the stitching was in simple straight and diagonal lines, but it was not long before it became more elaborate and decorative. Quilts appeared with central ornamental motifs surrounded with sprays and scrolls. The women of France introduced appliquéd ornaments in the forms of flowers, leaves, and vines done in contrasting colors of satins and velvets. Quilts of beauty and artistic design were by this time an integral part of home decoration.

France, Italy, and Spain

The materials for quilts varied greatly in different parts of Europe. Silks and damasks were popular in France and Italy, although records show that fine cotton was sometimes used. Spanish quilters used heavier brocades and velvets, and most of their work was found on ecclesiastical vestments of traditional patterns.

Quilting in Italy was concentrated in the island of Sicily, though the climate of the Mediterranean delayed the peak of popularity until the seventeenth century. Usually hand-loomed linen was the fabric employed for the covers, and the design and ornament were stressed rather than warmth and comfort. The special quilting stitch known as the Sicilian (or Italian) cable stitch was first developed in southern Italy and is to be found chiefly in spreads and quilts of that region. This stitch has cordings inserted beneath the fabric covers to emphasize and outline the design.

Mary Stuart learned to quilt while she lived at the court of Catherine de Medici; and there is to be found among old records of the French Revolution the description of a quilt that formed part of Marie Antoinette's wedding finery. This quilt was made of satin heavily appliquéd with patterns of flowers, doves and cupids skillfully quilted by hand by the ladies at the court of Maria Theresa of Austria. It was related to the detriment of the young French Queen that this quilt had been eight years in the making and the extravagance was criticized by the French Revolutionary tribunal.

Cottage and Castle Quilts

In the Low Countries and in Britain the craft flourished among farmfolk and gentry alike. As the need for and popularity of quilting grew with increasingly cold winters, the home craft took on the proportions of an industry, and the cottagers made quilts not only for their own use but for the even colder rooms of the great country houses of the nobility. Though the passage of time and the perishable nature of the quilts themselves have left very few pieces for the museums of today, we find account books and inventories of English homes which contain many records of such furnishings. We often find exact descriptions of quilted valances, side-bed curtains, and quilts with their bills in the account records of great families. So valued were these articles of comfort and home decoration, they were often left as legacies to relatives and friends bequeathed along with other heirlooms.

Most people today have heard that the great William Shakespeare left to Ann Hathaway, his wife, by his will in 1616, his "second best bed and furniture." It is less well known that in those days the "furniture" consisted of the quilted valances, the side curtains of the bed, and the quilts, as well. And to be quite fair to Master Will, it should be noted here that it was the usual bequest for a wife to receive the "second best bed." The "first" bed was put in the guest room. It was almost always more ornate but never so comfortable, and probably Ann Hathaway preferred her own bed with its "furniture" of quilts.

In England the early quilts were invariably hand woven linen, and varied for use of cottage or castle mainly in the quality of the weave, the gentry preferring the finer but less sturdy texture.

OLD PATCHWORK QUILT WITH HOUSE PATTERN

Each block in this many-colored quilt has the house pattern repeated in a different figured
material, and even the windows are made of contrasting patches.

THE STORY OF QUILT MAKING

TRADITIONAL PATTERNS OF BRITAIN

Refinements of the craft during the fifteenth, sixteenth and seventeenth centuries when the popularity was at its height, leaned toward intricate and artistic variations of the quilting stitch patterns. Three areas in the British Isles developed definite individuality in quilting patterns. Today in cottages and farms where the craft is still followed these same areas use the traditional patterns their great grandmothers stitched.

Roughly, these areas are defined as the Western or Welsh, the Northern Border, and the Southern or Wessex Downs patterns. The Welsh type inclines toward the use of straight lines enclosing geometric forms and these we know today as the Horizontal, the Cross Bar, the Double Cross Bar, Diagonal, Diamond, and Double Diamond. Along the west coast of England and in the mountain cottages of Wales, quilting frames still carry these traditional patterns.

Along the border country to the north of England, patterns were developed from the forms of nature, but the Border pattern makers were adapters rather than copyists. The Downs folks in the South copied nature as they saw it, using nodding heads of wheat, oak leaf clusters, and birds on the wing.

The women drew inspiration not only from the world about them but also from the life and times in which they lived. A fisherman's wife whose man was at sea often and long, designed one pattern that records for all time her life while he was away. Her thoughts of her absent mate, her longing for his return, even her ever present fear of the sea that haunts all mariners' wives, stands clearly stitched in the pattern of waves flowing about the borders of the quilt, while safe at the center is the horn of plenty, a visible hope for his safe return.

These "plain" quilts, decorated only with designs of the quilting needle, are chiefly notable for the quality of the handwork and the balance and precision with which the quilt space is covered with the design. On early quilts, geometrical designs cover the entire background. Later a theme was developed. There is a central motif with a border and the test of the caliber of the quilter lay in her ability to turn the pattern skillfully around the quilt corners. Between the border and the central motif are found the so-called "filling" patterns. Four dominant ones were used in England and Wales. They varied with the central motif. When that was in a circle or curved design, the filling pattern was stitched in straight lines defining squares and diamonds. When the quilter chose a square or rectangular central motif, the filling pattern used was the shell design or wineglass.

Around the Quilting Frame

In the cottages and farm houses of Britain, the wife was the keeper of the quilting frame and the custodian of the quilting designs. Quilting was usually routine. When daily chores were finished, the mother of the family ordered the frame set up and in the long, English twilight or even by candlelight, taught the growing girls the craft she had acquired from her mother when she was young. Even the youngest girls took their places along the quilting frame. With the mother as teacher, it was the juniors of the family who did the actual work.

THE BAKER'S DOZEN

Each daughter had a task before her. She must quilt the coverlets to use on the beds in her home when she was married. All the girls started early so that there would be a supply to last until each had daughters of her own to draw up a stool to a quilting frame. For each the goal to achieve was a baker's dozen—thirteen—quilts for the wedding chest. Usually twelve were carefully planned when the girl was just a tiny tot. Each quilt was different, though all were made along the lines of designs handed down in her own family. The first quilt was simple in design, easy for tender fingers. The designs increased in complexity as the girls grew older. Then when the day arrived when the daughter was pledged to marry the man of her own and family's choice, the thirteenth spread was specially designed and quilted. This was called the Bride's Quilt and was always the most elaborate one among the baker's dozen.

"At Your Quilting, Maids"

Sentiment was deeply rooted in the quilts which grew under the fingers of the young girls dreaming at the quilting frame of the days when they too would have homes of their own and be wives and mothers. Hearts were often incorporated in the designs for central motifs and border patterns were carefully plotted so that there would be no broken ends nor twisted lines of stitching. To the superstitious in England of those days, broken ends in the border were a certain omen of trouble to come, of married life shortened by disaster.

An old quatrain, crude but meaningful, can be heard quoted today among Devon folk. It reads:

"At your quilting, maids, don't dally,
Quilt quick if you would marry,
A maid who is quiltless at twenty-one,
Never shall greet her bridal sun!"

MIGRATION TO THE
NEW WORLD

By the time the seventeenth century rolled around, the fireside craft of quilting was at the high noon of its popularity in Britain, the Low Countries, and throughout northern Europe. In that same century a new ferment was stirring the same peoples—the English, Dutch, French and the Swedes. Having halted for centuries on the westward fringe of Europe, the migratory wave was restless again. Soon these same people would be boarding ships for western lands. With them would go their arts and crafts, among these their quilts and patterns, their skills and designs, to settle down across the sea in the new land of America. There the art-craft of quilting would change and be adjusted to the needs of living in the new home. It was this seventeenth century which was to usher in the Colonial era for quilts and quilting.

After the trip across the Atlantic, "quilts" could be said to have gone through a "sea change." In the new land bed covers were to be as varied and different from the quilts of Europe as the New World differs from the Old. The ancient craft of quilting acquired new vigor with the transplanting.

The high point of quilting popularity in Europe was the sixteenth century. From then on it suffered a gradual decline there. Overseas in America, changed and invigorated in the hands of pioneer women, quilting flourished mightily until the last quarter of the nineteenth century. So hardy, indeed, was the new growth of the craft, that it was not until numerous inventions brought about an evolution in manufacturing and the rise of the machine age, that quilting ceased to be a craft practiced every day in every home.

Settlers of the Far Frontiers

While women from every homeland brought their patterns and skills to the New World, those settling the extremes of the continent, the French in Canada and the Spanish in the South, contributed little to the growth of the craft in the new home. The climate was too mild in the South to make heavy bed coverings necessary, so Spanish needlewomen devoted their time to embroideries for church decorations.

In Quebec, though warmth was needed for protection during winter nights, two factors kept the quilting craft at a minimum. The wild character of the Canadian hinterland slowed growth of all domestic arts. The frontier there attracted a different type of colonist to New France —more men bent on exploration and adventure and fewer women to establish homesteads in the New World. The French found the northern woods teeming with wild life. The type of men who came to New France eagerly embraced the life of trappers and hunters. It was far easier to kill and cure skins of the plentiful game for protective coverings than to set up and operate looms and quilting frames.

COLONIAL AMERICA

Settlers along the middle Atlantic coast were a different breed. There were women on the earliest ships. The Puritans in New England, Dutch and English in New York, Swedes, Quakers and Pennsylvania Germans in Pennsylvania, Cavaliers and other gentry throughout the South, all must be credited with the growth, development and new artistic aspects of the quilting craft in colonial America. More especially they were responsible for its new characteristics—the definitely ornamental phases and the vigor of expression manifested before and after the Revolutionary War period.

FIVE PERIODS OF AMERICAN QUILTS

Five definite periods are clearly

SUNBURST PATCHWORK QUILT

Made entirely of diamond patches, this early nineteenth century Sunburst pattern is made in varying shades of brown and orange. The appliquéd border is composed of stars and streamers, with an oak leaf in each corner.

marked in American quilting. First, the Colonial period when the products most nearly resembled the craft of the lands from which the quilters had come; then the Revolutionary era with complimentary French accents, flower sprays cut from *toile* and appliquéd on the backgrounds, in tribute to gallant allies; then the pioneer period when the West was being won, and ending with the Gold Rush days of '49; the Civil War era including the 1850's and 1860's; finally the Centennial period. By the early 1880's except in remote villages and farmhouses of the Middle West, and mountain cabins of the Great Smokies and Blue Ridge Mountains, the craft of quilting had received its death blow from power machines and industrialized needle trades.

The first quilts used in America had traveled across the Atlantic in the hampers and boxes of Puritan and Cavalier alike. Can there be a doubt that the famous Boston maid, Priscilla Mullins, had quilted her quota of bed coverings back in her English home? Or that these came along with her in her boxes on the Mayflower, later to grace the beds in her home when she married the shy John Alden? The quilts that accompanied the Puritans were of sturdier fabrics and simpler design, as became plain living, than those which came ashore with the Cavaliers in Virginia, in the Carolinas and with Lord Baltimore's settlers in Maryland. Throughout the Colonial period the distinctions and differences remained true.

THE ORIGIN OF PATCHWORK

Many of the distinguishing characteristics of American handmade quilts can be traced directly to the conditions of the life which faced the colonists. There was no industry here —not even the cottage type they had known at home. Some years passed before enough flax could be grown or enough sheep raised and sheared to supply spinning wheels and looms with warp and woof of homespun fabrics. The hard climate and the generally rougher wear of a pioneer environment rapidly wore out the original quilts and necessary repair soon produced the so-called "patchwork" quilts. Lack of fabric for the backgrounds and the need "to make do" originated the practice of sewing together pieces of materials, mainly woolen for warmth, into a "patchwork."

In Town and Country

The type of quilt made in the early days was dictated in the main by the state of the family purse, but the location of the homestead also had much to do with it. Families living in towns along the sea coast were in touch with vessels sailing back and forth to Old World ports. These colonists could obtain more easily background fabrics in variety, in greater quantity, and of larger size than could those families who had pushed on westward into inland farmlands.

While townsfolk had lesser difficulties buying "yard goods" imported from England, Holland and

THE DECORATIVE YO YO QUILT

In its early American setting, the Yo Yo Quilt, with its variegated colors in calico,
adds a novel note to its prim surroundings.

France, the farm families were dependent upon their own efforts and the results of their own industry. The flax from their own gardens and the fleece from their own flocks provided the fibers which they carded, spun and later wove on their own looms. They dyed these fabrics with native dyes, butternut and other vegetables colorings, and even decorated the woven cloth with tying and dipping. These sturdy fabrics could be depended upon to give long service, appearing many years later in patches of New England quilts and the "squares" of the pieced quilts, so popular and so decorative, which marked the products of the colonists as they pioneered westward. The Ohio Valley quilts were their successors.

The Dutch and Germans

In New Amsterdam, later New York, the Dutch housewives were able to import stanch weaves for backgrounds which they decorated with patterns neatly stitched together and appliquéd upon the plain cover. Then the whole coverlet was interlined and quilted. The Germans who came to settle in the land of William Penn used the same style of quilt except that, going inland, these hard working settlers immediately set up their looms and wove the backgrounds for their bed coverings. Of all the early quilts those of the so-called Pennsylvania Dutch are the easiest to identify. The designs are bolder and more elaborate, the colors are gaudier and the quilts are always intricately and superlatively quilted. These designs are often pieced to-gether rather than appliquéd and their outlines are of the geometric type.

In the South

Farther south even in earliest colonial times, background materials were both richer, lighter in weight and wider in variety. Cotton and linen were favored over woolens and strength of texture was sacrificed to enhance the look and feel of the finished quilt. Even in the very early days, silk was often used for the coverlets on guest room beds in the great houses which soon rose along the banks of the James, the Potomac, the Rappahannock and along the famous eastern shore of Maryland. Here the patterns of the appliquéd designs were more graceful and delicate and the effect pictorial, executed in what today we would term "decorator's colors."

Mention of this style of quilt brings to mind an exquisite one owned by an old southern family. Though the quilt itself has now succumbed to time's ravage, recollection of its beauty is still vivid. There was the fine textured background of silk, a graceful all over design of iris—flags, as they were then termed—appliquéd in glowing orchid and purple tones with long spiked leaves of tender green, arching in graceful curves toward a feather-stitch quilting on the fine creamy silk background. Coverlets like this were frequently included in the trousseau of a southern girl when she left her own plantation home for that of a new husband's family.

In Historical Records

Over and over again in the records of old colonial days can be found wills and marriage inventories listing quilts often with detailed descriptions. In old account books and letters are traces of materials purchased so that a wife or daughter might start a new quilt. Sometimes the invoices of clipper ships recreate for us the days when the quilting frames waited greedily for the arrival of more and more fabrics to be stitched by agile, eager fingers of the womenfolk. There is an old inventory in Connecticut records about Sarah, the bride of John Kidd who later became the pirate, Captain Kidd. When she was married she took to her new home three newly quilted coverlets.

Another fertile source of quilting lore can be found in the records of sales of various estates throughout the colonies. At one of these, that of the Fairfax estate at Belvoir, Virginia, George Washington purchased nineteen "coverlids" or quilts to take back home to Martha in Mount Vernon.

GOING WEST

The gradual westward movement across the continent began in the very earliest times. People from New England moved from the coastal settlements into western Massachusetts, Connecticut and along the valley of the Mohawk River in New York. This westward population flow accelerated with the close of the Revolution. Men and women from the Eastern Seaboard, mainly from New England, left the homes they had built and fared forth, climbing the mountains, fording streams and rivers until they reached and settled in the lush lands of the Western Reserve and the fertile Ohio and Mississippi valleys. Packed securely within chests and boxes went the cherished quilts and quilting patterns of the New England housewife. With her, too, went her nimble fingers and the originality of her questing mind.

In the wide open spaces of the Middle West, these pioneers settled down for awhile, they built cabins and homesteads; their wives set up quilting frames and unpacked the treasured patterns. Farming the black fertile loam, richer than the stony New England pastures, these pioneers prospered. Out of the more bountiful land the women folk evolved the ornamental details which mark the special gift of America to the art of quilting.

Quilts and Rifles

At their quilting frames the women were often joined by neighbors. They set up and stitched the beautiful quilts we see today in collections and on museum walls. Often these women with fingers busy on quilting stitches, balanced a loaded rifle against the frame, ready alike for the lumbering bear, the thieving fox or the marauding Indian. The strength and quality, the decision and precision of pioneer women are preserved for all time in the vigor and integrity of their quilt designs.

"PIECED" QUILT APPEARS

The "patchwork" quilt of New England became the "pieced" quilt of the Middle West. Beyond the Alleghenies, perhaps under stress of scarce fabric, even small pieces and bits of goods were precious. Carefully cut out they were pieced together to form larger blocks and these in turn were joined to make the cover, backed and padded, and quilted on the frame. The smaller bits were cut of uniform size and shape and contrasting colors were used to give interest to the design which was usually geometric.

As the years passed, stimulated by the availability of more material, covers of the "laid-on" or appliquéd type rose to favor in that region. This type of quilt pattern has become the most important contribution made to the art-craft by American quilters of the late seventeenth and eighteenth centuries.

Many of these cut-out and appliquéd designs that are seen in collections of Ohio Valley quilts, have been given distinctive names. Many have come down the years in a community or a family just as did the quilting stitches of their ancestors hundreds of years before.

These patterns have been developed largely from the common flowers and natural objects of the region. Such are the Rose of Sharon, Tulip, Sunburst, Birds on the Wing, the Log Cabin and many other original designs and patterns. The proudest boast a woman of those days could make was to be able to say that she had originated a quilt pattern of her own.

AMERICAN HISTORY IN QUILTS

In these quilts, their patterns and fabrics, colonial and early American history can be traced. The ups and downs of financial conditions appeared in quilts long before the statistician came along with his graphs to plot the booms and busts of the American cycle. Here in the quilts can be seen the good years when scraps were cut from lengths of French challis imported for mother's go-to-meeting gown, or bits of London broadcloth from father's best suit. In stark contrast, in the very same quilt, can be found coarse calico or sacking dyed with home-made dyes and purchased, perchance, at the crossroads store with a dozen eggs from the housewife's hencoop.

Quilts were the family records of good days and bad—pictures of the past for younger generations to cherish. Here were squares enshrining grandmother's wedding dress; there were triangles of sprigged muslin prompting mother to tell of picnics and hay rides when father had come a-courting; here was a lavender challis, all that was tangible of Aunt Sue who had climbed into a covered wagon and gone on to the West before the youngest children were born; this square held bits of buff and blue, faded with the years that passed since great grandfather wore his Revolutionary War uniform. And these circles of rose muslin were the christening dresses of the twins who had died so many years before. Yes, quilts were family records during the winning of the West. They made real stories to tell around the glowing hearth on winter evenings. They were indeed the precursors of the photograph albums that came at the turn of the century, to stand on the parlor table in all American homes.

The Quilting Party

Particularly in New England from the days of the Plymouth landing, quilting was woven tightly into the social fabric of the New World. The bleak land into which the Puritans came, and the dour philosophy they practiced, eradicated all natural joyous living. In New England and later in the Middle West where the trail blazers swept on to their conquest of the continent, life was bound up in work. The rise in popularity of social events, such as quilting bees and singing parties in the winter and "house raisings" in the spring and summer and husking bees in the fall, knit the communities together and were all closely tied into the work picture. The quilting craft assuaged the natural loneliness of the women folk cut off in farm houses, distant from each other and a long workday from the men in distant fields and from the children at school miles away. Visiting just for social intercourse was not tolerated in their severe lives, but groups of women from farms miles apart gathered to busy themselves about a quilting frame.

Quilting parties became the high spots of the winter season. They were thoroughly enjoyed by the women during the whole day. In close and quiet intimacy around the quilting frame they gossiped of neighborhood affairs, of their families, the new minister or the latest sermon of the circuit rider, and all the while their nimble fingers covered the quilting spaces with perfect, tiny stitches. When dusk fell the men too, would gather. The frame would be shoved aside, the supper would be set out and the hostess would find her keenest joy in compliments on the quality of the work they had accomplished. Supper over and dishes "red up," with her husband and children about her, she would stand at the farm house door to speed her departing guests. She would watch the wagons with their flickering lanterns going bobbing down the road, and listen to lusty voices as they faded out, singing in the distance.

Courting and all social life of the New World centered about such homely pleasures as our American composer, Stephen Foster, writes in his well remembered ballad—

" 'Twas from Aunt Dinah's quilting party
I was seein' Nellie home!"

OLD AND NEW TRADITIONS

Carried over from Old World traditions were many of the old customs of the young girl preparing far in advance the quilts for the home she would have when she married. The custom that squares should be pieced, and covers made and stored until she had found the man of her choice, was

From Old-Time New England Bulletin

A QUILTING BEE IN THE OLDEN TIME
From a Drawing by H. W. Pierce

a carry-over from cottage life in England. Here in America a fresh note was added. The quilting party at which the bride-to-be brought out her pieced covers was the time when the engagement was announced while the neighbors quilted for the happy pair. These can be seen as fore-runners of engagement showers of today.

Quilting Today

Down the years, the surviving quilts have become the story books of our past. Especially for those who made them, they evoke vivid pictures of memories sewn tight within the pattern. For the woman of today with labor saving devices in her household to give her more leisure time, quilting holds promise of a daily increasing interest and gives opportunity for new and artistic expression. A modern "Aunt Dinah," or "Nellie" can cut out and piece her patterns both old and modern and can have them quilted for her or quilt them herself if her living space has room for a frame. And while her needle plies the quilting lines or adds blocks to an old-time pattern, the quilter of

OLD CRAZY QUILT BLOCKS IN MODERN SETTING

The blocks of silk and velvet crazy quilt pieces are set together with stripes of blue velvet, and a border is added in the latest manner with scalloped edge over a silk ruffle. Featherstitching decorates all the seams.

today can listen to a symphony concert, hear the news or follow the fortunes of her favorite soap opera on the radio.

WHAT'S IN A QUILT?

Then with the completed quilt on the re-finished antique four-poster she can run her fingers over the glowing, smooth stitched surface and remember the past as did one great grandmother back in Ohio. That kindly, ancient lady reminisced as she passed her work-worn fingers over a quilt she had pieced together while her family was growing up:

"It took me more than twenty years, nearly twenty-five, I reckon," she told me softly, "in the evenings after supper when the children were all put to bed. My whole life is in that quilt. It scares me sometimes when I look at it. All my joys and all my sorrows are stitched into those little pieces. When I was proud of the boys and when I was downright provoked and angry with them. When the girls annoyed me or when they gave me a warm feeling around my heart. And John too. He was stitched into that quilt and all the thirty years we were married. Sometimes I loved him and sometimes I sat there hating him as I pieced the patches together. So they are all in that quilt, my hopes and fears, my joys and sorrows, my loves and hates. I tremble sometimes when I remember what that quilt knows about me."

INDEX OF QUILT DESIGNS